village life in modern thailand

village life

UNIVERSITY OF CALIFORNIA PRESS

Institute of
East Asiatic Studies
University of California

in modern thailand

John E. deYoung

BERKELEY AND LOS ANGELES: 1963

University of California Press
Berkeley and Los Angeles
California
Cambridge University Press
London, England
Library of Congress Catalog Card Number: 55-9879

Copyright, 1955, by
The Regents of the University of California
Third printing, 1963

Designed by Marion Jackson

Foreword

This report is an attempt to present a descriptive account of the life of the Thai peasants who live in that vast area of Thailand which lies outside the Bangkok delta plain. It deals mainly with the north, the northeast, and those parts of the central area not in the delta region, but, except for minor variations, the pattern of life described is representative also of the villages of the southern peninsula. Thus, this account covers almost 80 per cent of the peasants of rural Thailand and over two-thirds of the entire geographical area of the country. In addition, most of the basic patterns described are applicable to the peasants of the Menam Plain, although there they have been modified by a differing economic structure.

The Menam Plain, which includes eighteen of thirty-two provinces of the central area, has a peasant population of roughly 3,800,000—a little more than 20 per cent of the total peasant population of the country—less than half of whom live in the immediate Bangkok delta area. Though having only one-fifth of the total peasant population, the Menam Plain is of tremendous importance, for from there come millions of tons of export rice, the basis of the nation's economy. Intensive, commercialized rice cultivation has wrought important changes in the social and economic life of the peasants of this area during the past fifty years. Compact village units have broken down—farmhouses are now scattered—and a rice crop raised for cash has brought about increasing dependence on a money economy.

An extensive study of peasant life in a rice-crop money economy now is under way. A team of American and Thai social scientists, headed by Dr. Lauriston Sharp of Cornell University, is at work on a detailed analysis of a commercial-rice-producing village community in the Bangkok delta. Only preliminary and fragmentary reports on this study have as yet been forthcoming, for the project is not scheduled for completion until 1956. Until the time when the final results of this study are made available, it would be pointless to try to depict the changes in the pattern of life for the peasants of the delta region. It is for this reason that I have not attempted to include the peasant of the lower Menam Plain within the scope of this study but have concentrated on those peasants who live in long-settled, compact village units, who practice a self-subsistent rice economy, and depend on secondary crops and other sources for their small cash income.

This account is not meant to be a detailed economic analysis of village life, such as the Zimmerman survey of 1930, which surveyed 41 villages by the questionnaire method and prepared numerous elaborate statistical analyses from the raw data collected. Here a synoptic account of the daily activities in a Thai village is presented, designed to give the lay reader a picture of how a Thai peasant and his family live and work in present-day Thailand, to show how the life of the peasant has changed in the last half century, and to point out some of the possibilities for his immediate future. This descriptive account has been based largely on direct first-hand field observations. I spent almost three years in social research in Thailand, one year

(1948–49) of which was spent conducting an integrated social study of a northern village community under a grant from the Social Science Research Council. Although many of the examples used for illustration have been drawn from this study, no generalizations have been made unless the pattern described was verified from field notes taken in other parts of the country on my frequent survey trips to villages in the central area, in the northeast, and in the south.

I wish to express special thanks for assistance in this phase of the study to former colleagues in the field, notably to the late John F. Embree and to Lauriston Sharp, under whose guidance my original field work in Thailand was begun.

The research following this field work and the first draft of the manuscript were completed as part of a Modern Thailand Studies Project of the Institute of East Asiatic Studies of the University of California, Berkeley, in 1952–53. During this period I held an appointment as Associate Research Anthropologist in the Institute, and I deeply appreciate the guidance of its director, Dr. Woodbridge Bingham, in the planning and execution of the study.

I am indebted to many persons who gave special assistance in preparation of the final manuscript: those research assistants of the Institute of East Asiatic Studies who helped gather source material, and the other staff members who aided in many ways; Walter Vella, my co-worker on the Modern Thailand Studies Project, whose work on Thai history gave me a fresh insight into the historical aspects of governmental and administrative patterns that touch on village life; Richard Marcus and Jean Esary of the Institute staff and John Gildersleeve of the University of California Press, for their painstaking work in preparing the manuscript for publication; and Dr. Choh-ming Li for his careful reading of the manuscript and valuable criticisms.

To Dr. Mary R. Haas I am particularly grateful, for the present book would not have come into being without her assistance, encouragement, and critical evaluation at various stages in its preparation.

JOHN E. DEYOUNG

Quezon City, The Philippines
January 5, 1955

Contents

1. VILLAGE ORGANIZATION 1
2. SOCIAL ORGANIZATION 22
3. LIFE HISTORY OF THE INDIVIDUAL 48
4. AGRICULTURAL AND ECONOMIC PATTERNS . . . 75
5. RELIGIOUS BELIEFS AND PRACTICES 110
6. CHANGING SCOPE OF THE VILLAGER'S WORLD . . 147

APPENDICES 205

NOTES 215

BIBLIOGRAPHY 219

INDEX 223

Maps and Illustrations

MAPS

GEOGRAPHIC AREAS OF THAILAND	2
TYPICAL RIVER VILLAGE LAYOUT	9
TYPICAL ROAD VILLAGE LAYOUT	10
TYPICAL COMPACT "ISLAND-TYPE" VILLAGE LAYOUT	11
TYPICAL COMMUNE ARRANGEMENT OF THE NORTH	15
TYPICAL PLAN OF A VILLAGE WAT	112

ILLUSTRATIONS

Facing Page

HOUSE OF BAMBOO AND THATCH	34
OLD-STYLE TEAKWOOD HOUSE	34
TEAKWOOD GRANARY OF THE NORTH	35
OUTDOOR RICE MILL	35
A MARKET PLACE IN THE NORTH	66
BOOTHS AT A TYPICAL WINTER FAIR	66
TYPICAL NORTHERN SPIRIT HOUSE	67
CREMATION SCENE	67
HARVESTING RICE	98
WINNOWING RICE IN THE FIELD	98
SHELTER FOR HARVEST WORKERS	99
TRANSPORTING RICE TO THE GRANARY	99
TYPICAL WAT OF THE NORTH	130
VILLAGE BOY DRESSED FOR ORDINATION	131
MONKS AND TEMPLE BOYS	131

1 | *Village Organization*

Bordered by Burma on the west and north, Indochina on the east and north, and Malaya on the south, Thailand consists of an irregular-shaped main body and a long, thin peninsular finger jutting deep into the Malay Peninsula. In crude outline the irregular shape of the country is not unlike that of the profile of an elephant's head; the main part of the country forms the head and ears, and the long, narrow southern peninsula represents the animal's trunk.

The country is slightly smaller than Texas or France, having a total area of roughly 513,000 square kilometers (approximately 200,000 square miles). The latest census, in 1947, set its population at 17,343,714; but taking its past annual increase of 1.9 per cent into account, the total population today should be close to 20,000,000. Considering the area of the country, this is a relatively low population. The official population density is

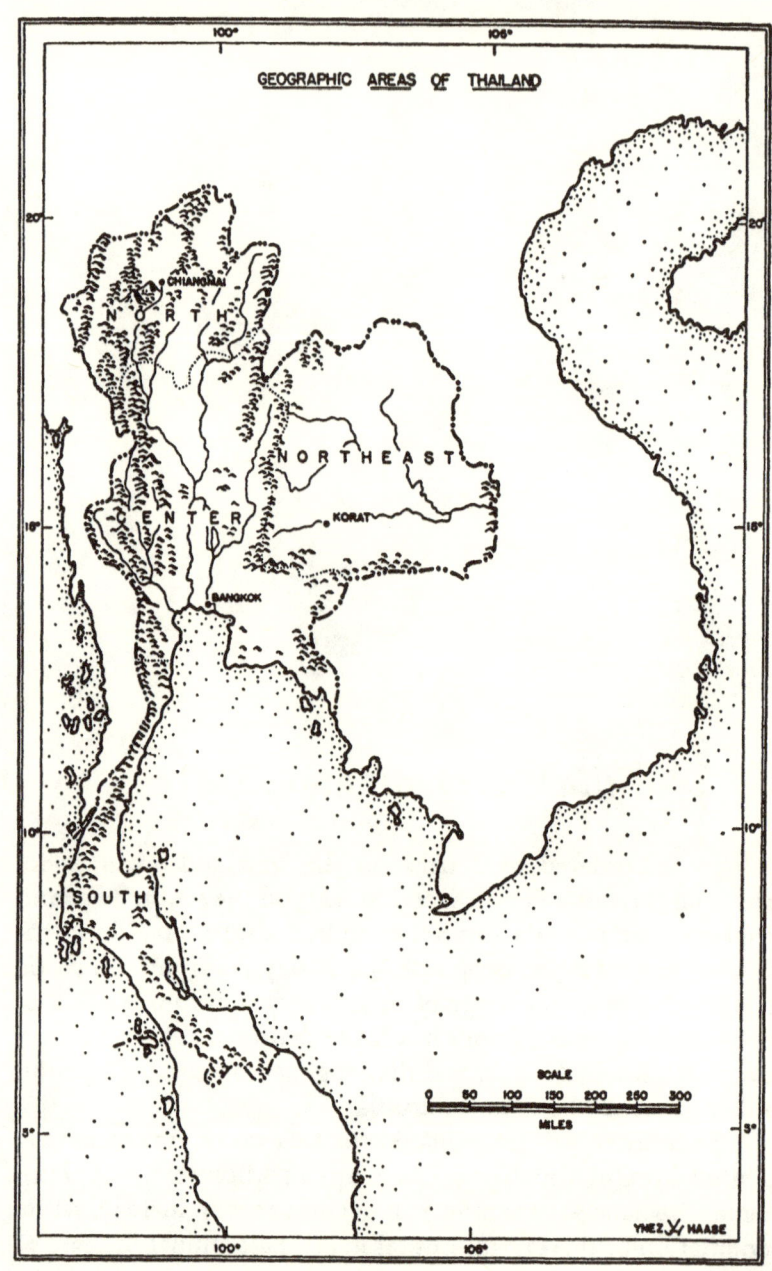

Geographic areas of Thailand

about thirty persons per square kilometer, which is one of the lowest population densities in all of Asia.

Though all of the country lies between the Tropic of Cancer and the Equator, stretching from 5 degrees to 21 degrees North latitude, its length of 1,020 miles and its extreme diversity of terrain have resulted in a marked variation of ecology and climate in the various sections of the country. Geographically, the country is divided into four major areas: South, Central, Northeast, and North Thailand. Within these regions climate, topography, and ecology vary, and minor cultural differences have resulted, mainly from economic adaptation to environment.

THE LAND

The heart of Thailand, the central plains region, is a vast alluvial plain whose upper reaches are drained by the four major rivers of the north which join at Paknampo, some 350 kilometers from the Gulf of Siam, to form the Chao Phya or Menam River, whose branches and channels intersect the fertile delta area. This vast alluvial area, often called the Menam Plain, consists of roughly 55,000 square miles of low-lying land, and makes up a little less than 25 per cent of the total land area of the country. The altitude of this alluvial plain varies only from a low of 1.80 meters above sea level near Bangkok to a high of 44 meters in its northern portions. The low, flat topography is characterized by yearly floods of the Chao Phya and other rivers and the flood depth may be as much as 3 to 4 meters in some parts of the delta. The Menam Plain today is the great rice bowl for all rice-deficient countries of southeast Asia, and the area under most intensive cultivation is the delta north of Bangkok, a fertile, triangular-shaped flood plain with each side some 200 kilometers long, containing some 6,000,000 acres of paddy land, or more than 55 per cent of the paddy land of Thailand. From this limited region come the millions of tons of rice that the country exports each year and on which the nation's economy largely rests. Approximately seventeen provinces of central Thailand are in the Menam Plain and it is here that roughly 20 per cent (about 4,325,000) of the peasant population live.

The confines of central Thailand have long been a subject of controversy: Credner and others limited the region to the Menam Plain proper and classified the portion west of the flood plain as West Thailand and the region southeast of Bangkok (the Chandaburi region running to the Cambodia boundary) as Southeast Thailand.[1] Zimmerman and Andrews include these areas under Central Thailand.[2] Thai government officials follow much the latter classification, extending the lower part of the central area as far as Prachuab-Kiri kham in the south; it is this classification that is followed here. All told, some thirty-two of the country's seventy-one provinces make up the central area, and about 41 per cent of the population of the country live here.

South Thailand is made up of the northern two-thirds of the Malay Peninsula, a section of the peninsula with a narrow, high mountain chain flanked by narrow strips of land. Rivers and numerous small streams create watersheds in the valleys on each side of the mountains, and it is on these valley floors that wet-land rice is grown. Heavy rainfall and abundant soil make this one of the most fertile areas in all Thailand, but it is not a commercial rice-producing area; the peasants grow rice only for local consumption. Since many villages are on or near the coast, fishing ranks with rice-growing in importance; much of the known mineral wealth of the country is in this peninsula; here most of the country's 665,000 Malays live, the population south of Pattani being primarily Malay, north to Songkla half Thai and half Malay, and beyond Songkla principally Thai. A large Chinese population is in this region, particularly in the Kras Isthmus; the Chinese work in mines and on rubber plantations or are shopkeepers and vendors, and do not compete as small independent farmers with the Thai peasant. There are 14 provinces in south Thailand and approximately 2,400,000 people.

Northeast Thailand, often called the Korat Plateau, is a huge saucer-shaped basin bounded on the north by the Mekong river and the Dong Phya Yen mountains, which rise about 1,000 feet above sea level; it is the largest of the four regions of Thailand, consisting of 167,000 square kilometers (64,500 square miles),

---

[1] For notes to chapter 1 see page 215.

or about one-third of the entire area of the country. Here in 15 provinces more than five and a half million peasants, or 35 per cent of the country's population, eke out a living. By far the greatest part of the plateau is undulating or flat, and in general is very poorly watered; the greatest part of the region is covered with jungles and grass plains. Some regions of the northeast remain unexplored. In the flood area of the river lowlands rice is the principal crop, and although the northeast lacks water and has poor soil, it does supply a small amount of rice for export. Dry-land rice is grown on jungle hillsides and wetland rice in the lowlands, and more cattle are raised here than elsewhere in Thailand.

North Thailand, geographically, begins north of Raheng, Utaradit, and Petchabun and extends to the Burmese and Indochinese border; it contains seven provinces and approximately 2,000,000 peasants. The terrain is hilly or mountainous, divided into four major valleys by the Ping, Wang, Yom and Nan rivers, all of which flow to the south. Rice, the chief product here as elsewhere in Thailand, is planted along the low-lying regions of the rivers, whose annual flooding provides water and enriches the light sandy soil. Since the northern rivers flood relatively late in the year and since the monsoons occur later here than in central Thailand, June rainfall is not enough to give the rice a suitable start. Northern farmers long ago developed well integrated irrigation systems, so that many valleys have a constant supply of water throughout the year and farmers can grow a secondary crop of tobacco or soybeans after the rice is harvested.

CLIMATE

Thailand has a tropical, monsoon climate. In central Thailand the temperature rarely falls below 15 degrees C (59 F) or rises above 32 degrees C (89 F). The mountainous topography of the north and northeast drastically affects the temperature there during the cool season; although the days will be warm, the night temperatures may fall as low as 10 degrees C (50 F); in the hot season between March and May temperatures during the day may rise above 38 degrees C (100 F).

For all of Thailand except the southern peninsula, the seasons are determined by the direction of the prevailing monsoon winds and fall into three periods—the hot season from February to May, the rainy season from June to November, and the cool or winter season from November to January. In the southern peninsula there are only two distinct seasonal periods, a hot season from February to August, and a rainy season from September to January, the heaviest rains coming in December. The climate of the peninsula is milder than the rest of the country and the temperature is not so variable.

The rainy season for Thailand, except for the south, falls mainly between May and November, slackening off by the end of September. In central and north Thailand, there is little rain after October. The rainy season begins when the southwest monsoon winds from the Bay of Bengal and Gulf of Siam bring in the rain-laden clouds. The rains occur mainly as heavy afternoon and evening squalls and only rarely will there be a day or days of continual rain. The vast northeast has a rainfall similar to central and north Thailand, except that this region receives relatively less rainfall because mountains to the southwest and west act partly as a rain barrier. The western part of the Chaipum province is semi-arid.

THE PEOPLE

Only the Thai-speaking, lowland, wet-rice agriculturists, who make up the bulk of the country's population, will be described in this report. These peasants, who are scattered throughout all regions of the country, are concentrated in the river valleys where they can practice their wet-rice agriculture, and the great bulk of the peasant population is located in the central plains and the northeast. Accurate statistics are not available but analysis of the crude population data of 1947 would appear to indicate that perhaps 80 per cent of all the peasants of the country live in these two regions. The north with its approximate 2,000,000 inhabitants is also predominantly peasant. The peninsula region has large numbers of Chinese who are non-agriculturists, yet except for this group the remainder, both Malay and Thai, are predominantly a peasant folk.

Regardless of what region of Thailand they live in, all peasants are Thai in language and origin. The peasants of the north and northeast, who are half of all the peasants of the country, have long been referred to as Lao, but this is an arbitrary designation used in the past by the central Thai to refer to northerners and picked up by European writers. The Thai-speaking peasants of the two northern areas do not refer to themselves as Lao but as Muang Thai, as do the rest of the peasants of the country; and these so-called Lao are as Thai as the central and southern groups, all having drifted into Thailand from the Yunnan provinces of China between the first and fourteenth centuries A.D., bringing with them a tropical wet-rice paddy culture adapted to the lowlands. Over the centuries, owing partly to geographic isolation and partly to external forces, minor cultural differences among the various Thai peasant groups developed—differences in dialect and costume, for example. In recent times, many of these have been erased; even the dialectical difference, which is always among the last to change, is being whittled away by the compulsory village school, in which the central-Thai dialect is spoken as the standard language of the country. Therefore, although the peasants of the north and northeast may still be called Lao by outsiders, the term has little real meaning any longer; by government order, this term is no longer used officially, and it lingers in Thailand only as a cultural remnant.

The last half century, particularly the years since the 1932 revolution, has brought about a remarkable degree of similarity in patterns of life of the peasants of all Thailand. Certain of the overt cultural earmarks, easily observable a generation ago, (e.g., the tattooing of northern men) have been completely wiped out among the present generation. The central Thai woman has given up her traditional *panung*, a diaperlike Siamese version of the Indian dhoti, in favor of the northern woman's skirtlike *pasin*, making for uniformity in women's dress. Only her distinctive hair style sets the northern woman apart from her southern sister, and today only older women retain this hair style.

This is not to say that regional differences exist no longer;

many minor differences remain, not only from region to region but even from one village to another. Among the four main regions of the country, decided cultural differences, many in agricultural techniques, may be observed, many of them due to differences in terrain and climate, and in addition, each village may have its own local variations within the basic pattern. What is important is that a basic cultural pattern can always be ascertained.

Any description of regional variations must also consider foreign influences on the Thai. North Thailand, which is next to the Shan states and has been under Burmese influence, has had borrowed cultural characteristics which did not exist in south Thailand—for example, the tattooing of men. On the other hand, the southern Thai peasant has been influenced by the practices of the Malay peoples; he has, for example, adopted the Malay method of reaping rice. Moreover, in south Thailand, Malay influence causes Thai women occasionally to carry loads on their heads, which is something strictly forbidden by native Thai custom and never done throughout most of Thailand, where the head is regarded as sacred, to be touched only in the most ceremonious manner.

All Thai peasants who live in small, long-established, self-sustaining villages have the same general culture; and this is 80 per cent of all the peasants of Thailand, that is, all Thai peasants except those of the commercialized delta region. The minor cultural variations which are found will be described in this report as contrasts to the general pattern of life of the present-day villager, and, wherever possible, the reasons for these variations will be explained.

TYPES OF VILLAGES

Villages in Thailand commonly fall into two main types: a group of houses strung along a waterway or road, or a cluster of houses set among fruit trees, coconut palms, and rice fields. Along a wide river, houses of the latter type of village are built on only one bank, but along a narrow river, a canal, or a road, houses may be located on both sides; the village may extend from one to several kilometers, houses often being only one deep along the road and rice fields starting at the rear of the house compounds.

Villages of the other sort, the cluster type, are set some distance (one-quarter of a kilometer to a kilometer) from a main thoroughfare—a river, a navigable canal, a railroad line, a branch road, or a main highway. A cart road or cart track leads

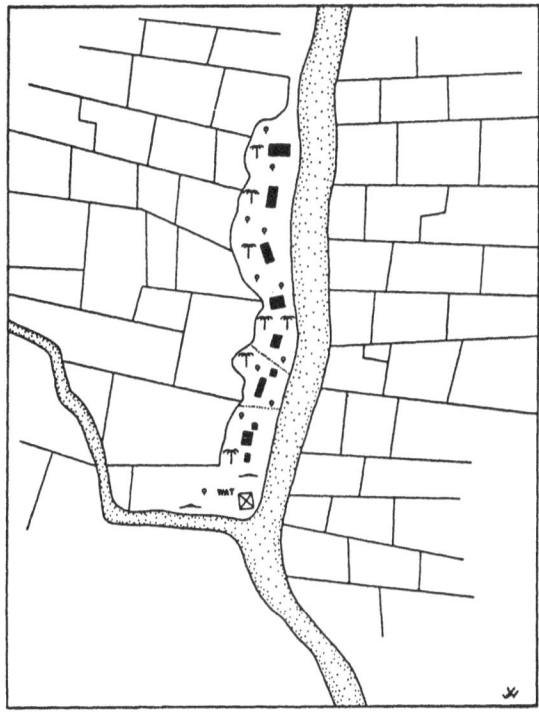

Typical river village layout

from these villages to the thoroughfare; these tracks are built and maintained by the villagers and, although impassable during the rainy season, can be used for at least eight months of the year. These crude roads are at the peak of their use in the dry season after the harvest, at which time even trucks can drive on them. (The bus and the truck are becoming increasingly important in Thailand, and traveling vendors drive into even isolated villages during the dry season.)

In parts of central Thailand, isolated farms or an isolated group of several households have become prevalent; the former have become dominant in the Rangsit irrigation region outside of Bangkok, and thoughout parts of the lower delta, the traditional compact, integrated village has given way since 1900 to small groups of farmhouses, each widely separated from its

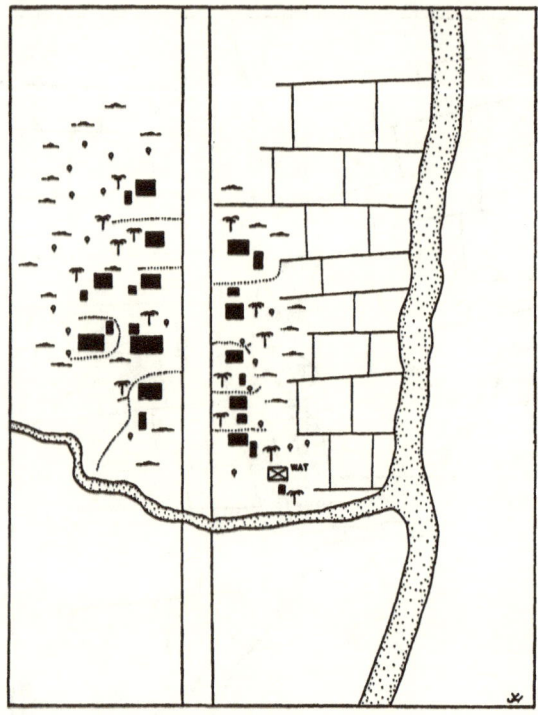

Typical road village layout

neighbors on its own tiny piece of high ground. This new sort of community is the result of intensive commercialized rice-growing in the delta region; anywhere from ten to fifty of these widely separated house clusters will be grouped together conceptually for administration purposes and each such "village" has an elected headman.

No records are available of how many of the central-Thai peasants are involved in this new type of community, but probably less than one-tenth of all the villages in Thailand fall in this category. Scattered households apparently are typical of only the portion of the delta near Bangkok. Isolated farm dwellings are also found in the rubber-growing districts of the South, where workers on rubber plantations must live close to the rubber trees to give them daily attention, but almost all of these households consist of Chinese families whose way of life

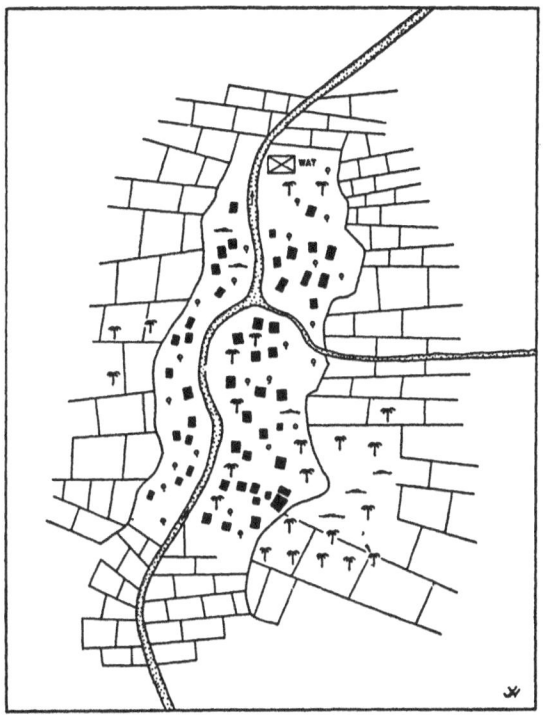

Typical compact "island-type" village layout surrounded by rice fields

is radically different from that of the Thai peasant. In the region directly south of Bangkok, where fruit growing is combined with rice farming, "villages" of the scattered, small-cluster type and isolated farm houses are grouped together to form a conceptual village unit, although the farmhouses may be distributed over several miles.

Historically, the village on a river or canal has been the most important to the Thai peasant, for the river or canal has fur-

VILLAGE ORGANIZATION 11

nished the essential water for wet-rice farming and has provided the only feasible communication and transportation; and although no census of type of village layout ever has been taken in Thailand, probably the canal or river village is still most numerous, for waterways still are the life blood for every community. In the past fifty years the railroad and road systems of Thailand have progressed steadily, so that it is a rare village today, except in some of the extremely low-lying areas of central Thailand, that is not within walking distance of a branch road leading to a main road running to the market town or provincial capital. Even river villages have been increasingly influenced by the ever-expanding road system, especially in the north and northeast, where the rivers are likely to be low during the dry season. River villages in these areas have cart roads that lead to a highway even though much transportation is still by water. The same growing influence of the road has been reported by Sharp for central Thailand.[3]

Villages tend to be set off from each other by large expanses of open rice fields, but occasionally in the extremely long narrow river village, whose households may extend several kilometers along the banks, the casual observer often cannot tell where one river village stops and the next begins, although administratively there is a sharp demarcation of village boundaries.

Villages vary in size, generally having a minimum of fifty families. Ordinarily, a concentrated-type village will have about a hundred households, and larger villages may contain up to two hundred. Size of a village is correlated with regional variations in soil fertility, with availability of irrigation water, with general population density, and other factors. Throughout the northern regions the average village consists of approximately 100 households, and from 450 to 500 inhabitants.

Usually only the larger, strategically located villages have an area for holding the morning markets; today, most villages do not have their own market, but help to support a central market area, often located on one of the main roads. The rotating village market system common earlier is giving way to a fixed market area for a group of villages.

THE ADMINISTRATIVE STRUCTURE

Until 1932, Thailand was divided for administrative purposes into ten large regional areas known as *monthons* (circles), with a lord-lieutenant or high commissioner appointed by the crown responsible for the general administration of a circle. The bloodless revolution of 1932, which created a limited monarchy in Thailand, abolished the *monthon* and made the *changwat* (province) the primary administrative division. There were then seventy *changwats* divided into 411 *ampurs* (districts); an additional province was created in 1947, and districts were redivided, so that today there are 71 provinces, 411 districts, and 80 subdistricts. The number of districts in each province varies from five to ten. The *ampur* is again broken down into *tambons*, a group of villages commonly called communes, of which there are 3,327. There does not seem to be any specific regulation about the size of a commune, which varies throughout the country and is apparently determined by topographical considerations and by ease of communication and transportation. The average commune contains at least ten villages, and some as many as twenty. These in turn are broken down into the smallest government unit, the individual village or *muban*. The total number of *muban* recognized as administrative units by the government was listed in the most recent census as 49,832; but the number tends to vary from period to period, depending upon consolidation of village units into administrative units, and the actual number of ecological village units is probably greater than this figure.*

The province is in charge of a governor appointed by the Minister of the Interior. He is assisted in the administration of his province by a staff of officials representing the other ministries of the country. The provincial governors report directly to the Ministry of the Interior. For supervisory purposes, the country has been divided into regions, each headed by a regional commissioner. There are now nine of these regions, the number having been raised in 1952 from five. The duties of the regional commissioner are mainly that of coördinating and supervising

---

* See Appendices II and IV.

activities within the provinces in his region. Each province, depending on the size of its population, elects one or more members of the assembly of people's representatives. Provinces vary widely in area and population; the largest, Ubon, in northeast Thailand, has a population of roughly 850,000; and the smallest, Ranong, in south Thailand, only 21,305. The southern provinces are generally smaller than those elsewhere. The average province has between 200,000 and 250,000 inhabitants.

THE DISTRICT AND DISTRICT OFFICER

A district officer who is under the direct supervision of the governor of the province is in charge of a district (*ampur*) and has his headquarters in the district seat; he has under his jurisdiction to assist him in carrying out his duties a group of civil service officials representing various ministries, such as education, police, health, agriculture, finance, and excise, and, in general, the district administrative system parallels that of the province on a smaller scale. The district officer is a civil servant and is appointed by the Ministry of Interior. District officers are moved about frequently from province to province so that their administration will remain impartial; this means that every three or four years the commune and village headmen are under the direction of a new district officer. His duties are varied and manifold: he is responsible for the collection of taxes, fees, and fines; he is the administrative officer and the chief local magistrate.

To the villager, the district officer is known as the *nai ampur*, which might be translated "boss of the district"; he is for them the closest and most real of all contacts with the central government. He may be called in to settle disputes between villagers concerning boundary lines of their rice fields; he judges disputes between landlord and tenant, and sees that the villagers obey government regulations. He holds monthly meetings with all commune and village headmen at his office to discuss routine matters and special business—for example: election procedures, if an election for national assemblymen is approaching; health information, if there is news of an epidemic in a neighboring area; diseases such as rinderpest that affect farm animals, an

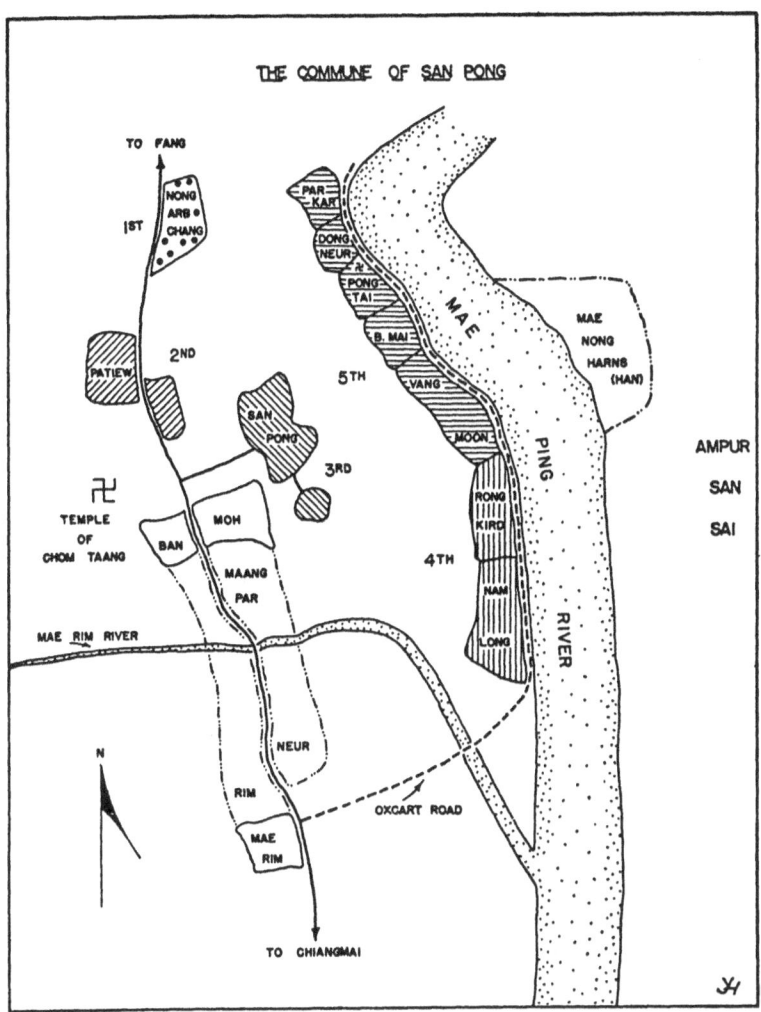

Typical commune arrangement of the north, showing grouping of villages into administrative units

almost constant source of discussion. If the school year is about to start, the *nai ampur* reminds the headmen of this, and warns them that all eligible children of school age must be registered and sent to school. If an important government holiday is approaching, the headmen are given instructions about services that might be held. In addition to the regular monthly meeting, district officers frequently call special meetings of the headmen; these may be occasioned by the visit of a central government official to inspect the *ampur,* or to explain a government program, as, for example, a new drive for credit coöperative membership. The *nai ampur* visits the villages of his district to see whether the headmen are carrying out instructions, particularly those about new government programs, and so the villager, even if he does not leave his village, is brought by these visits into contact with the *nai ampur.*

ROLE OF THE KAMNAN

Each commune or *tambon* has a supervisory headman known as the *kamnan,* who is a village headman chosen for the commune headmanship by his fellow village headmen. The *kamnan* can be called only semi-government officials; civil service status ends with the district officials. Administratively, they are under the control of the district officer, but they are not under civil service regulations, nor do they receive a civil service salary. Today *kamnan,* as well as village headmen, receive a monthly stipend from the central government, but this was begun only about 1938. Before, their only compensation was a few privileges such as being exempted from the old head tax and receiving a discount for railroad travel, and, in addition, a small commission for measuring taxable land and a small percentage of the fees they helped collect. In prewar days, *kamnan* drew a monthly allotment of five ticals, and village headmen, of one tical; after the war, these stipends were raised, so that in 1950 *kamnan* received forty-two ticals a month, and headmen twenty-four. (A tical at this time was roughly equivalent to five cents in American money.) It has been reported that these rates have been raised slightly since 1950.

Since the *kamnan* is also a village headman, he is allowed an assistant to help him administer the commune; this is the *sarawat* (secretary), who also receives a small monthly salary.

The *kamnan* must report each month to the district officer on events in his commune. Accordingly, he meets with his village headmen at his home to inform them of new government procedures or to settle minor disputes and commune affairs whose importance is not great enough to be brought to the district officer's attention. In the north, meetings of this sort often are held to discuss commune irrigation problems which still are handled largely by the peasants themselves. Most of the village headmen, unless an emergency arises, make their reports to the *kamnan* prior to the monthly meeting at the *nai ampur's* office.

In addition to his supervisory duties within the commune, the *kamnan* is in charge of vital statistics and health problems; he must report all births and deaths in the commune every month to the district officer. The head of a family is responsible for reporting the birth of a child within fifteen days to the *kamnan* of his commune; this he does by reporting the birth to his own village headman. By regulation, deaths must be reported within twenty-four hours. Reporting of deaths is handled by the registered village "doctor," who checks on the death and then officially reports to the village headman who passes the report on to the *kamnan*. The regulation that a report of death should reach the *kamnan* within twenty-four hours is for the purpose of notifying the district office at once in case a contagious disease was the cause of death; however, unless a death seems to have been due to a dangerous disease, it is seldom reported to the *kamnan* until the village headman sees him at the monthly meeting at the district seat.

VILLAGE DEMOCRACY

The village headman (*pu yai ban*) is elected by the men and women of the village. The fact that women participate in these elections is often pointed out with pride by Thai officials to show that woman suffrage in local affairs is far in advance of other countries. Zimmerman reported that a village headman was elected for a term of five years, but throughout rural Thailand, in the past and now, no fixed term for village headmen has existed.[4] A headman may serve continuously without election as long as he retains the confidence and respect of his villagers. It is not uncommon for a respected village headman to retain his position until his death or retirement. A headman usually retires at about sixty, an age the Thai peasant believes proper for retirement. Retired headmen, along with other old men of the village, serve as a sort of informal council to the headman, and wield great influence in village life; rarely will a headman initiate an important undertaking without discussing it first with this group.

A village headman automatically loses his position if he is imprisoned on a criminal charge; he can resign for reasons of health, old age, family or economic problems, or if he moves away from the village. Villagers can ask for the removal of a headman who has lost their confidence by petitioning the district officer, who has the power to dismiss headmen and to call for a new election. In voting for village headman, a meeting is held of all adults who wish to vote. Each household will be represented by at least one adult member. There is no campaigning; the retiring headman and his informal council of elders recommend one or two candidates from mature, respected men of the village, and the villagers vote for these candidates. Election of a headman is generally in open assembly, by a standing vote or a voice vote, with a simple majority electing. Secret ballot is rarely used. Commonly the most popular candidate will be the assistant to the retiring headman, and he is usually elected; he is familiar with the office, and will have gained the respect of the villagers in his dealings with them as assistant.

Headmanship confers prestige and honor on the incumbent, but it carries heavy responsibilities, and demands considerable time. The allotment paid by the central government is too small to be of financial gain to the headman; in fact, the office usually costs him money because he will be expected to make frequent contributions to the temple and for funerals, and to provide food, betel nut, liquor, cigarettes, and cigars for prominent visitors. Only a relatively prosperous villager can afford to be headman, so that a young man has little chance of being elected.

A village headman appoints an assistant who serves without pay—often an industrious young villager somewhere in his 30's. The assistant is chosen by the headman, nominally with the *kamnan's* approval. In previous times in the north, the assistant headman was called *sarawat*, but today this term is reserved for the paid assistant of the *kamnan*.

The election of the village headman and of the *kamnan* must be confirmed by the provincial governor through his representative, the district officer. This approval comes automatically, and rarely, if ever, is the candidate elected by a village challenged by the *nai ampur*. The extent of freedom in the election of the headman and *kamnan* is shown by the fact that neither the district officer nor any representative of this official is present.

Many smaller villages do not have their own headmen, but are under the control of a headman of a nearby village. Throughout the northern region, quite often a village of fewer than seventy-five households is placed under the jurisdiction of the headman of a larger neighboring village. In such villages the headman designates an assistant to act for him. The commune of San Pong is a good example of this type of consolidation of administration; the population of this typically northern commune is 4,093, and it contains eleven villages, the largest having 755 inhabitants, and the smallest 350. The commune is divided into five units, each with a headman; depending on the unit, a headman may be responsible only for the village in which he lives, or he may have several villages under his jurisdiction. In this commune only two of the eleven villages have their own headmen. One headman has two small river villages under his jurisdiction, another has five small river villages under his jurisdiction, and one headman, in addition to his own village, has a nearby road village to supervise. (See map of San Pong, page 15.) Proximity and contiguity, as well as size, are the factors determining whether a village has a separate headman; in this commune the villages which have their own headmen are separated from the others by more than a kilometer; the five villages under a single headman are contiguous.

The consolidation of several villages under one headman has apparently been encouraged by the central government as an economy measure. The central government has attempted to bring the headmen under more direct control by paying them a small monthly stipend, and putting several villages under one headman has enabled the government to reduce the number of headmen and at the same time to increase their stipend. Proposals to make the local headmen regularly salaried civil servants have been broached but have always met with defeat on the grounds that the civil service budget could not possibly carry this added burden.

This sort of consolidation is not possible in the delta region, where, as a result of commercialized rice farming, the concentrated village has given way to small groups of houses distributed throughout the paddy fields. In the Bangkok area, the headman setup must follow a somewhat different pattern. For example, in the village area of Bangchan (in the district of Minburi some twenty miles from Bangkok) some 290 households, with a total population of roughly 1,600, are widely distributed throughout the area either as isolated homesteads or as small groups of houses. Here the farms are larger than elsewhere in Thailand, ranging from 2 to 44 acres, or an average of 11.6 acres.[5] For purposes of administration, there are seven headmen, or one headman for an average of forty households. This is far below the number of households that a headman would have charge of in a concentrated village, but in the delta where distances between houses are so vast, taking care of even forty households is a major task for the headman. The rest of the Menam Plain, even though it is commercialized, tends to have more concentrated villages, and although these in general are not so compact as other Thai villages, the administrative pattern for village areas, with the exception of the Bangkok delta region, follows today that described for the commune of San Pong.

One other semi-government official on the village level should be mentioned—the so-called village "doctor," who is under the supervision of the district health officer and who receives a small monthly stipend from the central government. Before World War II the village "doctor" received a monthly allowance of one tical a month; this was raised to fifteen ticals in 1949, and is reported to be slightly higher now. "Doctor" is a very misleading term, for this man has no modern medical training, though he is versed in native medical lore. He is really a village quack who has been registered by the district health officer and who has been given some instruction in drugs and hygiene; however, the term "village doctor" is used in Thailand to distinguish this practitioner from the faith healer and spirit doctor, who also practice their arts in the village. Being under the jurisdiction of the district health officer, who is a trained medical man, the village doctor does have limited contact with modern health practices; he is used by the district health officer to spread information to villagers on health and disease, to vaccinate village babies against smallpox, to dispense Western drugs and medicine, to report cases of serious illness and deaths to the district health officer. Much the same consolidation described above for the headman is followed for the registered village doctor: villages within a commune are grouped into units and often one registered doctor is placed in charge of several villages. The usual custom is to choose a young quack doctor who seems intelligent enough to understand the rudiments of modern medicine and who is likely to coöperate with the district health officer. Quacks and faith healers are in every village.

2 Social Organization

The primary social unit in Thai village life is the family household. Basically, this household is the small-family type, which consists primarily of mother, father, and children, and sometimes one or more grandparents. At times the rural family household becomes a small extended family; for example, when a daughter's husband comes to live in the house, and when a child is born to this marriage—however, once they have become parents, the young couple usually start a household of their own. Only one daughter or, if there is no daughter, only one son will remain in the family household. If a household has no children, it is common to take in a boy or girl, who is sometimes a relative, as a helper in the house and fields.

The household is the smallest unit and the basic social unit of the village community. All village coöperative activities center around the family household rather than the individuals.

Each village household is given a number by the headman (*pu yai ban*), and a record of its members is kept by him.

The village community is not organized into formal neighborhood units, but informal neighborhood groups do exist for coöperative work in planting and harvesting; these groups are determined partly on a geographical basis within the village (proximity of households) for neighbors often work with each other, but the work group may also include friends and relatives from all parts of the village. Funerals, upkeep of the Buddhist *wat*, temple ceremonies, and repairing of the village school, roads, and canals are done by the community as a whole rather than by a group of neighborhood units. One exception to this is found in some villages of the north where geographically defined neighborhood groups with demarcated boundaries have been created to prepare food for the monks in the *wat*. For this sole purpose, the elders of the village may divide the village into specific districts, each with a designated leader or chief. Their role and function are described in the section on religious life. Such formal neighborhood groups are not found in all northern villages. In the commune of San Pong of Chiangmai province in the north, where eleven villages were studied by the author, roughly half of the villages had this special formally designated neighborhood unit for feeding the Buddhist monks. Such a pattern as yet has not been reported elsewhere, and it may possibly be a local innovation in this northern region.

FAMILY AND HOUSEHOLD

Family name and inheritance come through the father, who is the head of the family. Both sons and daughters inherit rice land equally, but the house and house compound frequently are inherited by right of succession by the daughter who with her husband expects to make her home in the family household. The custom of one married daughter remaining in the house of her parents and inheriting the family house is so widespread throughout the north that it suggests a system of specialized matrilocal residence at an earlier period, although at present the system no longer is consistent. Reports from central and south Thailand indicate that this system is even weaker there;

hence, a generalization for all of rural Thailand cannot be made.

Although the father is regarded as the head of the house and children are expected to obey him, the Thai farm family is not a strict, authoritarian one as is the farm family of Japan or China. Thai farm children are brought up to show respect and deference to the family head, but his orders are not obeyed as absolute commands. Early in life children learn to respect and defer to their father, but without an exaggerated sense of strict duty and obligation. Within the family it is the mother who inculcates the children with the proper family precepts, but these are taught as the proper way for a child to behave rather than as absolute, mandatory rules. Breaking of these precepts is not uncommon, and characteristically in Thai culture, the child or adult is forgiven, for early in family life a strong amount of individualism shows up in the peasant child.

The social position of the Thai peasant woman is powerful: she has long had a voice in village governmental affairs; she often represents her household at village meetings when her husband cannot attend; she almost always does the buying and selling in the local markets. (It is so unusual for a Thai male to do this that it elicits comment if he does.) Through their marketing activities Thai farm women produce a sizeable portion of the family cash income, and they not only handle the household money, but usually act as the family treasurer and hold the purse strings. Control of family finances by women is possibly even stronger in urban regions where a money economy is more intimately involved, but in village life, also, money brought into the household by farming is usually disbursed by the wife, and if she does not actually control the expenditure of the family income, she always has an important voice in the decision concerning its use. There is one exception: in the commercialized delta area where large amounts of money are brought in by the sale of rice, the farmer seems to keep control of this rice income himself.

The strong individualism of Thai life is seen in the handling of money brought into the family by teen-age children who earn shares or a cash wage by working for other farmers. If they come from a very poor family, much of their earnings, either in rice or cash, will go to support the family, but even then they are allowed to keep a certain proportion for their own needs. In families that are moderately well-off, minor children who work outside may turn their earnings over to the mother for safekeeping but they can spend them as they wish.

In contrast to that of other countries of southeast Asia, the social organization of rural Thailand does not revolve around a tightly integrated extended family or a larger kinship unit. The Thai family pattern can best be described as a loosely woven structure within which considerable variation of individual behavior is permitted.[1] This looseness of structure is evidenced also in the larger kinship groups: relatives tend to coöperate with each other in planting and harvesting work parties, but even in a relatively small village blood-relationship lines do not have the importance that they do in other areas of southeast Asia.

NAMES

Family names are recent in Thailand, for it has been only within the past half century that surnames have come into use. In 1916, King Vajiravudh decreed that every person must have a patronymic name; he bestowed names on the minor royalty and officials, but villagers were obliged to choose a name from a list prepared by the king. It is not uncommon to find several families in a small village bearing the same surname, even though nominally they disclaim blood relationship.

Few farm families can trace their ancestry back more than two or three generations unless a grandparent is alive, for family records have not been kept. The fact that only in the last generation has a family name existed is partly responsible for the loose kinship structure typical of Thailand. The looseness of the kinship relationship can be seen in the ease with which a person loses contact with his immediate family if he marries outside the village or moves to a new locality. Within one generation kinship ties among villagers tend to be broken, and

---

[1] For notes to chapter 2 see page 215.

contact is rarely maintained among family members in neighboring villages unless they are of the same generation.

Within the family, children address older relatives by their position in the household—"father," "grandfather," "mother," or "grandmother." Siblings address each other by given name. Thai kinship terms distinguish age differences and there are specific terms meaning "older brother" and "older sister," or "younger brother" and "younger sister." These are used strictly as kinship terms and not as terms of address. In speaking to an older sibling, one uses the more general term *pee* (elder sibling); in speaking to a younger sibling, on the other hand, one uses his given name rather than the word *nong* (younger sibling). When he is referring to a sibling to an outsider, the Thai villager always will use the kinship term rather than the given name.

Husband and wife use special terms for each other depending on the age group in which they fall. Couples from twenty to thirty ordinarily use the respect term for siblings in talking to each other, the husband calling the wife *nong* (younger sister), and the wife addressing the husband as *pee* (older brother). Some of the younger villagers today no longer follow this consistently but use each other's given name. If the husband has served in the Buddhist temple, a special term of respect denoting type of service is prefixed by the wife in addressing the husband, a man who has served as a novice being called *pee noi* by the wife. In some parts of Thailand, husband and wife after they have children refer to each other as "mother of ——" and "father of ——."

As the married couple reach the middle age level, they may begin to use a general term meaning "you" when talking to each other. As they get older and fall into the last age group, that above sixty years, they often begin to address each other by their given name. The minor dialectical differences in the various regions of the country affect kinship terms.

In speaking of relatives to outsiders, the villager uses the kinship term that expresses the exact degree of relationship. There are many kinship words in the Thai language, and exact shading of degree of relationship, whether of blood, marital relationship, or generation can be denoted by use of special terms.

Titles of respect based on religious service and age are used with a person's given name or the term that identifies him. Males are addressed by the term *nai* (mister). If a man has served as a novice or monk, his name throughout the rest of his life will include the term of respect denoting this service. Usage of this special respect term will be followed not only by outsiders but also by his close family.

As a villager reaches old age, he will be addressed by younger villagers in special terms of respect. All old people will be called by the kinship terms of "grandfather" or "grandmother" even though the speaker is not related to the old person. Often an additional respect word meaning "very old" is added to the general term of grandfather or grandmother.

Unmarried village girls are addressed as *nang sao*, and married woman are referred to by the term *nang*.

CLOSE FRIENDS

Friendship plays an important role in the life of the Thai peasant, being particularly strong for the men. Friendships sometimes are described in terms either of a "die" friend or an "eating" friend. The "ideal" or "die" friend is very rare, while "eating" friends will be common in a man's life. The pattern of the "die" friend is best illustrated among the *nak leng* or bandit groups of the past, where individuals made pacts to die for each other. For the village men, close friendships based on age are very important. Close friendships between boys of the same age are very common in northern village life. Such friends are not called "die" friends but *sio*, although the *sio* might at times fit this ideal classification.

SOCIAL CLASSES AND SOCIAL POSITION

All observers of Thai village life agree on the absence of servility and on the high degree of self-reliance of the Thai peasant. Much of this is due to the lack of a rigidly defined social-status system. In traditional times, class lines could be delineated to some extent within the rural framework: at the top of the rural hierarchy was the local prince, who ruled much like a feudal lord and exacted toll in form of produce and services from the farmers on his land; the peasant group then included slaves as well as free men. Today, rigid class lines do not exist in the Thai village, and although arbitrary groups based on economic and prestige categories can be set up, the complex classification (from upper-upper to lower-lower), so popular in recent years among sociologists and anthropologists, would be meaningless to describe a Thai village community. Ownership of land and certain occupational categories (some relatively recent, like the school teacher) can be used to delineate broad social groups within the village society.

Generally, the village headman is at the top of the village social structure, a landowner of some status and a man who has demonstrated leadership qualities. From the standpoint of social prestige and importance, the abbot of the village *wat* will outrank the headman, but although the abbot may possess the highest prestige status of the community, nominally he is regarded as being outside of the community and should be considered separately within the religious framework.

Every village has a group of prosperous farmers who are usually the largest landowners, moderately well-off families, and poor families. Ownership of land is important but not always essential, for in the north a successful sharecropper may be quite well off by village standards; moreover, prestige may be earned by other means than wealth. A poor man may be a highly respected person because he served many years in the temple as a monk, and one of the poorest men of the village may rank well above a rich farmer who has never had any temple service.

The Thai cultural pattern, especially in the Thai village, is noteworthy for its absence of status anxiety.[2] In the old days the peasant accepted the dominant position of the noble or prince of his area without question; today, he accepts the central government representative (the district officer), who has taken over this role. Within his own village the Thai peasant is self-reliant and rarely in sharp competition for status with his fellow villagers. His individual prestige will come from serving in the temple, by being a renowned story-teller, a good farmer, or serving the village community as a leader. He will not scheme or strive for this type of prestige.

THE PHYSICAL HOUSEHOLD

Peasant houses tend to be the same, regardless of the region of the country. The Thai farmhouse is raised on posts some five to six feet off the ground. In regions near rivers, where annual flooding may bring water to a depth of from one to four or more feet into the village, houses are built on taller posts than in the rest of the country. In such areas during the flood season it may be impossible to get from house to house without a canoe. Houses are raised on posts mainly for flood protection, and, in an earlier period, this practice provided protection from marauding animals and thieves. A ladder that can be drawn up into the house at night is still found occasionally, but more often than not at present the stairs are fixed.

The old type of Thai farmhouse consisted of three separate oblong rooms arranged along three sides of a central platform of split bamboo or teakwood planks. A narrow veranda, somewhat lower, skirted the three sides of this central platform. Apparently for ceremonial reasons the floor of the rooms opening off the veranda were slightly higher than the veranda itself. Many of the older teakwood houses of northern villages are of this type. Another common type of village farmhouse is roughly oblong in shape with an outside open veranda running the width of the house in the front. Opening off this veranda are two or three rooms raised slightly above the veranda.

The houses of very poor villagers may be built completely of bamboo and thatch, and may consist of only the veranda, a separate screened-off sleeping room, and, at the rear of the house, a partly open room which is used as a cooking room or kitchen.

The building materials used for village houses vary from bamboo and grass thatch to heavy teakwood, softer woods, and tile. Village houses to a great extent reflect the economic and social status of the owner, as well as regional variations. In the north, particularly in the past, when teak and other hard wood were plentiful and inexpensive, the entire house may have been built of teak (used for beams, posts, and planks) or of a combination of teakwood (for pillars and floors) and plaited bamboo (for walls). Along the rivers and in marshy places throughout Thailand, roofing of overlapping attap palm leaves is very common. If the attap palm is not found in sufficient quantity, thatch is made from the long, broad leaves of a certain kind of jungle grass. Thatch roofs of this type last about three years. In the north, in addition to clay tile roofs, a roof of *tung* leaves (a broad, thick, bastard teak leaf) is found. Regardless of material, roofs are always steep and pointed. A village house, depending on the wealth of the owner and the region, may range from a house made entirely of bamboo with a thatch roof to a completely wooden house roofed with clay tiles. In the old style of farm dwelling of the north, the house is built in two sections with two separate roof trees; in cross-section, the farmhouse seems to consist of two buildings, one larger than the other, placed side by side.

The farmhouses of central Thailand in general are not so substantial as those of the north. There is little hardwood forest left in the Menam Plain, and in the delta region the jungle has long since been turned into rice land. Commercialization of rice farming likewise has made the farmers here dependent upon professional carpenters, and even a bamboo-type house is much more expensive here than in other regions.

Individual house compounds do not differ materially from region to region. The house generally is in the middle of the fenced-off compound. Within the fenced house compound, there will be a vegetable patch, a few fruit trees, a group of coconut palms, a betel palm, various shrubs and flowers, and a clump of banana trees.

A village which is not on a waterway may have wells in some compounds, which several neighbors use, or less often will have wells in all of its compounds. If water is scarce and the village is small, many of the village families may use the well in the temple compound. In the delta region, a farmyard may have a small pond which doubles as a source of water supply and a fish pond for the farmer.

An earth latrine occasionally is found within individual compounds, although these are relatively recent and rare. A granary for rice storage, if the family has rice lands or raises rice on a share-cropping basis, will commonly be found somewhere in the compound. Throughout all of rural Thailand the layout of the house compounds tends to be the same, although a few regional differences will appear. In central Thailand, farmhouse compounds in the low-lying regions, which are deeply flooded during the rainy season, have animal platforms built on tall posts with a graduated incline. On these the buffalo sleep during the flood period. A foot-operated rice mill is almost an inevitable part of each compound, although near Bangkok home-milled rice is giving way to the commercial rice mills, many of which are run by Chinese. Outside of the Bangkok area, the monotonous pounding of the rice mill is still the characteristic sound of village life, from early morning to late at night.

Frequently, a small spirit house stands at the compound entrance; in the country, these are made of bamboo with a thatch roof, and often have a miniature bamboo ladder. Previously, it is reported, every houseyard had one, and today every village will still have a good number of spirit houses.

A small bathing enclosure is found in all house compounds except those along a canal or river. Usually, this does not have a roof, and the walls are made of plaited bamboo, or a thatch of *tung* leaves in the north, and reach only to a person's shoulders.

The open area under the house is utilized in numerous ways: formerly, the loom was kept here, and even though weaving has been given up, many households still have a loom half buried in debris under the house; it is here the pig is tethered and water buffalo stabled; part of the area is a storage place for the plow, harrow, cart, and other farm equipment. In rainy weather, the area becomes a playground for the small children, and often a homemade swing is put up for them.

Each house compound is surrounded by a bamboo fence which not only defines the compound area but also serves to keep stray animals out, and small children in. If there is a vegetable garden, it will be separately fenced to keep chickens and small children out of it.

A farmhouse will have an uneven number of rooms because

an even number is considered unlucky. Ordinarily, there will be a division of the house into three parts or rooms—the open veranda, the sleeping rooms, and the kitchen. Even a crude bamboo shelter of a very poor farmer, seemingly only of one room, follows this arrangement in principle, for a screen or a cloth will be used to curtain off the sleeping portion of the room. A fair sized village house will have a division into three or more rooms. The number of steps of the stairs or ladder and the number of windows and doors is always uneven, for it is held that an even number of steps or apertures will be unlucky and will direct evil spirits to the house.

All village houses have some kind of veranda open at the front: here the meals are eaten, here the family rests during the day, here visitors are entertained, and here the older boys sleep. Often, this veranda will have movable screens or shutters to close off the open front at night. Opening off the veranda are the sleeping rooms and the kitchen area. A large house of the newer style (in which the veranda runs only along the sides of the house front) may be divided into two sections by a center hall off of which two or more sleeping rooms open, one used by the parents and younger children, another by teen-age girls, and, if the house is big enough, a third by the older boys; the kitchen is at the rear of the house. In the older-style house (built in three sections around a central veranda), one of the side sections may be utilized as the kitchen. Usually, part of the kitchen area is built like an open lean-to to allow smoke to escape, for the clay stove or earth fireplace has no chimney, and the floor of the kitchen is built with wide chinks through which garbage can be dropped. Quite often houses have an attic above the main part of the house, where extra pots, mats, and other equipment are kept.

Traditionally, housebuilding has been a coöperative affair, friends and neighbors (often those who also help at planting and harvesting) joining to cut bamboo or trees in the forest, to weave the wall mats, to make the roof thatch, and to erect the house. Today, much of this coöperative building of houses is on the decline, especially in the Bangkok delta plain, where commercial carpenters, usually Chinese, are called in to build the house. Even the building of simple bamboo houses in this region has become commercialized, the farmer often having to buy the bamboo mats for the walls. Elsewhere in rural Thailand, when a farmer builds a substantial house, he must hire carpenters, whether from his own village or outside. It is no longer permitted to cut trees in the forest, so that most of the wood used in house building must be purchased. But a simple bamboo and thatch house, except in the Bangkok delta region, can still be built by the villager and his friends, who go off to the jungle to cut bamboo and attap for thatch, and can erect the house in a day or two. This house-building bee is followed by the traditional housewarming ceremony and a feast to which the neighbors are invited.

Throughout the north, where lumber now is relatively expensive, even a wealthy farmer salvages as much of the old teakwood as he can from his former house when he builds a new one. While the new house is being built, the family may live in temporary quarters underneath the rice granary. As a result of this practice, even new houses look weatherworn. When not enough teakwood can be salvaged, even wealthy farmers must now use cheaper soft woods for sidings and floors; and even if considerable lumber from an old house is used, the cost of a wooden house with a clay tile roof is high by village economic standards. For example, in 1949, the local headman of San Pong, who is one of the wealthiest men of the village, built a new house in which about half the wood was teakwood from his old house. Labor and new materials cost him 9,000 ticals ($450), and the cost would have been much greater if all materials had been new. His house can be taken as representative of a modern dwelling of a wealthy villager, large as modern houses go but only "medium" in comparison to the old, huge teakwood house of the north. Within the past fifty years all wooden houses are smaller because of the increase in cost of materials and the necessity of hiring carpenter labor. On the other hand, it is still possible to build a small bamboo and thatch cottage by coöperative labor at a cost ranging from 100 to 200 ticals ($5 to $10). Most village houses of the north are built today of a combination of wood and bamboo, and average at least 1000 ticals

($50) for materials. Smaller houses, generally of bamboo, are still built largely by coöperative labor; wooden houses are increasingly being built by carpenters, often Chinese from the nearby market town. In San Pong in 1949, a small wooden house costing 6,000 ticals ($300) was built completely by outside carpenter labor for the first time in the village's history. Labor costs for these outside carpenters was 1,200 ticals, or 20 per cent of the total cost. Building costs in the central plain, both for material and labor, are much higher. Even wealthy farmers in this area are content with houses built mainly of bamboo and thatch.

HOUSEHOLD BUDDHA SHELF

Every village house has a Buddha shelf on the veranda at head level, facing the entrance, where offerings of flowers and clusters of the male betel leaf are placed before a small statue of Buddha. The Buddha shelf altar varies a great deal with the economic status and devoutness of the household: a prosperous farm household may have a fine gilt lacquer statue of Buddha, artificial paper flowers, and other offerings on display; a poor household may have only a few sticks of incense and a handful of male betel leaves and flowers on the altar.

These shelves or altars are always on the right-hand side of the veranda as one enters the house, the spot called in the northern areas *hua tirn,* literally, at the head of the veranda. Since village houses often face south, the Buddha shelf is on the east side of the house entrance, but the rule is that it must always be on the right side, and the east position is true only if the house has a southern exposure.

The *hua tirn,* or altar area, is regarded as sacred. Women and small children are forbidden to walk below it; mats or mattresses laid on the floor at night must never be so arranged that the sleeper's feet point toward this shelf. (Peasant superstition also holds that the head, in sleeping, should never face the west, since this is where the sun "dies" and, hence, is synonymous with death, so that mats are aligned in a north-south direction, with the head to the north.) In sitting in the veranda living

House of bamboo and thatch

Old-style teakwood house

Teakwood granary of the north

Outdoor rice mill

room area, great care is taken that the feet do not point toward the Buddha altar. Small children are taught early to show proper respect to this sacred area of the house. However, the members of the family do not pray before this altar or conduct any kind of daily services before it. Very devout families may change the fresh flower and leaf offerings daily, but others may place offerings on the shelf only once a week, or only on the special Buddhist holy days.

Two selected posts or pillars in the main sleeping room also have religious significance, but this is animistic and directed toward the house spirits. These are the "lucky post" (*saw mongkol*) and his mate (*saw nang*). When a Thai farmhouse is built, the owner chooses a pair of posts which are new and free from blemishes, and which have not come from a cemetery or a deserted house compound. The larger of the two posts is designated as the dwelling of the house guardian spirit and is called the "lucky post"; the smaller post is known as his wife. Offerings of betel leaves, green coconuts, young bananas, and sugar cane are tied to the spirit posts at the time of the housewarming so that the spirit will guarantee good harvests, and bring happiness and prosperity to the housedwellers. Offerings to the lucky post and his mate are made only once in the lifetime of the house, at the time of the housewarming ceremonies, although the family will always know which is the lucky post.

In the northern areas, where houses are commonly built with two separate roof trees, there will be two sets of guardian posts designated at the time the house is built. Houses of this nature are in reality two separate sections, one slightly smaller than the other, and in such houses each has its own set of guardian posts.

Special spirit offerings are made also in the kitchen area at the time of the housewarming. Offerings of food, betel, cigarettes, and flowers are placed on the mud stove platform or on the portable clay stove as offerings to "Mother Earth." Bits of food, often make-believe, such as a piece of bamboo held by tiny tongs to represent a roasting fish, a tiny green leaf box of unhusked rice, and a bit of cooked food will be placed on the fireplace. The "Mother Earth" goddess will send luck to the house and will ensure that the new house will always be filled with rice and fish. Again, such offerings to kitchen spirits are made only at the original housewarming period.

HOME FURNISHINGS

There are few furnishings even in well-to-do farm households. Ordinary household furnishings consist of mattresses or mats for sleeping which are kept rolled or folded during the day, mats for sitting on, eating trays, a few pillows, betel boxes, and spittoons. A wealthy farm household may have a cupboard or two, a sewing machine for the women of the household, and other miscellaneous objects. Usually, the only tables and chairs in a village will be in the temple dormitory and the home of the headman. Even the poorest families have a mirror, and well-to-do families have large mirrors prominently displayed. The houses with the biggest and best mirrors are those where there are unmarried girls. Many village houses have cheap colored lithographs of Buddhist scenes with the animal representing the birth year of the individual. A colored lithograph of the boy King Ananda, who died under mysterious circumstances in 1946, is often found, as well as a photograph of Phibun, the present premier. These pictures were printed in great numbers and sold at low prices throughout the countryside before the war. A few ornaments, such as deer horns, or even a deer head molded in plaster, may be found on the walls. Almost every village house will have pasted to the walls of one of the rooms a number of national lottery tickets, for these are bought in large numbers in the rural areas. For safekeeping, these are pasted to the wall of the main sleeping room, where they remain as souvenirs. Families, if they somehow secure a newspaper or magazine, cut out the pictures and paste them on the walls. Village houses do not have closets, a nail or string in the sleeping room being used for hanging clothes. Extra clothing will be kept in cupboards or boxes.

FAMILY ACTIVITIES

The housewife and the girls of the family prepare the family meals. By the time a farm girl is ten years old, she knows how to cook rice and is helping in the preparation of meals. Farm boys also pick up the rudiments of simple cooking by watching and helping the mother. While cooking is not regarded as a man's task, it is something that every Thai peasant man can do if he desires or is forced to do so by necessity. At ceremonial feasts, men may do a large part of the cooking in addition to the hard work of cutting up pork, chopping vegetables, and grating coconuts for the special curries.

Some household tasks fall into a taboo category for men—milling rice (if the housewife is sick and there are no girls in the family, a neighbor woman will be asked to mill the rice), fetching water from the well (boys and men may do this if necessary), cleaning up after meals and washing of dishes. Ordinarily, women do the laundry for the household, but often boys and men wash their heavy work clothing themselves, and may also wash their own shirts and shorts, and are allowed to do the ironing. One very strong taboo exists regarding a man's washing of women's clothes, specifically the *pasin* skirt, which, because it might be contaminated by menstrual blood, is considered unclean and dangerous to a male.

The entire family lives and works as a unit, eating their meals and working in the fields together. All members of the family do some work. Small children help the mother around the house and act as nursemaids to younger siblings. Old people engage in many minor activities around the household, many of a handicraft nature, and look after the young children of the household. By the time a villager is fifteen years old, he will be carrying on full time adult work alongside the parent.

EATING MEALS

The number of meals taken by the Thai peasant varies. In the north and northeast, three meals a day are eaten at much the same time American meals take place. The peasant of central and south Thailand eats only two major meals a day, one between 7:00 and 8:00 in the morning, the other at about 5:30 in the afternoon. Occasionally, a cold snack may be taken around noon. While a good deal of "snacking" goes on during the day among the urban Thai, the eating of snacks is not as common among the villagers, largely because the itinerant snack peddler ordinarily is not available in the country regions. In the urbanized peasant area around Bangkok, the network of canals and waterways does provide a means by which snack peddlers can reach into the villages, and here in the delta region, the peasant eats more snacks than elsewhere in the country.

The morning meal is not started until rice from the main pot has been presented to the monks. In very devout Buddhist families a small offering of steamed rice is also placed on the Buddha shelf before breakfast, and in the areas where spirit worship is still important, a similar morning food offering may be placed in the spirit house in the house compound. Much of this daily food offering to the house spirit has died out in the peasant area.

The standard dish for all meals is curry and rice, the curry commonly being made of dried or fresh fish, and, on special occasions, of pork, chicken, duck, or wild birds. No dessert is taken; fruit, if available, is eaten between meals, as are sweetmeats. Water is never taken with meals. The family member, after finishing a meal, will, if he desires, drink a dipper of water from the water jar kept in the kitchen.

The family sits in a circle on the floor around the main rice pot and dishes of curry and vegetables. Meals may be eaten in the kitchen, but if the family is large, the veranda is used. Children eat with the family unless there are special guests; then they eat by themselves in the kitchen. Each family member has a special bowl in which he places his rice and curry, and from which he eats with his fingers, although spoons are used for soups and watery curries. Bowls used today are of cheap porcelain, though on special occasions a wealthy family may bring forth a silver bowl for the use of an honored guest. Cheap Chinese-style porcelain spoons or homemade wooden or coconut shell spoons are used to dip the curry from the main pot and for dishing out the rice. After the meal, the older members of the family may chew betel or smoke a homemade cheroot.

In northern Thailand, a special round tray table with seven carved legs standing about twelve to fifteen inches in height and about two feet in diameter is used for eating. The pot of rice, curry bowls, and other dishes are placed on this tray table and the family sits cross-legged around it. If the family is large, several of these tray tables will be used.

Although curry and rice form the staple dish of all Thai peasants, ingredients used in the curry as well as types of vegetables vary according to the season. Fish, fresh or dried, is used all year around. Meat and fowl are found as curry ingredients at planting and harvest times when special food is prepared for the cooperative work parties, at funerals, or on festive occasions. Usually, eggs are collected and sold in the markets by the women rather than being eaten at home.

During the planting and harrowing in June and July, when the fields are flooded, women and girls splash through the mud and water collecting pollywogs and small fish from which a curry is made. Later, the irrigation canals and ditches, as well as the flooded paddy fields, provide innumerable fresh fish.

Rice crabs, a great pest to the young rice plants, are collected by women and girls in large numbers. When the crabs are very small, they are ground into a crab paste which forms an integral part of many peasant curry dishes. As they grow larger, they are boiled and used with vegetables in curry. Common in the flooded rice fields in central Thailand is a small freshwater shrimp which is made into a shrimp paste sold in markets all over rural Thailand and which is used in almost every curry that is made by the farm women of the central plains.

At harvest time, fat frogs are collected, gutted, and roasted over hot coals. Another seasonal curry food found in large quantity in the flooded rice fields is an oysterlike clam.

Many of the common insect pests of the rice fields are utilized as delicacy foods by the thrifty peasant. The large rice grasshopper which lives on the rice leaves is caught, its wings and legs removed, and it is covered with salt and fried. Grubs of various species of ants are baked and eaten as are other insect larva.

PERSONAL HABITS

The Thai peasant is very clean in his personal habits, bathing daily and perhaps several times a day during hot weather. Where villages are located on rivers or canals, bathing twice a day is common. In some areas, as in certain parts of the Korat region where water is very scarce, this daily bath may have to be forgone during the dry season, but this is exceptional in Thai rural life. Most Thai farmhouses not directly on a river or waterway have a small bathing enclosure in the yard near the well. Bathing by both sexes is done without completely disrobing. Women use their *pasin* skirts as a bathing sarong, and men keep a bathing cloth wrapped around their thighs. After the bath is completed, the dry garments are slipped on and the wet bathing cloth dropped to the ground. So deeply ingrained by late childhood is this notion of bodily modesty, that an individual does not disrobe completely even when alone in the bathing enclosure. This modesty pattern also permits individuals of both sexes to bathe together in groups in the rivers and waterways.

Human evacuation is done away from the house compound unless a latrine is in the yard. If there are flowing irrigation ditches or waterways running through the village, latrines may be built overhanging them. Often there is no latrine, villagers simply squatting in a secluded spot at the edge of a waterway, or an unused part of the village. Earth latrines are not common; they are found usually only in the compounds of the village headman, the village doctor, the village school teacher, and other progessive-minded villagers. The village study of San Pong in the north revealed only seven pit latrines and three irrigation-ditch latrines for a village of 108 households. Approximately 90 per cent of the village families used either the open irrigation ditches or an unused section of the village. Yet, village sanitation was good, for the irrigation ditch flows continually and villagers did not use this ditch water for cooking or drinking. Children two to four years old use the area near the door stoop as a toilet. Since this door stoop area is constantly drained by splashing of water by family members washing their feet before entering the house, it does not become polluted.

Shoes are not worn in the house, and the feet are always washed at the door stoop. One of the first lessons a village child learns is to rinse his feet before entering the house. The floor of the ordinary village house, whether it be of split bamboo or polished teakwood, is kept clean, bits of food and refuse being carefully swept out of the house or through the chinks in the floor to the ground below where chickens and other fowl keep the ground clean. The floor of the kitchen area of the village house cannot be kept as spotlessly clean as the rest of the house, for cooking is done on an earthen platform or an open stove made of clay set directly on the floor. Cutting and chopping of food is done by the housewife on chopping boards that rest on the floor. The open fireplace or stove smokes up the kitchen area, often giving a misleading appearance of neglect to this area.

In villages situated on higher ground than the surrounding fields, the house site in the compound is chosen carefully for drainage, and while water may drain through the kitchen floor or from the door stoop, the ground space beneath the Thai farmhouse does not become a stagnant area. When pigs are kept tethered or penned beneath a section of the house, the pen area is changed frequently and is not the odorous spot that might be imagined.

The clean, well-drained village house compounds are in sharp contrast to the mud and filth of the crowded slum quarters of the city. Early writers observing these slum conditions in and around the Bangkok area often made the mistake of attributing the same lack of cleanliness in living conditions to the Thai farmer.

CLOTHING AND ADORNMENT

A generation ago both little boys' and girls' heads were shaven until they were four or five years of age. Then a lock of hair at the top of the head was allowed to grow out, which, in the upper class of the town, was cut off ceremoniously at puberty in the top-knot ceremony. Since the peasants rarely practiced the top-knot ceremony, in previous generations farm children at an early age adopted the prevailing hair style of the adults of the region. In lower Thailand this was the short brushlike haircut for both male and female, still to be seen on the older men and women. In the north, little girls put up their hair in a knot at the back of the head similar to the style used by the mother, while little boys wore the short brushlike cut.

Today, as the peasant girl reaches her teens, she lets her hair grow to semi-shoulder length, at which time she gets a permanent wave at the nearby market town. Settling down as a married woman, she adopts the hair style of the mature woman of the community. In the northern areas, this is still, for the older women, long hair fixed in a knot at the back of the head, but young married farm women of today are keeping their short hair styles. The short, bristly manlike haircut of the central Thai peasant woman of the past, although still worn by the older women, is fast giving way to a more westernized bob. The young married peasant woman here and elsewhere in Thailand has adopted a style that is not dissimilar to the present-day hair style of American women.

Today even the everyday clothing of the villager tends to be western in design, if not in manufacture. Some of the older villagers of both sexes of the central and southern regions may still wear the *panung,* the Siamese version of the Indian dhoti, which is a loose sarong whose ends are tucked between the legs and fastened at the waist in the rear, but the use of this old garment is fading fast. Village women all over Thailand have adopted the skirtlike *pasin* from the north, and men and boys wear Western-type shorts, trousers, and shirts. These are purchased from the stalls of Chinese merchants in the nearby market town. Men wear Western-type underwear consisting of a singlet and shorts. One old article of clothing that still persists for the men is a bathing cloth. This bathing cloth is a versatile piece of clothing, consisting of a narrow piece of cloth 5½ feet long by 27 inches wide, made in a variety of colors in large alternating checks. This cloth is wrapped around the waist, and serves as a sarong which village men wear over their undershorts in the privacy of their homes, and it is used in the same manner for bathing. With the ends pulled tight between the legs and buttocks and tucked in at the waist, it serves as a loin cloth for working in the fields or when fishing. It is used as a towel, a turban, and can be twisted to form an emergency rope for leading water buffalo and other animals if necessity should arise.

In northern Thailand loose baggy trousers of Shan origin

still are worn by the older men. Men wear hats both of local make and style as well as Western-type hats. For field work local-style sun and rain straw hats are used, but for wear to the temple, to the market town and to festivals, the Western-type hat made of straw or cheap felt, which is made either locally by Chinese factories or imported from Singapore or Hongkong, is found. Becoming fashionable and popular today as a dress hat for Thai peasant men is a European sunhelmet made of waterproof cardboard.

Villagers have canvas sneakers which wealthy farmers may wear even in the fields during the dry season. These cheap sneakers are imported from Hongkong or Singapore by the hundreds of thousands every year and are sold in every market stall in Thailand. Leading villagers such as the headman, village doctor, school teachers, and wealthy farmers may own a pair of leather shoes which are worn for very special occasions.

All villagers go barefoot about the house. Homemade wooden clogs may be worn around the muddy compound, but these are never worn in the house. Open sandals made of rubber or leather occasionally are worn, but these are more popular with the women than the men.

Village women have not adopted Western-style clothing to the same extent. The basic costume of the peasant woman is the *pasin* skirt. This is a piece of cloth sewn in a tube and folded at the waist and held in place by a belt. The *pasin*, once the identifying dress of the northern peasant woman, has been adopted all over rural Thailand. A European-type blouse may be worn on special occasions, but for everyday wear a bodice like a blouse without sleeves worn with the *pasin* is the common attire for women. European-type dresses may be found at times among the young unmarried women of the village, but this is a special costume, for the blouse and skirt can be called the national costume of the women of Thailand. Some regional variations are still found. In the north the *pasin* skirt for the older women is colored and patterned distinctively from district to district, but instead of being woven on the home loom, these special district *pasins* are made commercially in the provincial capital by Chinese weaving shops. Except for the older women of the north, most of the *pasins* of the peasant women are of brightly colored or black cloth, imported from Japan, India, England, or the United States.

The wearing of Western-style hats by all women of Thailand was ordered by Premier Phibun during World War II, and every Thai farm woman had to buy a hat, usually a cheap felt or straw model, locally made or imported by the Chinese. This forced wearing of a Western-type hat whenever a woman appeared in public met with great popular disfavor and ridicule, and the order was later dropped. Everywhere in the country regions a few of these wartime Western-style hats still remain, and can be seen at times worn by the women as sun hats when they are working in the fields. For field work the local sunshade hat is preferred. Village girls wear these local sun or rain hats in the fields, but few of them would consider wearing them to the market town as their mothers may do. Instead, the girls and young women wear a brightly colored kerchief over their heads much in the same way that a teen-age or college girl does in America. Some of the teen-age village girls also wear a bright kerchief for working in the fields, although usually a sun hat is worn over the bright modern kerchief.

Certain of the old customs of dress and personal adornment have changed drastically in the past generation. Ear piercing, once a common experience for all little girls throughout rural Thailand, is a custom that is fast dying out. Previously, a girl's ears were pierced by the mother, using a needle and a piece of thread, during the first month of the baby's life. The thread was pulled back and forth frequently to keep the hole open, and after it had healed, a tiny silver ear stud or earring was placed in the infant's ear. If, for some reason, this piercing was not done during the first month, at the age of five or six years the ear lobe was punctured gradually by exerting pressure over a period of days with a ring-like piece of metal.

At the present time, if a village girl does not have her ears pierced by the time she is six, in all probability it will never be done. Probably not more than a quarter of the village women of this generation have pierced ears. The village study of San Pong in the north, where ear piercing previously was universal for women, revealed that out of 234 village women of all ages, only 54 had their ears pierced, and of this group 50 were above the age of twenty-five. Out of approximately 120 females below the age of twenty-five, only 5 had pierced ears, and only half of the women between the ages of twenty-five and fifty had their ear lobes pierced. Above the age of fifty, all of the village women had pierced ears. Similar results were observed for the other 10 villages in this northern commune. Since the custom of ear piercing seems to have been stronger in the north than elsewhere in Thailand, it can be seen that this custom is rapidly disappearing.

A generation ago, the holes in the lobes were increased by inserting ear lugs of graduated size, so that an opening of more than half an inch was not uncommon. Village women often stuck a cheroot in the earlobe when working in the fields. This is rarely seen today, and where ear piercing is still practiced, only a tiny hole, just large enough for a thin silver wire to be pushed through the opening, is made.

Even boys of the northern areas previously had their ear lobes pierced, but this custom for the men died out about fifty years ago, and only village men above the age of sixty have pierced ears.

Tattooing on the thighs and belly, once a common procedure for all northern males, has almost completely disappeared within the past generation. Only village men above the age of forty-five possess this specialized tattooing, and those that have the traditional designs are well above fifty-five.

Betel chewing, once a universal custom among Thai peasants, is beginning to show signs of decline. Most villagers over the age of thirty-five still chew betel, although there are a few exceptions. Below this age very few modern villagers use betel. The younger villagers today very definitely have been indoctrinated at school against betel chewing, and in all likelihood many of the present school generation will not turn to it. Observers of Siamese life writing fifty years ago, all remark on the widespread betel chewing among the young and old, noting that the little girls, particularly, began to chew betel nut before their top-knots were cut at the age of twelve or thirteen. It would be almost impossible to find a child of this age chewing betel today in rural Thailand. School and health authorities frown on the custom, and during World War II, the Thai government went to the extreme of forbidding people to chew betel, a regulation which was ignored by the habitual chewers and finally was quietly dropped by the officials.

In addition to its stimulating qualities, betel stains the mouth and lips deep red, and in time, covers the teeth with a reddish-black enamellike coating. The Thai peasant of the past had a mouthful of black teeth, and a gleaming white smile in the old days was, to a certain extent, a mark of depravity. This attitude is now gone completely, and even habitual betel users of the middle age groups, men and women in the early forties, do not look upon black teeth any longer as a mark of beauty. Betel chewers of this age level, particularly women, will clean their teeth with leaves after a betel chew to prevent the black discoloration.

The use of betel is still very important in the daily life of the older villagers, not only as a habit but as a social custom as well. Anywhere in rural Thailand, the first mark of hospitality is to offer an older guest a tray of betel ingredients. The use of betel in some form or other has strong ritual associations: offerings to the spirits must always include betel-chew ingredients; only leaves from the male betel palm can be used for making offerings to Buddha.

Peasants say that while there is no particular time for a person to start chewing betel, generally, if he does so, it will be around the age of thirty to thirty-five. Since this is the period when a woman has had several children in quick succession and when men have been working in the fields for fifteen years or more, the loss of youthful vigor may have had something to do with adopting regular betel chewing as a habit at this time.

One final additional occupant of a farm household might be mentioned. A family may keep a dog or cat for a pet. In the isolated farmhouse area of the Bangkok delta region, dogs are kept as watchdogs. The north has a local chowlike species of dog, and here, if a villager has a dog, it is invariably a pet, sleeping in the house and having its own dish and pan of drinking water. The stray pariah dog so common in the streets of Bangkok or in the large market town is not found in village life. Accounts of early travelers in Thailand which describe packs of pariah dogs in villages either are based on the writers' Bangkok observations erroneously transferred to the village, or the pattern has changed considerably in the past fifty years.

Cats are kept to serve as mice catchers around the rice granaries and as pets. Unlike the farmyard cat of American farms, the cat, in the northern villages at least, is a household pet, living in the house.

3 Life History of the Individual

As in all cultures, the life of the individual in Thai peasant society is marked by a series of important crises: birth, maturity, marriage, rearing a family, old age, and death. In addition to these, all Thai males also attend primary school, and some serve as novices or monks in the *wat* and as conscripts in the military, and many become heads of households. Thai village women also attend primary school and may if they are widowed become heads of households; religious and military careers are not open to them.

BIRTH

The Thai villager, who is apt to talk freely and broadly about sex, has sexual intercourse as secretly as possible, always at night when small children of the household are asleep. The Thai reckon a person's age from the time of his conception rather than from the day he is born. Children are wanted and have a high position in the peasant's cultural and economic values, and attempts to prevent conception are rare. Village families in modern Thailand, however, are not large: surveys in the 1930's showed an average family size of five members,[1] and recent studies of Thai villages reveal that the size of the family has not changed appreciably since then. In north Thailand, the average family has about five members,[2] and in central Thailand about five and a half members, with ordinarily only two children younger than fourteen in each household.[3] Compared with the peasantry of other countries of Asia, Thai village families have a remarkably small number of children, a situation brought about by a relatively low fertility rate which unquestionably is linked with health and nutritional patterns, and a high infant-mortality rate. Deliberate abortion is not common in rural Thailand even though methods to induce it are known. Specific information about abortion is hard to obtain in any peasant area, but it may be assumed that since birth control is not practiced, any deliberate limitation of family size must be in the hands of women, and that abortion is practiced occasionally. Thai women, particularly midwives, know the abortifacient value of certain local drugs, especially quinine, which is used for this purpose throughout southeast Asia. In north and northeast Thailand, where malaria is an endemic recurrent disease, continual dosage of quinine may well be the cause of some unintentional miscarriages. Infanticide is so unthinkable by Thai Buddhist standards that anyone who committed it would be judged insane. The high cultural value attached to bearing children is shown by the belief that sterility is sinful, since a sterile woman has not been blessed by Buddha.

Almost always a child comes in the first year of marriage. A pregnant woman does not follow any special pattern of behavior, has no food taboos, and carries on her ordinary household duties until she is ready to give birth. A village woman bears her children at home, lying on a mat or mattress on the floor of the sleeping room or in a small screened-off portion of one of the main rooms. She is attended by a midwife who has

---

[1] For notes to chapter 3 see pages 215–216.

had no modern medical training, sometimes also by the older women of the household, and if the birth is labored perhaps by the village "doctor," who has been given the rudiments of medical training by the district health officer. But the assistance of a male at childbirth is not customary and occurs only when the birth is delayed and even then only in urbanized regions where emphasis on the use of semi-government officials in health matters has been drummed into the villagers. When the baby is born, the midwife cuts the umbilical cord with a sharp bamboo knife, ties the cord close to the infant's body, sponges him, and wraps him in swaddling clothes.

Many of the charms and spells formerly used to guard mother and child from evil spirits have been abandoned, but it is still customary in many villages for the midwife to stamp two or three times on the floor as soon as the child is born. Today, this custom is explained as being necessary to waken the baby so that he will not be so frightened by noises later, but earlier accounts[4] state that this was done partly to announce to spirits that a child was about to enter the family, and if the spirits wished to claim him as theirs, they must do so at once or give up any future claim on the child's soul. Another widespread custom was to string a cord, which had been given protective powers by the spirit doctor, around the birth area to ward off evil spirits.

Formerly, a Thai mother was expected to *yoo fai* (stay by the fire) after birth, a widespread custom in ancient southeast Asia. In central Thailand, after the birth of her first child, the mother lay for thirty days on a mat surrounded by hot charcoal fires in portable pot stoves, and for at least fifteen days after the birth of each other child. In south Thailand, only one stove was used, placed on one side of the mother to act as a stomach warmer, and in north Thailand the custom was never so widespread as in the central area; however, the hold this custom once had in Thailand was demonstrated by the unsuccessful attempt of King Mongkut to stamp it out among his royal wives. Within the past thirty years "roasting" has been practically swept away except in isolated villages of central Thailand, and even there the custom now requires only that a woman lie next to the fireplace or a portable stove for a day or two. The mother rests for several weeks or a month, much of the time in bed, before resuming active chores—a period called *yoo deun* (literally, "month's rest" or "month's stay") in north Thailand—during this period she drinks boiled water, eats only soft foods, and takes herb potions.

The placenta is regarded as "unclean" and is also considered part of the child, through which an evil spirit may gain possession of his soul; therefore, immediately after birth the midwife or the father of the child must bury the placenta. A favorite burying place is beneath the house ladder or stairs, for this is a place that evil spirits fear because it has become "unclean" by contact with the skirts of menstruating women and because it is unlucky for an evil spirit on account of the uneven number of steps.

EARLY CHILDHOOD

The baby, once he has been washed and wrapped by the midwife, is placed in a low tublike bamboo basket, where he spends his first month, being taken out only to be fed and cleaned. In former days, and still often today, a "sacred" thread was wound around this basket to keep off evil spirits. When he is a month old, he is put in a wooden or bamboo-slat cradle which hangs from the ceiling beams on ropes, and which can be swung by an attached string; he sleeps in this cradle until he grows too big for it, and often passes many hours awake in it as well, when he is frequently swung by his mother or some other member of the household.

Thai babies are nursed whenever they cry, the mother sitting on the floor and cradling the baby in her arms and lap. Like other rural women of southeast Asia, the Thai peasant mother does not consider her milk sufficient food for her baby, and when the child is three months old (six months in north Thailand), she begins to supplement breast feeding with bits of boiled rice and bananas which she mashes in her mouth. When the child is ten or eleven months old, he is fed mashed fish as well. Most Thai children are weaned by the end of their second year, but some are nursed into their third year if their mothers have not borne another child. Weaning is done gradually, and mothers frequently quiet an older child by letting him nurse for a short time even if she is nursing another baby. As a result the child does not feel cheated of his mother's breast, and little sibling rivalry is evident among Thai children. Children two years old are allowed to play freely with a new baby, and it is common in Thailand to see a child of two sitting on his mother's lap and helping hold a baby who is nursing.

A Thai baby is fondled a great deal by his mother and by other members of his family, all of whom share in taking care of him. He is fed his supplementary diet by his father, grandparents, older brothers and sisters, as well as by his mother; he is often taken out of his cradle and held and fondled by some member of the family. When he is nine months old, he is carried about everywhere straddled on the hips of an older brother or sister. One of the most frequent sights in rural Thailand is that of a baby being carried in this fashion by a small boy or girl. This constant fondling, jiggling, and carrying helps to strengthen his back and leg muscles, and most Thai babies develop excellent motor coördination at a very early age and soon learn to balance themselves on the unstable bamboo floors and to crawl up and down the ladder or stairs of the house. Although no particular emphasis is put on forcing him to walk, the baby is coached by members of his family, who hold him by his arms and around his body while he takes his first steps; by the time he is six or seven months old, a Thai baby can stand only partly supported, and it is not unusual for him at eight months to take a few steps supported by some older member of the household. By their twelfth or fourteenth month most Thai babies are walking without aid. Babies who live along waterways also learn to swim at an early age, although the frequent reports that Thai mothers throw a baby who is only a few months old into the water with a pair of water wings to teach him to swim are unfounded: Thai mothers teach their children to swim gradually and under constant supervision, but not until a baby is well over a year old and walking is he able to swim.

Children are not given proper names at birth, and often not until they are several months old. In north Thailand, a baby is called *noi* (little one) until he is named; boy babies are *ai noi* (mister little one) and girl babies are *ee noi* (miss little one). Babies in central Thailand are called by diminutive terms such as "little pig," "little rat," or "little mouse" until they are named, and may be called by this baby name by close relatives until they reach maturity. In earlier times, parents conferred with the local soothsayer, who drew up a horoscope for the baby and selected a suitable and auspicious name. Today, many Thai parents take their children to the *wat*, where the abbot selects an auspicious name from a book containing elaborate charts based on lunar calculations and the forty-four Thai characters: he notes the hour, day, month, and year of birth, and then studies the charts to find a lucky character. The child is given a name beginning with this character. Many younger parents decide on their child's name themselves, although they are careful that the name be auspicious. Naming a child is important, not only for the family, but for the village; he is now registered in the headman's records and officially recognized as a member of the community. Children are often named on an alliterative basis, that is, all siblings' names begin with the same syllable, often the syllable with which a parent's name begins; but this practice appears to be more common in urban Bangkok than in the villages. An individual's being given two first names also appears to be more common in urban regions, where upon reaching maturity he may choose another first name for himself.

Most of the traditional first-year ceremonies have passed out of usage among the present generation. Once-important rites, such as the ceremonial shaving of the head at four weeks of age and the ceremonies of name-giving, are no longer practiced, even among the urban upper class and the nobility. In 1952, when some of these ancient Brahmin rites were reintroduced for the infant crown prince, Thai newspapers carried articles by scholars to explain them to the present generation.

Babies in rural Thailand are toilet-trained gradually and without punishment. Thai infants go naked in the house or wear only a shirt, so that there is no problem of soiled diapers and diaper irritation. The messes they make on the floor or in somebody's lap are wiped up without fuss or scolding. Babies are accustomed to going outside for their bowel movements by being taken there, but no special point is made of toilet habits until the child can walk and talk. They are first taught to use the shallow ditch under the platform at the foot of the steps of the house; a child eighteen months old begins to go there by himself, and by the time he is two years old he goes to the toilet without help. Later, he is taught to use the regular family latrine, which may be the canal or an earth latrine. At three a Thai child is usually entirely toilet-trained.

The popular belief that Thai children are never punished has no basis in fact. Up to two years of age a baby is petted and appeased even when he is deliberately petulant. By then, there is usually a new baby, and although the older child still receives a great deal of attention, he must adjust to the fact that he is no longer the baby of the family. Ordinarily this adjustment is made with a minimum of difficulty. A child three or four years old begins to be punished for deliberate naughty acts, and although he is never subject to a great amount of corporal punishment, he may be spanked lightly on his buttocks or shoulders if verbal chastisement does not work, and may even be whipped lightly with a stick if he is excessively disobedient and unruly. Verbal chastisement is usually sufficient, and often Thai parents pretend to repudiate a naughty child, saying they found him floating in the canal or bought him from an Indian or one of the hill tribes. A Thai child learns early in life to respect his elders and to accept his place in the family hierarchy. He also learns very early to make the gesture of obeisance—palms together before the face—for his mother or some other family member places his hands in this position so often that by the time he is walking and beginning to talk, he makes the gesture automatically. Later, he is taught the proper degrees of obeisance—clasped palms raised to the forehead for monks and the Buddha, to the nose for elders of the village.

Village children do not wear clothes until they are two and a half or three years old, although they wear a shirt or dress when they are taken to the *wat*. Boys run naked around the house and yard until they are five or six, when they start to wear Western-style shorts. Girls are clothed at an earlier age; in central Thailand they wear a little heart-shaped shield of silver mesh called a *chaping*, which serves as loin cloth and bangle combined. The *chaping* is not worn in north Thailand. Girls three years old begin to wear the *pasin*, a saronglike skirt. Children's hair is clipped or shaved until their second year; boys of three and older wear a G.I. haircut; girls' hair is allowed to grow out between their second and third year, and then is trimmed into a short bob until their early teens.

The village child learns about sex early, for he sleeps in the same room with his parents until he is ten or twelve years old. Children often play with themselves, and boys are not punished for playing with their genitals, although if they continue to do this as they grow older, they are ridiculed by their playmates. Sex play between boys and girls is rare, for children segregate into their own sex groups at an early age and keep to this segregation until their early teens.

Until his third or fourth year, a Thai child stays completely with his family and plays in the house compound; thereafter, he begins to play with other children of his age in the village—often there are only two or three children of the same age in a small village—and gradually to roam freely throughout the village. Boys plow make-believe fields, fly kites, shoot arrows, or play at blindman's buff; girls nurse wooden dolls, make mudpies to sell in make-believe markets, and cook meals of weeds in toy clay pots. In general, childhood is a carefree, happy time, and children have no regular chores except caring for their baby brothers and sisters (and they do not look upon this as a chore, for the infant is to them simply another plaything) until they are seven or eight years old. At this age, girls must begin to help with household chores, and boys must begin such tasks as watching the family buffalo, which is usually a chore they can do in groups while playing games or swimming in the canal.

SCHOOL

A compulsory national primary school system came into existence in 1921, but did not become widespread in the rural areas until after the 1932 revolution. According to law, a child is expected to be enrolled at the age of eight and must attend school until he is fifteen, or has completed the required four-year primary course. Many of the government's primary schools are located within the *wat* compound, and since not every village has a school, children of three or four small villages may attend a centrally located school. Increasingly in recent years, the central government has built village schools on public land near the main thoroughfare. The school buildings range from crude open-air structures to standardized wooden buildings designed by the Ministry of Education, and since these schools operate under tremendous financial handicaps, with the government supplying only the teachers' salaries and a minimum of equipment, most of them leave much to be desired. Children's desks and benches are apt to be homemade, and classrooms frequently are not partitioned off. In spite of all these shortcomings, the compulsory primary school has had tremendous effects on the present generation. These effects are analyzed in detail in chapter vi.

School opens at 8:45 with a flag-raising ceremony in the school yard, after which the children file into the school building and go to their several classes—which often may be in the same room. Classes last anywhere from thirty minutes to an hour, depending on the subject taught; a lunch or rest period is from 11:00 to 12:00; and classes resume until 3:00. Unless the school is in his own village, a child does not go home for lunch. Children do not bring lunches, but usually eat after reaching home in the early afternoon. The noon hour is used for playing. Occasionally, a village woman will sell snacks during the noon hour, but most children have no money to buy them.

A child must stay in the beginner's class until he has learned to read and write, and knows the rudiments of arithmetic; then he passes into the first of the four classes or standards (*pratomes*), which are all much the same, except that subject matter becomes more advanced and training more intensive. The child is taught the rudiments of ethics, arithmetic, reading, penmanship, health and sanitation, geography of Thailand, composition, spelling, craftsmanship, and agriculture. Children are promoted only when they pass a standardized government examination for their standard or class, and some children may repeat the beginner's section or the first standard two or three years. As a result, there is great discrepancy in the ages of children in the same standard. The beginner's class may have children eight to fourteen years old, both because some children repeat the class and because others are not enrolled until their tenth or twelfth year.

The village school operates the year round on a three-term basis which is correlated with the planting and harvest seasons and which therefore varies from region to region and even in different parts of the same region, especially in north Thailand, where irrigation water may reach different areas of a district at slightly different times. A "planting" vacation of from one month to six weeks comes during the rainy season, when fields are plowed and rice is planted, because children are needed at home during this period, and often the schoolteacher, who is a young villager himself, has to help his parents in the fields during this vacation. At harvest time there is another vacation of a month to six weeks. School is not held on the weekly Buddhist holy day (*Wan Pra*), on the first of every month (when all village school teachers meet at the district office to collect their pay and attend a teachers' meeting), on national holidays, and on the frequent special holidays declared during the year by the government. School children are expected to participate in the special ceremonies or services that frequently are held at the district office on national holidays, and classes from outlying districts as far away as five to eight kilometers march to the district seat on these days to attend the exercises.

ADOLESCENCE

An important ceremony of earlier Thailand was the cutting of the top-knot to mark the transition from childhood to adolescence, but this has disappeared completely, and even in former days it was practiced mainly by the townspeople and nobility and seldom by the peasants. For a village boy, entering of the *wat* as a novice formally marks his departure from childhood. Not all boys become novices, nor does every male become a Buddhist monk, as has commonly been reported. Recent village studies of north Thailand show that only 46 per cent of the males of the villages studied had temple association either as novice or monk.⁵ Studies in central Thailand also show that a high proportion of adult males never have this important temple association.⁶ But whether a male goes through the temple service or not, the experience is important for all of them, for it represents the ideal that every male should follow, and even those who do not go through the experience find they are affected by the ideal. A man who follows this ideal acquires in later life certain privileges the nonfollower will never acquire no matter how rich or respected he may become.

For a village girl, entry into adolescence and adulthood comes in more gradual and less marked stages, but certain significant transitional steps can be observed: being allowed to mill rice with a girl friend at night in the compound, to go by herself to the early morning market in a neighboring village or market town, to have a permanent wave when she is fifteen or sixteen, and to receive suitors unchaperoned on the veranda of her parents' house.

Traditionally, a girl's entry into adult status could be said to be marked by the birth of her first child; for at this time, she underwent the rigorous "roasting" which literally aged her fifteen or twenty years. Though this "roasting" custom has been wiped out, the birth of the first child still may be said to mark the girl's real entry into adult responsibility. Often it is not until the first child is born that a young couple set up housekeeping by themselves; before this, even a married girl is still part of her family's household and is under the supervision of her mother. Even if a young couple do not leave the girl's parents' home after the birth of their first child, the girl nevertheless now takes the status of mother and her role within the household changes correspondingly. Her mother treats her more as an equal and she can behave with a freedom that formerly would have been frowned upon.

A few village girls aspire to become schoolteachers, and today roughly one-quarter of all village primary schoolteachers are young women, but at most only one or two girls from a village can expect to gain this position. Those who do leave the teaching field after marriage, for keeping house, raising a family, and helping in the fields is a full time job for any young woman.

Modern Thai girls are not isolated in their villages; market towns bring them into contact with the outside world, particularly with Western fashions, and except in very remote villages, there is scarcely a girl above sixteen years of age today who does not have, or does not aspire to have, a permanent wave, and at least one Western-style dress for festive occasions. Her wearing rouge, powder, and lipstick has long since been accepted by the elders of the family. The lovesick youth of a generation ago sighed and likened his beloved at the village well to the morning star shining on the horizon; today, the young village lover yearns to be reborn as rouge or powder so that he may always caress his sweetheart's fragrant cheeks.

CONSCRIPTION

Every able-bodied man in Thailand must register for military service at the age of eighteen, and at twenty-one must report to his district office for a physical examination to determine whether he is fit for conscription. Standards of physical fitness are simple: a height of more than 160 cm., a chest expansion of at least 87 cm., good eyesight, and an absence of obvious physical defects. Most Thai youths pass the examination. Conscription is held once a year, at a date (usually in April) determined by the governor and the military commander of each province, and each district must supply a specified number of conscripts—usually a quota much smaller than the number of available males. For example, in 1949 the small district of Mae Rim in Chiangmai province had 242 eligible conscripts, but its quota was only nineteen. Because of these relatively low quotas, districts may call for volunteers (although a drawing of numbers is often necessary), usually only one or two men from a village are called the same year, and if a man is not recruited during his twenty-first year he may escape military service altogether. In San Pong, for instance, only two of thirty-two eligible males between the ages of twenty-one and twenty-four were conscripted, and from 1926 to 1946 this village was not obliged to send any men to the service. Figures for conscripts from ten villages around San Pong were proportionately small.[7]

The term of peace-time military service is two years, and recruits may choose the army, navy, or police. Most Thai youths choose to serve in the army, where base pay is 112 to 118 ticals a month for privates, and 225 to 245 ticals a month for lance corporals and corporals (although few recruits from the villages earn promotion to corporalcy during their two-year training period). Army recruits are trained at barracks in the provincial capitals. Most village youths, unless they have served as novices in the temple, have been out of school six or seven years when they are recruited and must be taught again to read and write. Vocational training is also given to recruits, and magazines and newspapers are available to them during their brief periods of leisure.

Formerly, military service—*taharn*—was a dreaded duty in Thailand, which many youths tried to dodge by running away from their villages during recruiting periods. But reforms since 1903 in the conscription service and the emphasis on nationalism in primary schools have gradually changed the attitude of Thai youths.

For many Thai youths, the period of military service is the only time they are away from their native districts and in contact with metropolitan life—with such novelties, for example, as radios, sidewalk cafes, and motion pictures. During this period the recruits lose their greenness as country boys, and the experiences they recount when they are home on leave have a great effect on the behavior of their village age mates. At the end of their training period, the recruits return to their villages and soon resume the rural routine, but they are never again as insular as the men in the village who have not experienced military service.

COURTSHIP AND MARRIAGE

Villagers marry young. A girl is considered marriageable at sixteen, and a man at twenty, but most girls marry between the ages of eighteen and twenty-one, or sometimes not until their later twenties if their families are poor and need them at home, and boys between the ages of twenty and twenty-four. The spinster or bachelor is rare, and is likely to be a physical or mental misfit. The Thai village youth does his own courting and makes his own choice of a mate. There is ample opportunity for young people to get to know each other, for boys and girls attend school together, work together at planting and harvesting, and attend festivals in groups.

Courting takes place in the girl's home, at dusk around the rice mill while the girls pound rice for the next day's meals, and in the early evenings on the veranda. Men go courting in pairs or groups, but once a girl has indicated her choice, the boy's friends, who still accompany him each evening, later drift off, leaving the young couple together. During the preliminary courting period, young men serenade their girls, recite love poems, exchange compliments, and talk nonsense. The old love songs and poems, once such an integral part of Thai courtship, are giving way to modern love songs from Bangkok, and even in the most remote villages some young man, often a returned conscript, possesses a cheap paper book of the popular songs. Parents and children retire to the sleeping chamber, but since only a bamboo screen or a thin wooden partition separates this room from the veranda, parents can watch the girl's behavior. At the rice mills, girls do the milling in pairs, often the mother or some older woman working nearby.

Though young people have a remarkable amount of freedom during courting, casual caressing is not allowed. Traditionally, a young man was not supposed to touch a girl before marriage. To touch or hold her hand was tantamount to expressing a desire for sexual relations, and such action was considered extremely immoral. At festivals men and women dance together in the *ramwong*, and although the partners constantly weave close to each other and their hands seem to touch, they never quite do. Only the most daring young man would attempt to brush the hands of his sweetheart with his fingertips during this dance. Western dancing, which has been adopted by the sophisticated young people of Bangkok, has not penetrated into the village. Groups of young villagers will go chaperoned to neighboring villages for festivals, and as they return to their own village late at night, couples may walk together but they do not hold hands, although two young men commonly may do so and, less frequently, young women friends. Nonetheless, rough horseplay is engaged in, particularly at planting, when young men toss mud pellets at the girls, who shriek and show their interest by retaliating; and the peasant custom of rhyming-song contests between teams of young men and women at harvest and festivals sometimes produces bawdy songs; but this and other suggestive banter remain, at the courting stage, in a verbal form, for until marriage, strict chastity is required of the young people. There are no prostitutes in the villages. Men have access to prostitutes in the market towns or provincial capital, but they visit them only when they are in the army and then only in a group when they have been drinking. The almost complete absence of venereal disease in the villages has long been remarked upon by medical and health workers, and supports the statement that village youths do not patronize the market town prostitutes, who invariably are riddled with disease.

Ruth Benedict, in her penetrating study of Thai behavior,[*] points out that the strong male dominance in Thai culture was powerfully reinforced by Buddhist doctrines and the exclusion of women from Buddhist religious orders. Since by Buddhist definitions a monk is asexual, Thai men do not suffer from feelings of anxiety to prove their maleness; hence, chastity for the young men is regarded not as something out of the ordinary, but as natural and accepted, and men are not expected to prove their virility before marriage.

MARRIAGE CUSTOMS

In some regions of North Thailand trial marriage is permitted. Once a village girl has singled out a suitor who meets with her parents' approval, he may begin to sleep with the girl at her house, but does not move his clothing or other personal property to the girl's house nor take his meals there. After several nights together, the couple may decide they do not want to be married, and the young man simply stops going to the house. The girl does not suffer any moral disapproval but resumes being courted by other suitors. Ordinarily, the practice is for the youth to transfer his belongings at once into the girl's home, and to eat and sleep there; this is regarded by the village as a true marriage, and any separation must be done according to the customary pattern governing divorce.

There is no religious ceremony of marriage in Thai village culture, the fact of a young couple's living together being the seal of marriage in the eyes of the community. Since 1935, registration at the district office has been required, but this is left up to the individuals to do, and many marriages, particularly in isolated villages, never are registered. In earlier times, it was customary, after the young couple had been living as man and wife for several days, for the bride's mother to send presents of betel nut, candles, and incense to the bridegroom's home through an intermediary known to both households. If the bridegroom's parents were also favorably inclined to the match, they in turn sent gifts to the bride's house. The offerings to the house of the young man were to propitiate the "house spirits" for the loss of a family member, and the exchange of gifts signified to the community that both families were pleased with the marriage. This custom, while still observed by many older villagers, is beginning to die out among the present generation; poor families dispense entirely with this exchange of gifts.

Among prosperous village families, there used to be more elaborate marriage arrangements; the young man did not live with his betrothed immediately after they had decided they wanted to marry, but, instead, a go-between was sent by the young man's family to the girl's family to ask their consent to the match, and if this was given, an auspicious day was chosen for the wedding. Friends and relatives gathered at the bride's house, the wrists of the young couple were bound together in the presence of the village elders, and they were led to the marriage chamber while the guests feasted, sang, and danced. Gifts were exchanged between the families two or three days after the wedding, and sometimes included money and property for the young couple's use. Also, a small property settlement was made by the couple's parents, usually land and work animals if the couple left the girl's home and set up their own household. A small payment "for the mother's milk" was made at the time of the marriage to the girl's parents by the bridegroom or his family. Today, in the self-subsistent village these old customs have largely disappeared, and property settlement is found only among very wealthy farm families. It would appear that these old traditional marriage customs have been retained to a greater degree in the Bangkok region than elsewhere, for, according to Janlekha,[9] there is a fixed rate for the customary marriage charge in the Bangchan area as well as later marriage-property settlements. No indication is given, though, whether this is still the prevalent Minburi pattern or is found only among the well-to-do farmers.

Formerly, if a young man came from a different village or district and was unknown in the village of his bride, he was examined as to his intent by the village headman before the girl's parents agreed to the match. In certain instances security in the form of money for his good faith was required, but this was rare even in previous generations, for marriage outside the village was unusual.

Although the villagers choose their own mates, they seldom choose a mate who does not have parental approval; the young couple almost always live with the bride's parents for a time, and for this the approval of her parents is necessary. Thai parents, like parents everywhere, encourage their children to marry into families of similar economic status, and a prosperous family rarely approves of their child's marrying into a poor one; for even though there are no distinct social classes in modern Thai village culture, wealth, occupational status, and other factors always set off a few families. Elopement occasionally occurs if the young man is able to set up his own household at once. There are no restrictions to marriages of a blood relation outside the immediate family; marriage of cousins is not improper, and in small villages, where blood lines are much mixed, it is common for bride and groom to have some degree of blood relationship.

There is no fixed rule where the young couple shall live, but the common practice is for the young man to take up residence for a time in the house of the bride's parents. Later, the young couple may move to a house built by the groom, or to the husband's family home. In north Thailand one of the daughters and her husband remain in her family's house, and an only daughter and her husband make their permanent home with her family, for the girl will inherit the house compound, and her husband will become head of the household when his father-in-law retires or dies. If there is more than one daughter, the eldest daughter and her husband remain in her father's house until the next daughter marries, and then they build a house elsewhere, either on part of his family's compound or in a compound that the husband buys in the village. If there are several daughters in the family, the youngest daughter and her husband stay permanently in the girl's household. Whether the son-in-law lives a few weeks or many years in his bride's family's house, his position is not uncomfortable; he is accepted as an additional adult male in his wife's family, and if his wife is the only or youngest daughter, the position as head of the household will eventually fall to him. Much the same pattern seems to have been common in Thailand in former times, but lack of data on the central area makes it impossible to judge whether it is still consistently found there today. If the bridegroom's family is poor and needs his services, or if his father is dead and he is the sole support of his widowed mother and younger brothers and sisters, a young man may take his wife to his home soon after marriage. Quite often in such instances, when one of his sisters marries, the elder brother and his wife set up an independent household, either on a portion of the family compound or elsewhere in the village. With marriage, a young man takes on adult responsibilities, but he will not be regarded as head of a household while he lives with his wife's family until his father-in-law retires or dies.

When a married daughter and her husband live with the girl's parents, the two women get along well together, but there may be some strain between mother and daughter-in-law if the bridegroom must bring his wife to his parents' home. If the young man's father is dead, he is regarded as head of the household, and his wife ordinarily will not be subordinate to her mother-in-law. If his father is alive, the young man is still only a minor member of his family, and his wife takes a subordinate position to her husband's mother and his teen-age sisters. Often in this situation the young couple, even if the youth's family is well-to-do, have to live temporarily in makeshift quarters under the family granary or in a small bamboo hut in the compound. A teen-age daughter may have a room to herself in the main house, while the eldest son and his bride live in a squatterlike condition somewhere in the house compound. Generally, this young man is dependent upon his father and works in his father's rice fields. It may take several years for him to save enough money to buy a piece of village land and to build a house for his bride and children. Although a young man is regarded as an adult once he marries, it is not until he begins to farm on his own, either on shares or as a farm owner, and takes on the active duties of a head of a household, that he will participate in village affairs as a householder. Until then he will be considered a part either of his father's or his father-in-law's household.

Polygamy was always exceptional in Thai villages, for only a prosperous villager could support two families; today polygamy is even more rare among Thai farmers, but it is still practiced in Bangkok.

Divorce is effected by mutual agreement between husband and wife. If a marriage has been registered at the district office, the divorce must also be registered. When a couple separate, each takes the property they brought to the marriage and joint property is divided equally. Children accompany their mother to her family's house and are supported by her and her family. An ex-husband rarely contributes to the support of his children. He, too, goes back to his parents' home until he marries again. Divorce among couples with children is rare; often the fact that a couple have no children will be one of the major factors in bringing about a divorce.

OLD AGE

When an individual reaches sixty, he is considered as having reached the last and oldest age group, i.e., to have completed the fifth of the twelve year cycles of the Thai zodiac calendar. At this age, most village men will have retired from active farm

A market place in the north

Booths at a typical winter fair

Typical northern
spirit house

Cremation scene

work, turning over this responsibility to a son, a son-in-law, or sometimes a tenant. Old men are not idle; they make fish traps and baskets, do small repair jobs around the house, and act as baby sitter with their small grandchildren. They seldom leave the house compound except to visit the *wat* or a neighbor. Younger men of the village who want their advice call upon them, and they are shown the high measure of respect due to their age. Women also retire from active household management at this age level, although they still spend much of their time taking care of the small children of the household, helping with the cooking, and with other household tasks.

Elderly persons are addressed by their families and by outsiders in special terms of respect; younger people wait upon them, prepare their betel chews, make their cheroots, and fetch and carry for them. Men and women in this old age group become freer in behavior and manner. In warm weather old women often go about the house compound with their breasts uncovered even when outsiders are present, a pattern of behavior that is not found among middle-aged women, young married women, and unmarried girls of the village. The old can break many language prohibitions and speak among themselves of things that younger men and women would not mention in a mixed group.

As they approach the end of their life span, the Thai turn to religious faith and are the most faithful worshipers in the temple. Their concern with Buddhism and the afterlife is demonstrated strikingly during the Buddhist Lent, when they spend the entire *Wan Pra* in the *wat* compound, sleeping two nights in the temple or in the *wat* salas. They are the only villagers who wear the prescribed all-white clothing that a devout Buddhist is supposed to wear on *Wan Pra* during Lent. (These white garments will be their grave clothes.) Old people frequently hold special ceremonies in the temple. Formerly, there were special Buddhist ceremonies for a person who turned sixty, but these "merit-making-for-age" ceremonies were rarely practiced among the peasants.

Most aged Thai villagers face death with resignation, and spend much of their time in the temple praying and preparing for the next life, but they also resort to means of postponing death. One method (which is now rarely used) was for the family of an aged person who was failing to prepare a coffin, a custom that originated from the old belief that to have a coffin waiting was a good omen and would prolong life. In north Thailand, a Buddhist ceremony for extending life is to invite a chapter of monks to the house to recite one of the Jataka tales which Buddha read to his disciples when they were ill and which they read to him when he was ill. According to Wells, this was an ancient Brahmin rite which was taken over by the Buddhist monks.[10] A bowl of water with a candle of beeswax placed on the rim is prepared, and the priests chant the service around this bowl of water causing it to become lustral or holy water. The psychological effect on the patient is strong, and he is also washed with the holy water which is believed to have strong curative powers. If an elderly or sick person dies soon after this ceremony, the explanation according to Buddhist doctrine is that the proper time for life to end had arrived and nothing could have prolonged it. The folk belief, strongly tinged with animistic interpretation, is that the *pi* (body spirit—as distinct from the soul) had already left the body and thus nothing could have prevented death. Folk belief also holds that the spirit hovers around the body for some time after death. When a person dies, a family member may cry out the name of the dead person several times in an attempt to lure the soul back into the body. Formerly, in north Thailand, a family member might even climb out onto the roof and call out the name of the decreased hoping to entice the spirit back. An ancient custom still practiced by older Thai villagers who believe in the transmigration of the soul is to make a mark with soot on some part of the corpse; if a birthmark appears in the next baby born in the family, this indicates that the soul of the dead person has been reborn in the infant.

DEATH

The corpse is bathed as soon as possible by family members and prepared for final anointing with holy water by relatives and friends. It is clothed in clean clothes, generally white for an old person, laid out on a mat or bed, and wrapped in white cloth, one hand left extended from the wrapping, so that the relatives and friends can sprinkle it with holy water which has been blessed by the Buddhist priests. During the three nights that the body will be kept in the house, a homemade oil lamp or wax candle is kept burning at the head of the corpse or coffin. This light demonstrates how animism and Buddhism have become interwoven. The Buddhist monk explains the light as an allegory of life: when the wick of the candle burns out, the light dies; so is a man's life extinguished, and the mourners are thereby reminded to achieve merit before their own end comes. The villager, while accepting this Buddhist explanation, also holds firmly to his own folk belief that the "death light" is to guide the soul so that it will not be lost on its way to heaven and be doomed to wander the world as an evil spirit. In earlier times in rural areas death was announced to immediate neighbors by the wailing of the family; today, one of the family reports a death to the headman, the village doctor, and the head priest, who arranges for a chapter of monks to go to the house that night to chant services for the dead.

Funerals are the most elaborate of all village ceremonies. Preparations for cremation take from three to seven days, although most commonly cremation is held on the third day. In rare instances cremation may be held sooner, even on the first day after death, but in all such exceptions a three-day mourning period of Buddhist ceremonies follows. On the first night an evening service led by a group of monks is held at the home attended by friends and relatives. After the service the mourners gossip, smoke, chew betel, and play chess throughout the night. To help the bereaved family with funeral expenses, the callers bring small gifts of money which are tucked into a cone of flowers or folded in a neat packet. Some member of the family receives the money offerings and keeps a rough record of the families who contribute, for at a later time a reciprocal funeral gift will be made. Not all the villagers who visit the house bring money offerings; these will be made mainly by heads of neighboring households and other villagers who have worked with the family in planting and harvest work parties. But, if the family is poor, small gifts of money may be presented by all the heads of households who come as mourners. The second day is devoted to preparing the casket, gathering wood for the cremation fire, and making food for the forthcoming funeral feast. Another service by a chapter of monks is held at the home on the evening of the second day, followed again by a wake of a group of faithful mourners.

On the morning of the cremation day, friends and relatives gather early, the men to complete the casket, finish the carrying frame and canopy for the coffin, and set up the funeral pyre. The women start preparing the special food which will be presented that noon to the monks. These activities take up most of the morning. About eleven o'clock trays of special food are prepared, and a group of the mourners carry them in procession to the temple where they are offered to the monks for their noon-day meal. While the monks are eating, this group of mourners retire to the *vihara* ("preaching temple") where later the monks hold a special service for them. Then the mourners return to the home of the deceased where they partake of the special funeral meal that has been prepared. After all the guests have eaten, a chapter of monks from the *wat* arrive at the house compound and a final ceremony is held. By this time the corpse has been placed in a crude wooden coffin. After the ceremony in the house, the monks descend and wait in the house compound for the procession to the cremation ground to form. The coffin is brought from the house and placed on the elaborately decorated bamboo canopy which was made and decorated by the village men. In the old days it was held to be bad luck to take the coffin through the door and down the steps, for this would enable the spirit of the dead, who might turn evil, to find its way back to the house. Hence, the coffin was often taken out through a window or a hole cut in the wall. This old custom is no longer practiced, although a modern survival of it is seen occasionally in that the house stairs may be carpeted with banana leaves, which serve to make the coffin route unusual and satisfies the requirement of confusing the spirit. A sacred cord, blessed by the monks, is fastened to the carrying frame at the foot of the coffin. The novices who participate in the procession carry the cord, while the monks lead the procession. Some six to eight men carry the coffin on its gaily decorated bamboo canopy followed in procession by the rest of the mourners.

At the cremation grounds, which ordinarily is an unused area some distance from the village, an inverted pyramid of six or more layers of planks or logs has been built by the men. In the thickly populated delta region of central Thailand, the cremation area may be within the *wat* confines, for there often is no other unused space available. The coffin is removed from the bamboo canopy and placed on top of this pyre. Pine-wood tapers and tapers made of sandalwood fiber in the shape of flowers are distributed to the mourners. Now the chapter of monks chant another service during which water from a young green coconut is poured on the ground near the coffin. The pouring of this water is to ensure that the deceased will be reborn in a land where the soil will be fertile and where there will be ample water for drinking and for growing rice.

Attached to the sacred cord and placed also on the foot of the coffin is yellow cloth or already completed robes for the monks. During the ceremony the monks pull these robes off and let them fall to the ground, where they are collected by the temple boys who will take them to the temple. By this procedure the monks follow Buddha's injunction that they were to make their robes from the cast-off clothes of the dead in the burial grounds. The temple boys also carefully roll up the sacred cord which will be used later in the temple for making candle wicks.

Depending on how strong the old customs are, a variety of special procedures now may follow. In north Thailand, a ripe coconut may be opened and the water poured over the face of the corpse to ensure that the soul will be fresh and clean when entering the gates of heaven, for coconut water is the purest water that can be obtained. Another old northern custom is for one of the family members to rap on the coffin before the monks begin reciting the final commandments so that the soul may be warned and listen. It is commonly believed that the soul lingers around the body until it is consumed by the flames.

The priests leave the cremation ground before the fire is lit, returning to the house of the deceased where later a final ceremony will be held. A small fire has been kindled near the pyre and the mourners now light their sandalwood tapers at this fire. Usually the lid of the coffin is removed before the funeral pyre is ignited. As they approach the pyre the mourners place their flaming tapers on the wood until the pyre ignites. In central Thailand the mourners may walk three times around the coffin before lighting the fire, but this is not usual in the north. As the fire mounts, most of the party leaves, returning to the home of the bereaved family where the monks await them. A dozen or so of the men will remain to see that the corpse is consumed. At the house of the deceased the monks chant the service of *Sankaha*, popularly called the "myth of Hades." While chanting this service, the monks sit around a large bowl of warm water in which a kind of dried sour bean has been dissolved and which is changed into lustral or holy water through the chanting. After the *Sankaha*, the monks chant a blessing in Pali and return to the temple dormitory. The family members take leafy branches and sprinkle the holy water throughout the house to purify it, and all the mourners who have had some contact with the corpse dip their hands into the lustral water and brush their hair and face with their wet fingers to purify themselves. A final evening service in the house is held on the night of cremation. In earlier times, it was customary for the family to go to the cremation ground accompanied by a monk a few days after the cremation to gather the ashes. These were taken home and a short service was held at the house. In many villages today this custom has been discontinued, for the modern Buddhist abbots do not approve of the family keeping the ashes of the deceased in the home.

Four days after the cremation, or seven days after death, a special morning service is held at the house to ensure happiness for those still living in the house. Special food is prepared for the group of monks who come to conduct the service. Friends and neighbors join in making offerings of food, betel nut, tobacco, candles, and incense, which are presented to the monks at the close of the service. After the temple boys carry the trays of food back to the *wat* for the monks' breakfast, the friends and neighbors eat a special breakfast. This ceremony of holding a service seven days after death and offering food and gifts is not done if the deceased has been buried instead of cremated. Burial is rare and, if found today, is for the death of a child or for a death in a very poor village family that cannot afford the expense involved in the elaborate cremation ceremonies. In traditional times, cremation was denied for persons dying suddenly from a plague disease or for women dying in childbirth, it being held that death of such nature was caused by evil spirits and cremation which endows merit to the soul could not be permitted. Dying from these causes no longer prevents cremation, the old belief having been discarded. If the body has been buried, the family does not hold this last memorial ceremony at the house. Instead, a tray of special food is prepared on the seventh day and sent direct to the *wat*.

This memorial ceremony seven days after death marks the final rite that is held for the dead. The town custom of holding memorial services on the fiftieth and hundredth day after death even in the past rarely was followed by most peasants. Elaborate mourning and postcremation ceremonies of prosperous townspeople and nobility might extend for months or even years. Such a pattern never has been part of village funereal customs.

Village cremations vary in elaborateness depending on the age and social and economic position of the individual and family. For the funeral of a baby, cremation is rare, and few of the rituals and ceremonies described are held. Like other peasant folk, the Thai peasant does not regard the death of a baby as a loss. A baby has not yet become an integral part of the family or community; its death does not produce a social or economic gap. Even though the parents mourn the lost child, another child will soon be born to take its place.

Thai villagers do not wear mourning clothes, although custom decrees that bright colors should not be worn at the funeral or at the later ceremonies. Women wear black skirts with a white or black jacket, while men wear their ordinary trousers with a white shirt or grey or black jacket. Wearing of a black mourning arm band by the men often is seen today.

Of the three great crises of a Thai peasant's life—birth, marriage, and death—the village is most vitally concerned with death. Birth and marriage are important, for birth brings a new member into the community, and marriage ensures continuance of the family. But from a social point of view these are family affairs, and involve no social ceremonies that include the village as a whole. Death is a calamity to the family and to the community. Group concern is shown by the village turning out to aid the stricken family and to mourn the loss of a member of the community. The elaborate ceremonies held at this time can be accomplished only by group activity. Further, by participating in these important ceremonies, the villager can store up "merit" for his own afterlife.

4 Agricultural and Economic Patterns

Except in the area around Bangkok and Rangsit, most Thai peasants are independent farmers living in a subsistence economy. It is estimated that 80 per cent of the farmland of Thailand is owned by small, independent farmers.[1] Zimmerman found that the average farm holdings per farm family in 1930 was, in the Menam Plain, 24 *rai* (9½ acres); in the north, 10 *rai* (4 acres); and on the Korat Plateau and in the peninsula 6 or 7 *rai* (2½ acres).[2] Holdings today are similar: Sharp[3] reports that the average farm in central Thailand (excluding Bangkok) has 29½ *rai*, and the author's survey of northern Thailand indicates an average holding of 10 *rai* there. However, even though most Thai farmers own at least part of the land they cultivate,

---
[1] For notes to chapter 4 see page 216.

tenant farmers are also common throughout the kingdom. Zimmerman's survey revealed that, in 1930, 27 per cent of the farmers in northern, 18 per cent in northeastern, and 14 per cent in southern Thailand, owned no farmland.[4] The author's study of San Pong in 1949 found 27.7 per cent of the farmers of the region to be tenants, a figure so close to Zimmerman's 27 per cent for northern Thailand generally that one may conclude that the proportion of tenant farmers there had changed little since 1930, although one must bear in mind that the percentage of tenants varies from province to province and from village to village.

The Menam Plain has a higher proportion of landless tenants than any other part of Thailand—an average of 36 per cent of the farm families there in 1930, according to Zimmerman;[5] 34 per cent, according to a recent study of the delta region[6]—but the proportion of farm tenants varies so much from one part of the plain region to another that any "average" figure for the whole region is rather meaningless. For example, 94 per cent of the peasants of the Dhanyaburi district were landless tenants but only 12 per cent of the peasants of the Lopburi district, which is also an important rice-producing area.[7]

In the Dhanyaburi district (near Bangkok) more than 85 per cent of the peasants are tenants, farming an average of 40 acres on the large estates of absentee landlords. Tenancy contracts in this district are on a yearly basis, and the tenant usually moves on to a new farm each year or so in a vain attempt to improve his standard of living. Enormous farms, migratory labor, and a lack of settled community life in the Bangkok area have destroyed the reciprocal labor groups so that agriculture here is on a cash basis: wages, rent, and taxes are paid in cash, and the farmer of this region must concentrate on producing a crop that will give him sufficient income to meet these disbursements. In the Bangchan area tenancy is the lot of 34 per cent of the farmers; here rent is often paid in kind (from 3 to 8 *tang* per *rai*) and less commonly in cash (from 12½ to 50 ticals per *rai*)—this is a little under one-fifth of the average yield of 32 *tang* per *rai*.[8]

In all areas except the delta, tenancy is generally on a sharecrop basis, usually half of the crop, or perhaps less if tenant and landlord are close relatives. Tenants and landlords live side by side and work coöperatively in each other's fields; the tenant always owns his house compound and perhaps a *rai* or two of paddy land. In this kind of arrangement, typical of northern Thailand, the tenant will farm the same paddy land year after year, having only an oral contract with his landlord. Farms around the provincial capitals are often owned by men who live in the towns, but these owners are not absentee landlords in the usual sense of the term (properly "absentee landlordism" in Thailand may be applied only to the Bangkok area); instead, the arrangements between the town landlord and his tenants are much like those between the village landlord and his tenants. In addition to tenant farmers and owners, there are likely to be several peasant households that neither own nor rent paddy land but work for shares of rice in other farmers' fields; several members working in this way can earn enough rice to feed the family for a year.

THE FARM AND EQUIPMENT

The peasant's work schedule revolves around one major crop of wet-land rice a year: he sows his seedbed early in June, transplants the young shoots a month or six weeks later, tends his dikes and weeds his fields in August and September, harvests in late November or December, and threshes in December and early January. Rice growing requires most of a farmer's labor, and any secondary crops are grown between the rice cycles. A relatively well-developed irrigation system enables villagers of north Thailand to grow secondary crops of tobacco, soybeans, peanuts, vegetables, or occasionally a second crop of rice; lower Thailand depends entirely on one crop of rice a year.

The only appreciable difference in the rice farming of the various parts of Thailand is the type of rice grown. In the north almost all is glutinous (70 per cent in the northeast); in central and south Thailand, nonglutinous rice is grown exclusively. Since glutinous rice has little export value, the surplus glutinous rice of the north and northeast is sold in the market towns and provincial capitals of these regions. Today the people of the north and northeast prefer glutinous rice as a food, but the original reason for their exclusive development of this variety probably was brought about by its shorter growing period (from 4 to 4½ months). In the northeast area, where the rainy season is unreliable, a fast-maturing rice is essential.

Farm layout is similar all over the country: fields are divided into many small plots, each surrounded by small bunds or dikes, and water is let into the fields from numerous small ditches that connect with a larger irrigation ditch, which in turn runs to a canal or river. Throughout the north and northeast, water runs through the paddy fields by gravity; in the central plains hand-powered machines, wind mills, or gasoline pumps must be used.

Except for the use of his water buffalo for plowing, the peasant depends entirely upon manual labor and primitive tools. (In the delta region wealthy farmers may use gasoline engines for pumping water into the paddy fields.) Except for steel or iron parts, most farm tools are made at home by the farmer himself or by a carpenter of the village. Iron parts are purchased in the market town or from traveling vendors. Threshing by machine is also unknown except for occasional hand-operated winnowing machines in the delta region. In the past few years there have been attempts to introduce tractor plowing in the rural areas near the larger provincial capitals. A small tractor owned by a townsman may be hired out to farmers living nearby. This was done in Chiangmai in the north in 1952 and 1953, but the farmers' reaction was mixed; some who had plowed their fields by tractor one season refused to do it the next because, they said, the tractor plowed too deep.

COÖPERATIVE WORKGROUPS IN VILLAGE LIFE

The outstanding form of economic coöperation in village life is the exchange of labor in rice farming, although in many of the intensive rice growing areas of central Thailand the reciprocal work group has died out. For instance, in Bangchan, a typical delta village some 20 miles from Bangkok, the reciprocal work group is used to a limited degree and only at harvest. But in most rural areas reciprocal work groups help to prepare seedbeds, and to plant and harvest the rice. This group activity has various names; in the north it is known as *mua torb*, literally "repaying work in turn," and in central Thailand as *long kag*.

The exchange labor groups, as we noted earlier, are not necessarily composed of neighbors, although it is the tendency for households that live close together to work together. If a farmer has only a few paddy fields, his work group consists of perhaps ten or fifteen persons, mainly his immediate relatives in the village; the reciprocal work group for an average northern farmer, who plants 8 or 10 *rai* of paddy, consists of perhaps thirty-five or forty-five members, representing fifteen or twenty families. No record is kept of how many workers or how many hours of work a family contributes. Here as elsewhere in Thai rural social organization the arrangement is loose and informal. The principle of exchange is primarily the number of workers: if household A provides two workers for household B at transplanting time, household B in turn sends two workers to A's fields. Reciprocal obligations are seldom if ever evaded.

Since even under this system farmers with larger areas of fields need extra help, poorer families who neither own nor rent fields have a chance to hire out for temporary employment for a daily rice-share wage during the transplanting period. They may work for as many as twenty or twenty-five families during the year, at a fixed daily rice wage. In any large work group there may well be several workers who are working for a share of the rice, payable at harvest time.

Many accounts of Thailand err in supposing that the exchange labor group for planting and harvesting is the only sort of communal labor in Thai villages.[10] This notion, however, is quite erroneous and probably comes from too great a reliance on descriptions of the Bangkok region, where the adaptation of farming to an intensified rice agriculture has developed an economic pattern that is quite unlike that of most Thai villagers. Actually there are several other communal work projects, some of a civic nature, some more specifically agricultural; these affect the village as a whole and many are less tightly organized so that the groups that perform them may not strictly be called reciprocal work groups even though a similar principle underlies them. Cart tracks and village streets are repaired communally under the direction of the headman; necessary work on the grounds and buildings of the *wat* is also done communally. For these tasks each household supplies as many able-bodied men as it can. In the north the need to maintain the elaborate irrigation systems has resulted in a rather formally organized communal task: villages in a given area are assigned responsibility for their part of the feeder canals and the smaller ditches in their section; in addition, each village must from time to time send a labor force to work on the main irrigation system. In San Pong and two neighboring villages—a "section" that embraces some 2,000 *rai* of paddy fields—two chiefs are elected to supervise the irrigation works of the section; it is the duty of these chiefs to see that the water is kept flowing and is properly regulated at the main feeder branches, and they have the authority to order communal labor for any necessary repairs. During the growing season this involves a considerable amount of work, for the chiefs must continually inspect the many branches as well as the main irrigation ditch; therefore, the villagers pay them a fixed amount of rice for their work. In San Pong, in 1949, this amounted to a levy of one liter of rice per *rai* of paddy farmed by each villager, so that the two chiefs received 50 *tang* of rice apiece, with a monetary value of 350 *ticals*, for their supervision during the growing season of that year.

THE RICE FARMING CYCLE

Preparing the fields.—At least 80 per cent of all rice grown in Thailand is transplanted. In the north and northeast, except for a small amount of upland dry rice, all rice is transplanted. The method of transplanting is much the same throughout the country. Fields are plowed soon after the rains begin, but not until water from the early rains, or from canals or irrigation ditches, has been allowed to stand in the paddy fields for several weeks to soften the ground and kill the weeds.

Water buffalo are used to plow in deep mud; in parts of the north and northeast where the soil is lighter bullocks may be used. The plow is a homemade wooden affair weighing about twenty-eight pounds, fitted with a steel plowshare; ordinarily, a single buffalo is sufficient to pull it, but in the Bangkok delta, two buffalo in double harness are used sometimes for deeper plowing. The plow is attached to a simple wooden yoke fitted onto the buffalo's shoulders, and the animal is guided by means of a long string attached to the halter and running through the left nostril of the animal. Plowing in rural Thailand is done to the continual chant of *"kwa! kwa!"* (right! right!) for the plowman can guide the water buffalo only to the left with the nose guide.

The paddy field is plowed several times, in the morning between six and ten o'clock and in the afternoon between three and six o'clock; water buffalo are not worked during the intense noon heat. Plowing is done by men and older boys, except in the commercialized rice area near Bangkok, where the size of holdings may force the women and girls of poorer families to take over some of the plowing.

After the paddy field has been plowed, water is allowed to settle for four or five days to soften the soil further and rot the weeds before the field is harrowed. A heavy wooden plank with pointed wooden teeth is pulled seven or eight times through the field to screen out the larger weeds, break up mud clods, and churn the mud for aeration of the rice seedling roots. The harrowed field is left under water for several more days; then the farmer smooths the mud by scraping the field with a heavy bamboo log attached to the harrow. The paddy field, now a pond of clear water above a smooth mud surface, is ready to receive the rice seedlings. Most of the farmers of the south prepare the fields in the same way as the other peasants of the country, but in a few parts of southern Thailand, for example, Jumbor and Surastra Dhani, which are low-lying areas where tall marsh grass grows, plowing is omitted. Here the farmers cut the long grass down to the soil line, remove the foliage, and drive water buffalo continually through the field to trample the mud. The trampled grass roots are allowed to ferment under water for about ten days, after which the rice shoots are transplanted directly into this mixture. As the grass springs up among the rice, the farmers cut it off to the soil line below the water.

Preparing the seedbed.—For transplanted rice, seedlings must be grown in a nursery bed, which is prepared when the first water begins to reach the fields. The farmer selects one of his most fertile fields, often one on the edge of the village; this is plowed and harrowed in the usual way, but the mud is not smoothed. The farmer informs his coöperative work group of the day the prepared plot is to be seeded, and on the morning of the designated day his helpers—anywhere from ten to forty-five in number, depending on the size of the seedbed—turn out. Men and boys hoe channels in the soft mud; women and girls follow, scraping up mud with their feet; this work forms six or eight flat mud beds about three feet wide, separated by foot-wide channels of water. The men then drain the water from the field, and the owner and several of his helpers walk up and down the rows sowing the rice seed in the soft mud. The work is finished before noon and the workers return to their homes immediately after the work is done.

A temporary bamboo fence is built around the seedbed to keep out water buffalo, and if the field is near the village, a bamboo lattice is put up to keep out ducks and chickens. For the first few days someone, often one of the youngsters of the family, stays near the bed to shoo away birds; sometimes scarecrows are placed in the field. Sprouts begin to appear on the second day, for the seeds are germinated before they are sown by soaking them for twenty-four to thirty-six hours and then covering them with straw which is sprinkled frequently to prevent overheating.

Transplanting.—About a month to six weeks later, usually early in August, the seedlings are ready for transplanting and the paddy fields are ready to receive them. The owner of the fields makes certain preparations in advance; he erects a leaf or straw thatch shelter to protect the seedlings from the sun after they are pulled and prepares many bundles of thin bamboo strips (*tork*) for tying the seedlings into bundles. His work group begins to gather about two o'clock in the afternoon of the day the farmer has designated for transplanting. Since many other farmers still have their own plowing and harrowing to do, about two-thirds of the transplanting group are women, in contrast to the seedling and harvest groups, which have an equal distribution of men and women.

Transplanting is usually done in the afternoon so that the transplanted seedlings will not be subject to the noon sun on the first day. Seedlings are pulled up by the roots with a rhythmic circular motion, the right hand swinging in an arc and uprooting several seedlings at a time. After several hundred seedlings have been pulled, the bunch is slapped against the foot or dipped in the irrigation ditch or standing water in the next field to clean the roots of any clinging mud. The bunch is tied together with a thin bamboo strip, and the tops of any very tall seedlings are sometimes cut off. Because considerable skill is needed to pull up the seedlings without damaging their tender stalks and roots the more experienced workers do this job; less-experienced workers gather the bundles together, place them in the shade of the temporary shelters, and prepare them for transportation to the paddy field.

When most of the seedlings have been pulled, the bundles are readied for transport to the paddy fields, which may be some distance from the seedbeds. In the north, bundles may be placed in baskets or hung on carrying poles and carried to the fields by the men; in central Thailand, where deep canals are frequent, the bunches may be attached to a pole and floated along a canal or transported by shallow-draft boats.

Transplanting commonly starts in the center of a field, although occasionally the workers start at one end and work across. Both men and women plant together in a long line; each takes steps about a foot and a half long and at these intervals pushes three or four seedlings into the mud. A fast worker can plant a hundred feet in a few minutes. It is monotonous, back-straining work, but is done with a great deal of laughing and ribald joking. Young men hold contests to see who can finish a row first. Frequent rests are taken to chew betel, drink water, and smoke cigarettes and cheroots supplied by the host. Food is not provided, since transplanting is done after the midday meal.

The number of transplanters to a field varies. Farmers who have a large area to plant will have, in addition to their reciprocal work party, several helpers who are paid in rice at harvest time on the basis of a day's work. Ordinarily, the workers break up into small groups of ten to twenty to a field, but a very large field may be planted by the whole party. A work party of thirty-five members can transplant an area of eleven *rai* comprising about fifteen paddy fields in two and a half hours. Hence, though transplanting does not start until late afternoon, it is finished by dusk. A corner of one field is planted thickly to serve as an emergency seedbed to replace any shoots that die in the fields.

Transplanting takes place regardless of the weather on the appointed day, though the work will be carried on in a more subdued manner if there is rain. The work will go on until all the village fields have been planted in turn. On August afternoons the village is deserted except for old people and children. After the fields have been planted, each farmer can do his own weeding, regulate the water in his fields, and repair his dikes; exchange labor will not be necessary again until harvest time many months later.

Floating rice and broadcast sowing.—In the commercialized agricultural areas of central Thailand about one-third of the rice is grown in deep water and must be sown broadcast rather than transplanted, for floating rice has a long, brittle stalk that is too fragile to be uprooted when the plant is young. In the Bangkok and Rangsit regions, on the huge farms of 40 to 100 or more *rai*, transplanting would require too much labor to be economical even if it were possible. Fields are prepared for floating rice in much the same way as for transplanted rice except that they require less plowing and harrowing. Seeds which have been germinated by soaking are cast over the flooded fields once the mud in the water has settled (floating mud particles choke the sprouts). Sowing is usually done in June or July; the deep flooding from the rains begins in August and lasts until November; the rice is harvested in December, after the water has receded.

Ordinary wet-land rice may also be sown broadcast, but to be profitable it must be grown where water conditions are favorable, that is, in the areas where the fields are inundated by a river or large canal. Only such water has sufficient oxygen for the extensive root system of broadcast rice, and if irrigation water or rain water is used, it must be changed frequently to refresh its oxygen supply.

Broadcast rice does not produce so good or so uniform a quality of grain as transplanted rice, and many agricultural officials in Thailand agree that the broadcast method is less desirable because of its much lower yield. Recently, however, one agricultural economist held that this argument was inconclusive, since, he contends, no systematic comparison between these two methods of growing rice has been made.[11] In central Thailand, whenever possible, the farmer transplants his rice, but in the delta area, he must use the broadcast method if his holdings are more than four hectares, for there the widely scattered houses and larger holdings no longer permit reciprocal work parties of neighbors, and all work must be done by the family.

Shifting-crop farming.—This is a type of agriculture which consists of clearing a patch of jungle and raising dry upland rice, corn, or vegetables in the clearing. It forms an important means of livelihood for many peasants of the Korat region. There is no suitable term for this "shifting-crop" farming, but sometimes it is referred to by rural economists by the Filipino term *caingin*.

In much of the Korat region, particularly in the foothills, shifting-crop farming supplements wet-rice farming and stock-raising, and often determines whether the peasant will make ends meet. The number of Thai peasants who depend partly or mainly on this type of agriculture varies from year to year, since lack of water in the northeast lowlands may at times force the peasants there also to resort to this method. It has been estimated that, not counting the hill tribes, about a million Thai farmers, most of whom live on the Korat Plateau, use about half a million acres a year for shifting-crop farming.[12] Only peasants living near the jungle hillsides can farm this way, for only here has the forest eliminated the insidious cogan grass and other noxious weeds, and here the soil is fertile, for the plant nutrients have not been leached from the top soil.

Farmers who employ this method select a suitable area at the beginning of the January dry season, at which time they cut forest growth and leave it to dry for several months. In late April or in May, before the rains begin, the area is burned over; burning the slash provides additional nutrients for the shallow-root crop which will be planted. After the rains have moistened the soil, the burned-over ground is planted simply by poking or digging shallow holes about an inch deep and an inch wide with a pointed bamboo stick or an iron-tipped tool, dropping in seeds of dry upland rice, cotton, peppers, corn, or vegetables, and covering the seeds with loose soil. The crop requires little tending other than perhaps one or two weedings to prevent it from being choked by the weeds and suckers from the burned-off slash. Since the *caingin* plots are some distance from the village, once the crop gets a start the farmer visits it only rarely until it is ready to be harvested. Only one crop can be grown on a single clearing, for the first planting exhausts its fertility; the next season the farmer burns off another clearing and repeats the process.

Harvesting.—Harvest time varies from region to region according to the time of planting and the type of rice planted. In northern and central Thailand harvesting comes in late November or in December; in southern Thailand, where rice cannot be planted until September, the harvest is in March or April. Harvesting, like transplanting, is a coöperative affair among neighbors and friends, and the work party that helped a man plant his fields works for him in the harvesting. Each farmer determines the day on which he wishes to start harvesting, but in a small village this is set in consultation with the friends and neighbors of his work group to avoid any conflicts in schedule. A farmer who needs more help than a work party can supply recruits hired labor from among the villagers who have no land and who do not work as sharecroppers, but work instead at planting and harvesting times for other farmers. These workers are paid in rice at the end of the harvest, the usual pay in the north being one official *tang* (a basket of paddy rice weighing about eleven kilograms) for each day's work; a slightly higher rate of one and one-third *tang* is paid for the heavy work of carrying sheaves of rice from the fields to the threshing area.

In highly commercialized rice areas the reciprocal work party has been replaced by migratory workers who flock to these areas at harvest time from the northeast. In other central areas at least part of the harvesting is done on a coöperative basis. In the Bangchan area, where farmers adjust the time of harvest of their fields by planting species of rice that mature at different times, there is some informal reciprocal coöperative harvesting, but some 70 per cent of the farmers must use piece-work laborers at harvest.[12] (In San Pong only 35 per cent of farmers with similar large holdings need to use piece workers at harvest, for the reciprocity pattern is strong there.)

In paddy fields where its level can be controlled, water is cut off some ten to fifteen days before harvest time to allow the fields to dry. Once the fields are dry, the work party gathers on the appointed day at half-past eight or nine in the morning, after the sun has dried the dew on the fields. The reaping party works until one o'clock, when, in northern regions, they stop for a noonday lunch that is supplied by the host and brought to the fields. (In the regions where a noon meal is not customary a rest break is taken at this time, and workers chew betel, smoke, or perhaps eat snacks.) After this respite, work is resumed and continues until dark, when a second meal is served. For these meals the women of the household cook chicken and pork curries, and other "special-occasion" dishes, and the householder supplies tobacco, betel, and native liquor.

In the central plains, and the northern parts of Thailand, grain is cut with a sickle and tied into sheaves. The reaper stoops down, holds the stalks of rice in one hand and carefully cuts them with a short curved sickle; after three or four stalks have been cut, they are gathered together and carefully laid on the stumps of the rice plants to dry in the sun. Reaping must be done carefully so that the grains of rice will not be dislodged. In the north reapers leave about a foot of the stalk attached to the ears, in the central plains, somewhat less. Reaping in the south is quite different; instead of a sickle, a small, comblike knife is used to cut the grain (a method similar to that of the Malays), and reaping is done almost exclusively by women.

Once the grain is cut, it must dry in the sun for several days, generally three to five, before it can be threshed, and if it rains during this time, much of the grain may be spoiled. In this period, the farmer prepares his threshing ground and helps to harvest the crops of other members of his exchange labor group. On the fourth or fifth day after reaping, the farmer and about half of the reaping party return to the fields and tie the stalks into clusters of eight or nine with thin strips of split bamboo. About five or six clusters are tied together to form a bundle or sheaf. A number of these sheaves are then hung on a carrying pole (a stick with ends that curve upward) and carried to the threshing ground. The time it takes to do the reaping depends on the number in the work party and number of fields. In the north an average farm has about 10 *rai* (4 acres) of rice, an area that can be reaped in three days by a work party of fifteen members; another two days are needed to tie the stalks into sheaves; the threshing itself, done by the complete work group (anywhere from thirty to forty-five workers) requires one day and part of the evening—ten days to two weeks, in other words, for the average farmer's rice to be harvested and stored.

In the central plains and other areas where water cannot be drained off, rice must be reaped in the flooded fields. If the water is shallow enough, the reapers may stand in the water to cut the stalks of rice; in deeper water, reaping is done from flat-bottomed boats and canoes. In some deep-water areas, bamboo racks that rise above the water are made and the sheaves are hung on these to dry in the sun; in others, the sheaves are taken by boat to the higher ground of the house compound to be dried either on racks or on the ground. When reaping is done from a boat, the reaper leans over the side and cuts the stalks half a foot or a foot below the water, leaving the rest of the stalk attached to the bottom. Later, during the dry season when the water subsides, these stalks are burned off.

Threshing.—A threshing floor is prepared while the reaped rice heads are drying; in the north, in a small part of a dry paddy field, in the central plains, in the house compound. The floor, about ten or fifteen meters in diameter, is flattened by pounding with heavy wooden mallets or paddles and plastered with a mixture of buffalo dung that dries in several days to a hard, smooth surface; in the north, huge, closely woven bamboo mats are used sometimes instead of buffalo-dung plaster. A post on which offerings to "Mother Earth" will be hung is erected in the center of the floor.

In the north and in the peninsula, where threshing is done by hand, sheaves of rice are stacked in a circle around the edge of the threshing floor so that the floor takes on the appearance of a small circular fort with one entrance. Within the circle, the workers strike sheaves of rice against the ground until all the ears are dislodged. After dusk, the thresher carefully feels each sheaf before he tosses it outside the threshing ring. Some peasants place several wooden planks on the threshing floor against which the rice sheaves can be beaten to dislodge the kernels. In central Thailand, where animals are used for threshing, three or four water buffalo or bullocks are tethered side by side to the center post, rice sheaves are heaped on the threshing floor, and the animals are driven round and round until the grain is threshed.

Winnowing is done in the same way in all parts of the country. The grain is tossed into the air with a wooden spade or woven bamboo tray to let the wind blow away the chaff. If there is no wind, a large, round bamboo fan one-and-a-half feet in diameter with a foot-long handle is used to blow the chaff away. Traditionally, a winnowing dance was performed by young men with these fans, and winnowers today still manipulate them in a somewhat ritualistic fashion.

Threshing continues into the evening; after it is finished, bonfires are lit and young people sing and court around the fires. Threshing time all through the country is one of much festivity and celebration, but many old customs are fading away. The rhyming-song contests, for example, are giving way to popular songs from the towns, and where a generation ago every harvest had a native orchestra and rhyming-song contests, often led by a special "song leader," today these folk customs lack general appeal.

There is some division of labor between the sexes at harvest, especially in the south, where only women do the reaping and threshing and only men carry the threshed rice to the granary.

In the rest of the country both men and women reap, thresh, and carry the rice in baskets from the threshing floor to the granary, although men do most of the heavy work, such as preparing the threshing floor, carrying the sheaves to the threshing floor, and carrying the heavier baskets of rice. An important job for children is to keep birds away from the ripening grain and from the sheaves with slingshots or bamboo clappers. If animals are used to trample the grain, a boy often is in charge of the animals, driving them round and round the threshing floor. Old men and women stay at home in the harvest season to take care of smaller children and help prepare the workers' meals.

Finally, the threshed rice, or paddy, is transported to the farmer's granary; in the northern areas by oxcart. Every village has several farmers who hire out their carts at harvest time to neighbors who do not own one. The charges for haulage range from 5 to 20 *satang* (a *satang* equals one quarter of a cent) per *tang* of rice, the exact charge depending on the distance from the field to the granary.

In the south and in upper central Thailand, the common type of granary is a beehive-shaped cone of woven bamboo plastered with mud and buffalo dung and roofed with thatch. In the north three types are characteristic: a family that gets all its rice from hiring out to work for other farmers has only a makeshift granary, usually a small beehive cone, similar, except for size, to that used in the south, and often attached under a lean-to shelter to the house; farmers with relatively small rice yields have several granaries of this type, but they are more substantial structures separate from the house; prosperous farmers have large, oblong granaries of wood raised on teakwood pillars, and roofed with clay tiles. In this last type rice is stored in elaborate wooden bins, and a balcony encircles the building. These imposing granaries of wealthy northern farmers are often larger than the houses of the poorer villagers. All types of granaries stand on posts three to six feet high, and are reached by means of a ladder; wide extending eaves protect the storage bins from the rain.

In parts of the northeast, where the rice yield is very low, or in the south, where rice farming is combined with fishing, no permanent storage granaries are built; instead, rice is kept in crude basketlike containers made of mats set on several layers of straw under the house. These are covered with mats or bamboo trays, but chickens and other animals have easy access to the grain. The same sort of crude storage bin has also been seen in the delta area.

WORK ANIMALS

Almost every Thai peasant needs at least one water buffalo to work his land. If he does not own one, he must rent one, for throughout Thailand the buffalo is essential for plowing and harrowing, and in central Thailand is used also for hauling. In 1930, Zimmerman found that in northeast and central Thailand the average number of water buffalo per farm family was two, in the north 1.41, and in the south slightly more than one for every two families.[14] The larger number of water buffalo in central Thailand is due to the larger average farm acreage, and in the northeast reflects the greater importance of cattle raising.

Bullocks are kept as cart animals. The north and south average more than one bullock per family, in the northeast more than 2.60, but in central Thailand less than one for every two families, with most of the bullocks in the western part of the region.

These averages give a somewhat erroneous picture, for they suggest a rather even, widespread distribution of work animals. Actually, quite a few peasant households own neither buffalo nor bullocks, and few own both. In a representative northern village (one with about 100 households) only three or four families own bullocks and carts. A farmer who owns a pair of bullocks will do the carting for his neighbors on a contract basis.

Although bullocks are used almost exclusively for transportation, in a few places in the south, north, and northeast, they may be used occasionally to plow light, sandy soil. They cannot work in the deep mud of the ordinary paddy field and are rarely, if ever, used there. In southern Thailand they are sometimes used for sport—fights between two matched bullocks.

The bullocks and cattle raised in large numbers in the northeast supply almost all of the local beef of the country, but in no village area, even in the northeast, are cattle or water buffalo slaughtered. The villager eats pork, purchased in a near-by market town. And although the milk of the water buffalo is rich in butterfat, it is not a part of the Thai peasant's diet, for southeast Asia obeys the ancient taboo on milk products. There is no dairy farming by Thai peasants.

CARE OF WATER BUFFALO

The care of the water buffalo is the task of men and boys; women look after work animals usually only in an emergency. When the animal is pastured in the fields, a small boy of the family always accompanies the beast, sitting or even sleeping on its broad back; if a family has no small boy, the farmer usually hires an attendant, or he may watch the animal himself.

Water buffalo are often stabled under the house, or, in the north, under the large wooden granary. In the Minburi region near Bangkok separate buffalo sheds are built in the yard, and poor families stable the water buffalo in the house.[15] At least once a day during the dry season the water buffalo is allowed to wallow in a waterhole or canal, the attendant often scrubbing the buffalo.

When the rice is planted, the water buffalo can no longer graze in the fields, and the farmer must provide food for the animal. If the buffalo is stabled in the house compound, the farmer must go out every day and cut grass from the edges of his rice fields and along the main irrigation ditch or canal. If the farmer has more than one buffalo, or if his fields are too far away from the village to allow him to fetch grass daily, he tethers the buffalo on a piece of high ground some distance from the village where he has built a small shelter for himself and his animals. Usually, several farmers use the same piece of high ground. Animals are tethered so that they will not get into the rice, but even so a watcher stays with them day and night. A family member will bring hot food once a day to the shelter. A young boy may be left alone with the water buffalo during the day, but at night the father or an elder brother stays in the shelter with the animals. Throughout the growing season, the rice fields around a village are dotted with flickering lights from the torches and fires of these camps. During the day one boy or young man may tend several buffalo, allowing the other watchers to return to their homes in the village.

CATTLE RAISING IN KORAT

In the Korat Plateau with its scanty watershed, insufficient rainfall, and large areas of savannah and forest, villagers have turned more intensively to cattle raising than anywhere else in the country. It was estimated that in 1939 there were five million head of cattle on the Korat Plateau, or 3.2 head of cattle to an acre of farmland, as contrasted with less than one head per acre in the Menam Plain.[16] This averages about five head of cattle for each of the million families of the plateau. Cattle raising, even here, is still subordinate to agriculture; only a few peasants have herds of more than six or eight head, although every peasant has enough cattle to be able to sell one or two each year. Cattle are bought by local dealers or by itinerant Indians who drive them in caravans southwestward to the Menam Plain, timing their arrival to coincide with the June planting season when the demand for work animals is highest. Farmers who can afford to do so keep a few water buffalo for use in plowing.

In areas where cattle rustling is a problem, animals are kept stabled in corrals under the house at night, and are taken to the forest to graze only in the day. After the rice has been harvested, cattle are pastured on the stubble and rice straw is fed them. Where there is no cattle rustling (parts of the Maharsarakam province, for example) farmers have several corrals in the forest clearings. During the dry season a family stables all of its animals in one corral; when the rains come, the animals are moved to the next corral, and the first, which has become fertilized by manure, is planted with tobacco or vegetables. By this rotation the fertility of the corral is maintained, and constant and extensive destruction of the forest by slash-and-burn agriculture is avoided.[17]

USE OF FERTILIZER BY THE PEASANT

In all regions of Thailand except the Korat Plateau the peasants make little use of animal manure in their rice fields. The low-lying areas have no need of it, for their soil is fertilized by the annual floodings. Animal droppings are of no value as a fertilizer in these regions because the weather quickly leaches all nutrients from the droppings. Manure is used to a limited extent to fertilize vegetable gardens and other plant beds of the house compounds in northern Thailand, but only in the Korat region is it used systematically and extensively. Here, because animals are relatively numerous and because they are corraled, there are large manure heaps. Without this fertilizer the Korat peasant could not grow the vegetables, cotton, tobacco, and other crops that are so necessary to supplement his livelihood. Tobacco, for example, has become the second most important crop of the Korat region; nearly every family has a small tobacco patch, and except for those on the fairly rich silt banks of large rivers all tobacco plots must be fertilized with manure.

Cattle manure, as well as ashes and garbage, is used to fertilize the mulberry trees in the house compounds. Raising silk worms is still quite an important occupation in the northeast even though recent importation of cheap cotton cloth has greatly reduced the amount of local silk-wearing. Banana, palm, and other trees, and all edible shrubs, are also fertilized with manure.

The peasants of the Korat Plateau have had through the centuries to adapt their agriculture to poor soil and inadequate rainfall. Only some 7 per cent of the area is under cultivation, and of this small area much of the usable paddy land is left fallow in alternate years. Yet here more than five and a half million peasants farm for a living. In the northeast a sizable number of large trees are left standing in the paddy fields, the peasants having learned that the fertility of the field is better maintained if not all the trees are cut. The poorer the field, the greater the number of trees left standing. That this folk belief has scientific validity is borne out by agricultural specialists who point out that the tree roots reaching down into the zone of weathering rocks get nutrients which eventually are added to the top-soil as plain offal.[18] In the area south of Bangkok and down through the peninsula, sugar palm trees are left standing on the *bunds* (dikes) separating the paddy fields, but they are not in the field itself, nor do they help fertilize the soil as do the trees in the paddy fields of the northeast. They are kept for their sap, from which brown sugar is made.

The poverty of the soil in the northeast has led the peasant to utilize another natural fertilizer—termite nest mounds, which often reach 2 to 3 meters in height and may be 5 to 7 meters in diameter. These nests, made of a sandy clay brought up by the termites from a depth of a meter or more below the sandy top soil, are fairly rich in plant nutrients and are further enriched by the termite activity. In those areas of Korat not near hill slopes or river banks, termite mounds often provide the only land available for secondary crops. The farmers flatten the mounds and spread the rich soil to form a bed in which they grow vegetables, tobacco, peppers, mulberry plants, and other crops.

SECONDARY CROPS

The dry season is not the time of idleness for the village peasant that early observers often reported it to be from their casual observations of life in the Bangkok delta. In the Menam Plain the peasant depends on one crop of rice completely and does not grow a second crop in the dry season, so that his work in the dry season is not so heavy as that of other Thai peasants. Like all Thai peasants, he must repair his buildings, fences, and tools, and he must take care of his vegetable patch, but he has more leisure in which to do these chores.

In the rest of the country, the raising of secondary crops in the paddy fields and on other land is an important part of the farmer's activity. In the north, tobacco is grown as an important cash crop. The tobacco industry in Thailand is controlled by the government's Tobacco Monopoly, under whose guidance the country now produces all the tobacco it needs. Paddy fields are sometimes used, but for commercial tobacco growing, river banks, edges of forested hills, or house compounds are preferred. The upland ground of the northern valleys is well-suited to tobacco growing; here, a fine grade is cultivated under careful supervision of government inspectors. Farmers who grow tobacco only for their own use or to barter locally need be less discriminating in the soil they use. To ensure suitable tobacco for its factories, the Tobacco Monopoly supervises the local farmers, for instead of raising tobacco on plantations, the government has fostered a system of tobacco raising adapted to the small, independent farmer.

The Tobacco Monopoly has seedling farms on which types of tobacco suited to the northern soil are grown. These seedlings are furnished without charge to the farmer, but on the stipulation that the grower follow the instructions on growing the tobacco and sell his crop to the government. When a northern farmer decides to raise tobacco commercially, he informs the nearest Tobacco Monopoly station and a trained inspector comes to inspect the land the villager plans to use. If the soil is not suitable, he will refuse to allow the villager to join in the Tobacco Monopoly's program; if it is, he gives detailed instructions to the farmer on how to prepare the ground. If the prepared fields meet with the inspector's approval, the villager is sent to the Tobacco Monopoly's seedbeds to get seedlings. Tobacco is planted about the middle of September, and the first leaves are ready to be sold a month or six weeks later; if the crop is good, leaves can be cut every week until the end of December. The villager takes his leaves to the Tobacco Monopoly barns where they are cured. Northern tobacco planters generally plant from 1,200 to 2,500 plants, it being possible to plant from 1,200 to 1,500 seedlings in one-half *rai* of ground. The Tobacco Monopoly pays for the leaves by weight. In the village of San Pong, in 1948, 17 farmers grew tobacco under the government's program; they planted a total of 29 *rai* and received severally from 30 to more than 1200 *ticals* for their crop. In the northeast, and even in central and south Thailand, farmers grow small patches of tobacco for home and local use, but they are not part of the Tobacco Monopoly's program and must develop their own seedlings.

Soybeans are another important cash crop of the two northern areas. Soybeans grow well in the paddy fields and require no plowing nor tilling. Seeds are planted in December in the open spaces between the dry rice stalks, and the ripe vines are cut in May. Stalks are bound into sheaves which are allowed to dry in the sun for several days before they are threshed. A farmer who has a large crop may thresh his soybeans in the field on a small threshing floor similar to that used to thresh rice. The pods are thrown on the threshing floor and beaten with sticks until all of the beans are out of them. The beans are sold by weight to dealers in the market towns, and the stalks and pod husks are piled in a corner of the vegetable garden. After the rains begin, mushrooms sprout from the mouldy heap and supply the family with a delectable food for several months.

In the north, onions, garlic, cabbage, and groundnuts are grown after the rice harvest, partly for home use, partly for sale in the market. Vegetables for family consumption are grown in the house compound throughout the year.* If a villager plants these crops in his paddy field, he first tills the ground by hoeing or spading. In several parts of the country, farmers raise small quantities of cotton, both for sale and for home use.

Dry-season farming necessitates a great deal of labor, for the plants must be watered every day. In the north, water is available from the irrigation ditches, but watering must be done by hand, for the level of the water is not enough to allow flooding of fields nor is the crop planted in a way that permits this even if it were possible. Hence, the crop area must be limited.

RAISING PIGS

Formerly, pig breeding in Thailand was controlled almost entirely by Chinese, but in the north, pig breeding on a limited scale is now done by Thai villagers. In the commune studied by the author, for example, most of the pig handlers were Thai, but whether this is true elsewhere is uncertain.

Thai peasants buy piglets about one-and-a-half or two months old from traveling vendors (most of whom are still Chinese), fatten them up for some eight or twelve months, and sell them to a dealer (who also will probably be Chinese). Pigs are sold by size rather than weight. In 1949, in San Pong, a baby pig fetched anywhere from 20 to 30 *ticals,* a ten-month old pig from 150 to 200 *ticals,* and a year-old pig from 220 to 250 *ticals.*

* Appendix III gives a list of the vegetables and fruit trees commonly grown in farm house compounds.

Taking care of the pigs is entirely woman's work, although the money they bring in is considered part of the general household funds. A household that lacks a woman able to tend them does not raise pigs. In one year 80 per cent of the households in San Pong sold one or more pigs.

In northern villages pigs are usually tethered by a rope and halter under the house; in northeastern villages, where more are raised, they are put in pens. Since a farm household has little garbage, pigs are usually fed messes of coarse vegetables, weeds, banana-plant stalks, and rice chaff cooked in a large clay pot over an outdoor fire; usually enough of this mess is cooked at a time to feed the animals for a couple of days.

Villagers do not slaughter their pigs because the Thai farmer is a Buddhist whose religion forbids the killing of animals and because he cannot afford the relatively high slaughtering fee (5 *ticals*). When a villager wants pork, he buys it from the Chinese butcher at the nearby market town. On very rare occasions—usually only for a festival when a great deal of pork is needed—a wealthy farmer may arrange to have one of his pigs slaughtered. Village headmen have a book of permits for slaughtering of pigs, issued by the district office, and a villager who wants to slaughter a pig must buy a ticket for 5 *ticals* from his headman; but local slaughtering is so rare that most headmen have sent their books of permits back. The death of a pig through accident, disease, or old age must be reported at once to the village headman or to the village doctor, one of whom must inspect the carcass. All animal deaths must be reported to the district officer. Villagers are forbidden to eat an animal that dies of disease.

Villagers usually dispose of their pigs by selling them to dealers who come to the village; the dealer either drives the pigs to a nearby market town or hauls them there in an oxcart. In the northeast, one of the villagers often drives several pigs, his own and his neighbors', to the pigpens of the nearest dealer, whence they are shipped to Bangkok. A villager in the remote parts of Ubon may drive a herd of hogs as far as 100 kilometers to the nearest hogpen.

In 1930 Zimmerman found in central Thailand an average

Harvesting rice

Winnowing rice in the field

Shelter for harvest workers

Transporting rice to the granary

of only one pig for every two families, and there is little reason to suppose that this proportion has increased in this area. Many pigs are raised here commercially by Chinese who live near the rice mills, and comparatively few by the Thai peasants. Zimmerman reported an average of one pig per family in the north and 1.23 pigs per family in the northeast,[12] but these figures may be too small since a census of pigs made at any one time fails to take into account the fact that families may raise two a year but only one at a time. In 1948, only 80 per cent of the households of San Pong raised pigs, and the proportion of pigs to peasants there is about the same as it was twenty years ago. In the northeast, pig raising has apparently increased considerably since 1930, if one may believe the 1939 census of animals, which reported some 4,250,000 pigs in this region. This figure, divided by the number of farm families, gives an average much higher than Zimmerman's average (1.23) for 1930.

RAISING POULTRY

Nearly every farm household in Thailand raises some poultry, but the northern and southern regions have a higher proportion of poultry per farm family than central Thailand. Chickens are raised primarily to sell at the market. Few Thai farm families eat more than four or five chickens a year. The native chicken is a hardy fowl, but its egg yield is low. This and the fact that eggs are saved for market sale by the women of the household means that eggs are rarely eaten by the family except on special occasions.

Farmers also raise a few ducks, for duck eggs bring good prices in the local markets. Duck raising on a large scale for eggs, meat, and manure, which is highly prized by market gardeners, is monopolized by Chinese poultrymen who live near Bangkok and other cities. In central Thailand, where duck raising is entirely commecial, only about half of the farm families engage in it because of the expense and trouble it entails.

The duck is a useful means of controlling pests in the rice fields. A familiar sight, particularly in northern and southern regions, is a line of ducks waddling along a village path early in the morning in the rice-growing season on their way to the rice fields; here they feed on rice crabs, snails, and insects that infect the fields. These flocks are unattended. (In Indonesia, where there is more intensive use of the duck as a pest controller, flocks are sent to the fields in care of boys who have trained them to stay within areas marked by bamboo flags.) The importance of ducks in controlling rice pests has not been adequately observed nor appreciated by foreign agriculturists who have studied farm techniques in Thailand. It may be pointed out that in villages where ducks work over the rice fields farmers do not have to resort to draining their paddy fields to kill the rice crabs, as they frequently have to do in some areas of central Thailand.

Chickens and ducks must forage for much of their food, though chickens are fed some paddy and rice-mill leavings. In the central area, chickens more often help themselves from the open rice-storage bins. Janlekha estimates that in the Minburi village area, a chicken of an average farm family helps itself to up to 40 kilograms of rice (4 *tangs* of paddy) annually.[20] Ducks in the central area are fed bran and broken rice.

The cost of raising chickens for the farmer is entirely in paddy. The average hen lays about 143 eggs a year, or 36 eggs for every *tang* of paddy she eats. Most of the eggs are sold, for approximately 4 *baht* per dozen, and since a *tang* of paddy costs about 7 *baht*, the clear profit is nominally 100 per cent. This means a steady, cozy little income for the Thai peasant, even if he has to spend it at once on other foods.

FISHING IN THE FARMER'S DAILY ECONOMY

The Thai proverb, "Rice on the land and fish in the water," sums up the dependence of the peasant on these two foods. The Thai consumption of fish is reputed to be the largest in southeast Asia. Every farm family devotes part of its time to fishing—fish is the most important source of protein in the peasant's diet—and the peasant family eats some fish at every meal. Every market stall and village shop carries dried fish, which is one of the most regular purchases of the Thai peasant woman in her morning market excursions.

Most peasants fish in inland waters—lakes, rivers, canals,

swamps, ditches, and fields—and eat most of the catch as fresh food. In some areas at certain seasons fish may be preserved by fermentation or by drying with salt. Thai peasants fish with bag, scoop, cast, and gill nets as well as traps, baskets, poles, and spears. Fishing with dip or scoop nets is the work of women and girls. Men and boys, who weed the fields and repair the dikes in the growing season, usually take charge of the traps; later, in the dry season, they fish in streams or canals. Young men go spear or pole fishing late at night by torchlight.

In the Chao Phya river system of the Menam Plain the annual upstream migration of a tiny fish of the cyprinid species, known to the peasant as *pla soi*, is caught by the millions in scoop and dip nets. When the *pla soi* are running, every household along the waterways spends most of its time netting the tiny fish. Much of the yearly catch of *pla soi* is fermented into the familiar *nam pla* paste, a basic ingredient in curry in the central plains. In northern Thailand the annual floods bring millions of carp and other fish into the paddy fields and irrigation ditches where they are trapped; these fish are caught throughout the farming season, with nets or scoops before planting begins, with line or pole afterwards; by the middle of the rice-growing season, the fish in the fields and ditches have grown as long as six or eight inches, for there is an abundance of insects for them to feed on.

The cost of fishing equipment varies considerably from region to region. In the north and northeast, peasants make their own nets, traps, and other equipment and buy only fish hooks; men make fish lines from the cocoons of silk worms. In the central regions, because of the commercialized rice economy, fishing costs are higher than elsewhere. Near Bangkok, the pond in the farmer's house compound is his main source of fish. He catches them with poles, nets, and by draining the pond once or twice a year. Fish ponds are subject to a tax of .60 *tical* for each cubic meter of water drained, which in a large pond amounts to a considerable sum; as a result, many drainings are not reported. In 1949, draining a pond 40 meters wide by 5 meters deep cost more than 780 *ticals* (a fish tax of 240 *ticals*, 150 *ticals* for rent of pumping engines, 365 *ticals* for labor). The pool had a yield of 60 kilograms of fish, all of which were preserved and consumed at home.²¹ This was the pool of a village headman, and without doubt entailed a much larger cash outlay than a farmer with a small pond could afford.

VILLAGE "SPECIALISTS" AND VILLAGE HANDICRAFTS

Every village has a few people who are trained in some livelihood other than farming, although nearly all of these "specialists" are also part-time farmers. School teachers, village doctors, and shopkeepers (usually Thai women) are about the only specialists who rarely or never engage in agriculture; the others—the handicraft specialists—are regularly part-time farmers who pursue their specializations during the dry season when others are growing secondary crops. Of these latter the carpenter is the most important. Nearly every village has a few men who, during the dry season, hire out to build or repair for the other farmers, and who train younger men (often their sons or sons-in-law) as carpenters in a sort of informal apprenticeship.

Handicrafts important enough to rank as cottage industries, i.e., those that produce important cash income, are not significant in the life of the average agricultural village; but throughout the northern areas, there are a few villages that specialize in one or more handicrafts—tilemaking, broommaking, papermaking, hat weaving. The Zimmerman and Andrews surveys gave an exaggerated picture of the importance of handicrafts as a source of income in the ordinary agricultural village: Andrews reported that 32 per cent of all annual cash income in the northeast, 26 per cent in the north, 30 per cent in the south, and 18 per cent in central Thailand came from handicrafts.²² In other words, according to the survey, in three self-subsisting areas of the country, handicrafts accounted for more of the total cash earnings of a farmer than agriculture. Even in central Thailand, where a rice cash crop is raised, this early survey indicated that handicrafts produced a fifth of the total cash earnings of a family. Andrews admitted these averages were computed by including villages that specialized in handicrafts. The inclusion of cottage-industry villages produced an average which did not give a true interpretation of the role of handicrafts in the wholly agricultural villages, which make up about 99 per cent of all the villages of the country. In these only a tiny fraction of family income is from handicrafts, for the products are largely for home use. At present in the Bangkok region, handicrafts are reported to be thoroughly moribund.[23] Here most handicraft products formerly made at home are purchased.

In the other areas some domestic handicrafts are still important, although all over the country in the last twenty-five years many important handicrafts have dwindled. Those that remain, like the making of mats, baskets, and hats, are in the hands of the men; spinning and weaving, except in the silk-raising areas of the northeast and a few localized spots in the north, has all but vanished. In the eleven villages of San Pong, only one operating loom to a village was found—a small loom for making scarfs. During World War II, a shortage of imported cloth brought out a few of the old spinning wheels and looms, and some cotton thread was spun at home by old women (young women today do not know how to weave), but the end of the war and the return of cheap textiles quickly banished the loom again. The day of cloth weaving is gone for village women.

A few old women in the northern areas still weave tiny cotton-wicks for homemade tin oil lamps, girls are taught how to weave twine fish nets by their mothers or grandmothers, and many other small household objects are still made at home—wooden spoons, torches, brooms, fans, coconut shell dippers, wooden clogs for the rainy season, etc.

Thai men have always woven baskets, mats, floor mats, and bamboo fish traps. Today weaving with cane, bamboo, or straw fibers is almost completely in the hands of the men; women help only in weaving floor mats. Basket weaving is the task principally of old men; younger men weave fish traps. Hat weaving is a more specialized skill practiced by only a few men in each village. Teen-age boys who want to learn hat weaving well enough to sell their products often apprentice themselves to an expert weaver.

HOUSEHOLD MARKETING

Throughout Thailand markets are held every morning in the larger villages and in the squares of the larger market towns.

Here village women bring eggs, vegetables, fruit, fish, and many other items to sell or exchange. Nearly all marketing is done by barter, but there are also enough cash transactions for women to earn trivial incomes. In 1934 Andrews estimated that every farm household within reasonable distance of a market sent at least one of its women to the market every morning.[24] Women from more distant villages go somewhat less frequently. In the San Pong commune, for example, only about ten out of a hundred households sent women to market on any given morning, although in the course of a week or ten days every household with an able-bodied woman was represented at the market. During the busy planting and harvesting seasons attendance at the morning markets falls off.

The permanent stalls in the markets of the larger towns operate from early morning to dusk. Stalls where meat and other quickly perishable foods are sold close out before noon. In the square surrounding the shops and stalls, the women who come from nearby villages carry on their buying and selling between six and eight, and are back in their villages by nine o'clock.

Poor women, many of them widows with children to support, peddle food or household commodities in their own village. Kerosene is a popular item with these local peddlers. It is used in every village for illumination; poor families burn it in cheap tin lanterns and wealthy families in expensive pressure lamps. Village women buy the fuel a little at a time (usually in a small bottle about the size of a soft-drink bottle, which costs 75 *satangs*, or 3½ cents), and their being able to get it from door-to-door vendors saves them having to carry the smelly stuff from the market with their food purchases. Village peddlers also sell bamboo shoots, mushrooms, peppers, garlic, and salt, or often barter these for rice, tobacco, betel, and vegetables. A few women sell food snacks, mainly around the crowded market centers in the larger villages of lower Thailand, and occasionally to village school teachers and children during the noon recess. Thai men of the northern villages engage in a seasonal, itinerant peddling. In May and June they go through the village selling steel plowshares, hoes, knives, and other farm implements; they often travel in groups for protection and usually sleep in *wat* resthouses and display their wares in *wat* compounds. Others peddle home-cured tobacco, rain- and sunshade-hats, or some other product of home industry. All of this Thai peddling is local and occasional, and offers no serious competition to the more aggressive and wide-ranging Chinese vendor.

ROLE OF THE CHINESE IN RURAL THAILAND

The Thai peasant knows the Chinese residents in Thailand chiefly as retail merchants and rice brokers—two activities over which the Chinese have acquired extensive control. His chief contact is with the Chinese merchant, especially the traveling vendor, who plies even remote villages; he sees rather less of the rice broker, for mill owners and their agents live only in towns or in larger villages that have rice mills (of which there are less than eight hundred, most of them in central Thailand). Both have an important influence on the economy of rural Thailand, and in general there are good relations between them and the Thai peasantry.

It has been reported that nearly every village in Thailand has a few Chinese families, but this report is false—nine-tenths of the villages of rural Thailand have none. The typical small village of the north and northeast has no Chinese, and Sharp's account of central Thailand notes that villages of the delta area commonly have no Chinese. Skinner's statement that many villages have Chinese residents[25] may have arisen from his impression that Chinese peddlers from the market towns, so frequently seen in the villages, resided there.

Most of the shopowners of the larger villages and towns are Chinese, but although increased roads and bus lines have now made it possible for more villagers to shop in these market centers, the principal merchant so far as the villager is concerned is still the itinerant Chinese vendor who regularly makes his village rounds, by small boat in central Thailand, on foot or by bicycle or bus in the rest of the country. A typical traveling vendor carries two trays made of soap boxes suspended from ropes on a carrying pole; these are stocked with needles, thread, buttons, soap, matches, belts, plastic bags, powder, hair pomade, and many other small drygoods. His largest sales come during the planting and harvesting seasons, when the busy villagers cannot get to the markets. The improved roads and increased bus lines have cut into his business but at the same time they have enabled him to extend his range of vending so that much of what he has lost in quantity of sales to a given customer has been compensated for by his being able to reach an ever greater number of customers. That itinerant peddling is still profitable is attested to by the fact that even remote villages are plied by the soapbox merchants. On a good day in the planting season a peddler can sell about 80 *ticals* worth of goods in the course of visiting several villages (the average in 1948 given by several peddlers who regularly ply the San Pong commune). Vendors are reluctant to discuss their profits, but it is obvious from the difference in retail and wholesale prices that at least half of each sale is clear profit. Vendors of more special items such as cloth and lottery tickets visit the villages during the dry season.

In recent years the highly profitable vending of pharmaceutical supplies has been opened up by Chinese firms in Bangkok and the provincial capitals. Mobile units in buses and motor launches are sent by these firms into the villages. In the north the visits of the large units from Bangkok occur usually only in the dry season when the roads are passable, but smaller units from the provincial capitals visit villages on the main roads at least once a month and villages on cart tracks some six or eight times a year. They play phonograph records over loudspeakers to attract the villagers, and sell aspirin, quinine, aralen, sulfa, and several local and foreign patent medicines. Villagers usually buy only in small quantities unless someone in the family is ill, but the village doctors often buy large quantities.

The Chinese own more than eighty per cent of the rice mills of Thailand. They have a virtual monopoly on the sale of all surplus rice, for every Thai peasant who sells rice deals either directly with a mill owner or with his agent who comes to the village as middleman. Chinese rice dealers are especially important in central Thailand.

To the peasant, the Chinese, whether peddler, miller, shopkeeper, or rice broker, is an essential link to the larger economic pattern of the country and a means of providing necessary and beneficial services. As aliens, as businessmen, and as townsmen, the Chinese of course come in for the inevitable garrulous depreciation of their rural clientele; the Thai peasant calls all Chinese peddlers *chek,* a somewhat derogatory Thai word for "Chinese," and the villager describes the peddler, when he is not present, as a sharp dealer who will try to cheat the village buyer whenever possible. But little of this is seen in face-to-face dealings with the peddler; in isolated villages, he is a welcome visitor, for he brings not only necessary goods but news and gossip from the market towns and from other villages. In larger villages where Chinese shopkeepers or mill owners live, they are likely to have married local Thai women, and their children are considered Thai by the villagers. Pretty girls of poor families often aspire to marry Chinese shopkeepers or rice-mill workers, for by village standards they are prosperous and can assure her and her family of economic support.

Throughout the country many handicraft and other domestic industries have been invaded by the Chinese. In northern Thailand, tanning, weaving, lumbering, and sugarmaking have been almost completely usurped by them. A great deal of local weaving in the north and northeast is done today in Chinese shops in the large market towns and provincial capitals; all lumber, both for local use and for export, is controlled by Chinese. In justice to the Chinese it must be pointed out that they have greatly expanded these crafts and industries. Carpenters and other specialized laborers of the market towns are also largely Chinese today, and almost without exception pig breeding and butchering are in the hands of the Chinese. Recent royal decrees have attempted to stop some of this encroachment by excluding Chinese aliens from certain occupations. In 1952, Chinese aliens were excluded from barbering, women's hairdressing, and dressmaking because these occupations, long held by Thai, were beginning to be taken over by them.

The Chinese money broker is a controversial figure in Thailand. As an alien cultural group controlling the Thai retail economy, the Chinese have provided a convenient scapegoat for rabid nationalistic-minded politicians of the 1930's and early 1940's. The Chinese moneylender has been presented as an "unconscionable usurer" charging exorbitant amounts of interest and bleeding the Thai peasant mercilessly. Reliable data on debt and interest rates are lacking, but incomplete information suggests that the Chinese moneylender is not any more avaricious than his Thai counterpart. In 1934, Andrews attempted to demonstrate that the Chinese moneylender in reality was likely to charge lower rates of interest than the wealthy Thai farmer or townsman. The moneylender has little importance to the Thai peasant except in the delta; elsewhere villagers seldom have occasion to borrow large sums.

Except for a few truck gardeners near Bangkok and a few laborers on the rubber plantations in the Kra Isthmus, the Chinese in Thailand do not directly engage in agriculture. To prevent alien Chinese from gaining control of farmland, the Thai government has systematically tightened the restrictions governing land ownership since the early 1940's. In 1943, aliens whose governments had not signed treaties with Thailand permitting reciprocal ownership of movable property were forbidden to purchase land. This regulation was directed specifically against China, which had no such treaty with Thailand.

In some localities regulations prohibit sale of land to children of Chinese aliens unless the buyer can prove Thai ancestry for at least three generations.[20] The Royal Estates Department also no longer renews alien-held leases of farmland.

The only appreciable amount of rice farming by Chinese has been in the Patalung and Tung Song districts of southern Thailand, where in 1930 an experimental coöperative rice farm was started under the sponsorship of a firm of Chinese merchants of Malay.[27] Chinese families moved into this area and cultivated several thousand acres with motorized equipment. This experiment demonstrated how thirty men working with modern machinery were able to cultivate an area of 600 acres of paddy which, by Thai methods, would have required 300 men. Within the next ten years, commercialized large scale rice farming expanded; the Chinese had their own rice mills and marketing outlets, and developed a completely independent farm colony. But the experiment was stopped by the anti-Chinese laws of the late 1930's and early 1940's. At present, further development of

Chinese rice farming coöperatives is prevented not only by the alien land law, but also by a royal decree of February, 1949, which specifically excluded Chinese from rice farming. Other restrictions of 1949 forbid Chinese aliens to engage in forestry and saltmaking.

5 Religious Beliefs and Practices

The Thai peasant practices the Hinayana form of Buddhism, which through the centuries has become so blended with Brahmanism and with elements of an earlier animism that it is impossible to segregate pure elements of each. Buddhism and Brahmanism have become so closely interwoven as to be indistinguishable to the ordinary Thai worshipper. The animistic or spirit worship which is so important in the peasant's daily life has infiltrated into Buddhist practice, invading even the temple. As a means of storing up merit for life in the next world the villager turns to Buddhism; for protection in his present world, the peasant looks to the host of good and evil spirits that affect his every undertaking. In the north and northeast a few villages have been converted to Christianity. In the south, there is an Islamic group of Malays.

THE WAT, OR TEMPLE COMPOUND

There are scores of thousands of Buddhist *wats* or temple compounds throughout the country, many abandoned and in ruins, for in the old days merit was gained only by building new *wats*, not by repairing old ones. According to a recent census, there are more than 18,000 *wats* in use. Nearly every village has its own *wat,* but small contiguous river villages often share one, and in the delta, where widely separated small house groups are common, a centrally located *wat* may serve a large outlying region. For example, in the Bangchan community area 1,600 villagers are loosely grouped into seven hamlets for administration purposes; all seven share one *wat* which is more or less centrally located.[1] The social life of the village revolves around the *wat.* The first sound in the village is the predawn chant of the head priest to awaken the temple dwellers, and the last is the chanting of the monks before they retire.

A large *wat* may contain a temple for lay worshipers (the *vihara),* a sacred temple for monks (the *bot),* a dormitory for monks, novices, and temple boys, a library, a number of rest houses (*salas*), a stupa (*chedi*), and, frequently, the public primary school; but not all of these are necessarily in every *wat.* Set off from the rest of the village by a wall and surrounded by tall coconut palms and fruit trees, the *wat* stands in a cool, inviting grove. Within the compound are more trees—the graceful coconut, the betel palm, and the sacred *bodhi* tree. Most temples are located on the outskirts of the village, to provide a measure of isolation for the monks and novices. The temple grounds are sanded and always kept free of grass. Every year at the New Year festival fresh sand is brought as an act of merit by worshipers so that in time the level of the temple grounds is raised above that of the rest of the village.

The temples with their colorful glazed tile roofs loom above the banyan, betel, and coconut palms. The *vihara,* or preaching temple, and the *bot,* or *bo-sote* temple, are rectangular, have a portico over the entrance, and two rows of columns inside to help support the roof; they are usually brick, plastered and whitewashed. The altar with its image or images of Buddha

[1] For notes to chapter 5 see page 217.

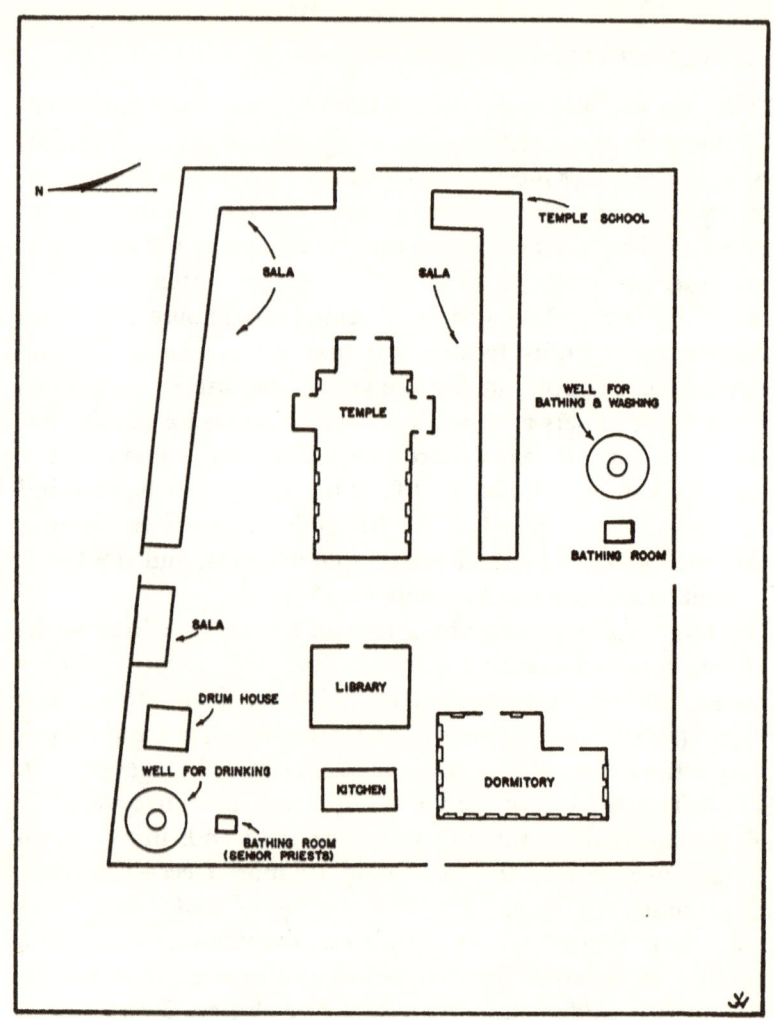

Typical plan of a village wat

always faces east, since this is the direction Buddha faced when he received enlightenment under the *bodhi* tree. The size of the *vihara* and *bot* varies considerably according to the size of the village, the only stipulation being that the *bot* must be large enough to seat a congregation of twenty-one monks. The *bot* is frequently on a separate piece of land some distance from the *wat* proper. If it is within the *wat*, it must be some distance from the other buildings, away from the distraction of the compound; for the *uposatha* (ordination) ceremonies are held in the *bot*, and its separateness ensures that women do not accidentally enter it, they being forbidden this consecrated area.

Legally all temple lands belong to the government in the name of the Buddhist order, and by ancient law it is held that land once part of a temple becomes consecrated ground and cannot be used for anything else even if the temple should have fallen in ruins or disappeared.[2] As a result, throughout rural Thailand plots of high ground on which temples formerly stood dot the paddy fields; these plots are regarded as belonging to the *wat*, but the villagers' belief in the sacredness of these old temple sites does not prevent their putting them to practical use as grazing areas for water buffalo, sites for rest houses, and fields for growing vegetables and tobacco. If a *bot* is outside the *wat* proper, often part of its land is used for grazing or farming. Villagers who use old temple areas must get permission from the abbot of their *wat*, but they do not have to pay rent for the use of the land.

In the north, each village designates one of its men who has been a monk as the leader of the community in matters concerning the *wat* and the villagers. He leads the congregation in making responses at the temple ceremonies because having been a monk he knows the proper procedure; he officiates at funerals, helps make arrangements for the ordination of novices and, assisted by the village headman, raises money for maintenance of the *wat*.

THE RELIGIOUS SERVICE

Wan Pra, the weekly Buddhist holy day, is a day of rest for all villagers. Farm work is done on *Wan Pra* only if it cannot possibly be postponed. In the past, the temple drums were beaten by young men on the eve of *Wan Pra* to announce to the villagers that the sabbath would fall on the next day; this old custom is followed now only during the Buddhist Lent or before a special holy day. During Lent, services are conducted by the monks on *Wan Pra;* during the rest of the year the villagers, led by the older men, conduct services themselves in the *vihara* after morning food offerings have been made.

All observers of Thai religious life have remarked on the sociability and air of festivity that permeates every religious ceremony. The congregation visit, gossip, chew betel, and smoke during the service. All the important Buddhist holy days are festive occasions and even the serious ceremonies, such as ordinations and funerals, are accompanied by feasts, music, and games. It is through the social aspect of the religious service that the peasant finds satisfaction for many of his social and recreational needs.

DAILY CONTACT WITH THE WAT

Every villager, even though he may not go to the *wat*, comes in daily contact with the monks, for it is one of the duties of the monk to beg for his daily food. Every morning the streets, lanes, and waterways are filled with a stream of yellow-clad monks silently going their way with their begging bowls of iron or brass. As they stop at the dooryards of the houses, women and children put offerings of rice, curry, and fruit into these bowls. Usually in a city or town the food gathered by the monks on their early morning rounds is not eaten by them but taken back to the temple to feed the temple boys, beggars, and dogs that throng the *wat;* the monks' meal is prepared by the temple boys from supplies sent by wealthy Buddhists who wish to gain merit. In villages, however, most of the food gathered by the monks on their begging tours is eaten by them; therefore, villagers place only cooked rice in the large begging bowl, and put curry and other cooked foods in special containers carried by the temple boys who accompany the monks. Frequently, households send additional food to the *wat* for the monks' midday meal, since they know that often not enough food is collected on the begging rounds for this meal. A temple drum is sounded at eleven o'clock to warn those who intend to send food that noon is approaching. This warning is called *pheen* or *nong pheen*. In central Thailand, where most villagers do not eat a noon meal, food is cooked at this time only for the *wat*.

In northern Thailand some villages have dispensed with the morning begging of the monks. Instead, the village has been divided into sections of from 16 to 20 households, each with a designated chief. Each section provides food for the monks on a fixed day. A bamboo bell is passed from section to section, and the chief's responsibility is to ring the bell at dusk of the day before it is his section's turn to prepare food for the temple, to warn his households to prepare extra food. Women and girls of these households carry baskets of food early the next morning to the temple. A few women stay in the *wat* to arrange the food on wooden trays and put the rice in the brass bowls of the priests. Novices or monks are served by the temple boys. Occasionally, men or boys bring the household's food offering, and devout old men may bring food offerings for the monks every morning.

The system is sponsored by the elders of the village, the old men and women who regularly attend all Buddhist ceremonies at the *wat*. This group selects a captain for each section, one, if possible, who has served as a novice or priest in his earlier days. Under this system a section of households prepares enough food for both the morning and noon meals of the monks. In addition, any other household can send food whenever it wishes. Should there not be enough food offered for these two meals, temple boys will be sent by the head priest to make the rounds of the village to procure additional rice and curry for the monks' midday meal. This occurs very rarely, for it means that a section did not meet its obligation; to avoid this, sections prepare more than enough food for both meals, and leftovers are fed to the cats, dogs, and pigeons that live in the compound.

The custom of dividing a village into sections responsible for providing food for the *wat* obtained in half of the villages of San Pong and in about half of some fifty villages in neighboring communes. This custom has been in effect in this area during the lifetime of the present generation, but it has not been observed elsewhere in rural Thailand, and may be strictly a northern innovation. On the other hand, similar customs that have never been reported may well exist in other regions, for no previous account of northern Thailand mentions the custom even though it obviously existed and even though much of the scanty literature on peasant life deals with the northern Thai farmer. The custom is not unknown even in northern villages that do not practice it. The term used to designate these food sections, *hua muad song kow,* is known throughout the general area, indicating that the custom is more than just a localized undertaking of the Chiangmai region. In villages where the daily begging of food has been dispensed with, the head priest or abbot may send young novices or even monks out to beg to teach them humility.

RELIGIOUS LIFE OF THE PEASANT MAN

Theoretically, a Thai male may enter the Buddhist monastery any time during his life, but if a villager does not do so while he is young and before he marries, in all likelihood he will never do so, for once he takes on family duties, he will seldom be free of them until he is middle-aged. Later in life, he may yearn to enter the monastery, but by then he will no longer be able to meet the academic requirements, and will be too old to adapt himself to the strict regime of monastic life. In urban Thailand, a married man may temporarily renounce his wife and children to become a monk, for here a woman can support herself and her children by any of several jobs. But in the self-subsistent rural economy the family cannot exist unless the head of the household works in the fields.

A representative village monastery contains young men who have entered the priesthood for only a few years, others who will stay in the monastery for many years, and a few who will remain priests all their lives. In time, the more intelligent of this last group will become abbots or teachers in the temple school for novices. Ideally, all Thai males seek to be ordained novice or monk at some time, but many do not achieve this ideal.

Although it is hard to estimate the percentage of men who never serve in the temple, either as novice or monk, the figure for northern villagers appears to be well over 45 per cent. In the commune of San Pong, roughly 46 per cent of all males older than twenty had no temple service. A survey of some fifty other villages in the north and northeast revealed the same ratio. Sharp's study of a central Thai village notes that in village life not every male followed the "ideal requirement" of spending some part of his life in the *wat*.* Significantly, the village study of San Pong demonstrated that this is not a recent development, for the ratio of nonservice appears to be even higher for the older generation of males than for the present generation.

Males who do not serve as either novice or monk are not accorded the same respect in later years by the community. Such men are called *khon dib* or "raw men." Males who have served in a monastery are given extra respect and deference, denoted by titles of greeting used by family members as well as outsiders. A man who has served as a novice is given the respect term of *noi*, and this prefixes his name and other terms of address all his life. A man, once a monk, later in life will be called *narn*. These men will be the leaders in the religious life of the community, and their words will carry weight in village council meetings. For the village man to become a monk, it is essential that he serve first as a novice, for this is the only way a young man can acquire the knowledge of Pali and of the Buddhist scriptures he must know to qualify. To become a novice, it is essential that the village boy serve an apprenticeship as a temple boy. This apprenticeship starts early in life.

BECOMING A TEMPLE BOY

Village boys usually become temple boys at about the age of ten. Parents are reluctant to allow boys younger than ten to live away from home, and a boy should be able to read and write so that he will be able to follow the daily services in the temple. Most boys are unable to read before they have finished the beginners' primary class and entered grade one of the village school. In a village *wat*, temple boys may range in age from ten to eighteen years, but the majority tend to fall between ten and fifteen. If they stay on in the *wat* after fifteen, they usually become novices.

Devout Buddhist parents encourage their sons to serve in the *wat* if they can be spared from farmwork, for the family earns merit by their sons becoming temple boys, and the boys are taught Buddhist ethics by the monks. Village surveys in the north have shown that about half of all village males spend some time in the *wat* as a temple boy. Those that do not do so generally come from families that cannot spare the boys from farmwork. No attempt is made to force a boy to serve in the *wat,* and some boys after a few days or weeks of service ask permission to return home.

The temple boys serve as attendants to the novices and monks in the *wat,* carrying the monk's bag when he leaves the temple, running errands, and keeping the dormitory clean. The boys sleep and eat in the *wat* dormitory but attend the public schools and usually go home for the evening meal, since the monks do not eat in the evening. Afterwards, they return to the temple dormitory to study their school lessons and join with the novices and monks at the evening service in the dormitory.

Most village boys are glad to become temple boys, for they are exempted from work at home. Although they are under the jurisdiction of the abbot, they have more free time to play than other village boys. Being a village temple boy is also advantageous from a scholastic point of view. Temple boys have a place to study, and are supervised to some extent by the monks. Often, the only suitable lamp for reading at night in a village is in the temple dormitory. If a village boy is making good marks today in the public primary school, he is probably a temple boy.

BECOMING A NOVICE

To qualify for novicehood a village boy must meet two requirements. He must have successfully passed grade four of the required primary school curriculum if he is below the school-age limit of fifteen years, or he must be able to read and write if he is fifteen years old but has not completed school; and he must pass an examination in Buddhist scriptures and precepts given under the direction of the head abbot of the district in which the boy's village is located; if he passes the primary examination, he is given a certificate signed by the abbot of the district.

To pass this examination, a village boy must usually have spent a year or more as a temple boy, for it is only in the temple that he can learn enough of the Pali scriptures to do so. In the cities, a male above the age of twenty years may study with a monk for a time to acquire enough background to pass the primary test. Under certain circumstances it is possible for a young man to enter the priesthood for a short period, usually during Buddhist Lent. In the larger towns and cities also, a young man may enter the monastery as a novice or monk for a special three-day funeral period when a parent or grandparent dies, in order to gain merit for the deceased. For this special short period of monkhood, the passing of the primary test is not required. These exceptions seldom apply to rural Thailand.

If the boy passes the required primary test, a consultation with the boy's father (or mother, if the father is dead) is held by the abbot; at this conference, arrangements are made for the robes and other supplies the novice will need. An invitation is sent to friends and relatives notifying them when ordination will take place. Often, a wealthy villager or relative asks to be the boy's sponsor, which means he must provide for the novice's upkeep in the temple. This custom enables even a poor boy to join the monastic order. Even when a family is able to meet the expenses itself, it is common to allow an outside sponsor to gain merit in this way. If a youth has a sponsor from another family, he is known as the "gem son" (*luke keo*) of the sponsor, and from this time on he will call his sponsor "uncle."

The novice-to-be becomes a special individual and an object of festivity and rejoicing. The festivity acts out in a dramatic manner episodes of the Buddha's life when he was still the young prince, Siddhartha. Village observance of ordination ceremony is not so elaborate as that of the towns and large cities, but it is still the most colorful and imposing ceremony of village life.

On the day of the ordination, the boy has his head shaved either at home or at the *wat*. Elaborate leave-taking ceremonies in the boy's home are held in urban Thailand but seldom in the villages. In northern villages there is, however, a blessing ceremony in either the boy's or his sponsor's home, conducted by the elders of the village. The boy is led before the group of old people, his hands are tied with a sacred cord, and one of the old men, who formerly was a monk, chants a blessing in Pali over the boy. This is called *pan porn* (giving a blessing).

The boy is then dressed in an elaborate costume of silk with gilt spangles, and a tall decorated headdress, to represent the princely garments of Siddhartha, and his face is painted like that of a classical actor, with dead white face, painted eyebrows, and beauty spots. The rural boy often wears a *likay* costume, which is the costume used in the Thai classical drama. In some parts of northern Thailand old costumes which formerly were worn by nobles of the region are rented out for these occasions. If the family or sponsor is poor, the costume may be made of white gauze, decorated with silver and gilt spangles. A horse is hired and the boy rides in procession to the temple. If a horse cannot be obtained, the boy often is carried on the shoulders of a village man who acts the role of Prince Siddhartha's steed. A ceremonial umbrella owned by the *wat* is borrowed for the occasion and held over the boy's head by an attendant. An orchestra with drums and cymbals leads the procession, which often makes a triumphal tour of nearby villages. Upon arriving at the temple, the procession marches triumphantly three times around the walls. The boy then says farewell to his parents, who deliver him to the monks.

At the temple the boy lays aside his princely garments and dons a white loin cloth and tunic which he will wear until he receives his yellow robes at ordination. In the north, ordination is delayed until the next morning, the young lad sleeping the first night in the temple as a candidate. The procession disperses, and villagers return the next morning for the ordination ceremony. Although accounts are vague on this point, it appears that elsewhere in Thailand ordination may take place on the same day.

In the temple the novice stands between two monks whom he has chosen as his guides. The candidate in his white garments, carrying his robes, incense, and candles, approaches the chapter of monks, bows three times to the abbot, and requests that he be allowed to become a member of the priesthood as a disciple of Buddha. He makes this request three times in Pali and presents his yellow robes to the abbot. The abbot instructs the candidate in the precepts he must follow as a novice and hands back the yellow robes, telling him to don them. After the candidate is robed, he presents gifts to the two monks who have agreed to act as his instructors and asks them for the Buddhist precepts. After the candidate has repeated the ten precepts of Buddha, he bows three times, takes up his begging bowl and, kneeling before the abbot, begs three times to be allowed to serve as a pupil. When the assent is given, the ceremony ends for the novice.

This ceremony is held in the *vihara* or preaching temple so that friends and relatives of both sexes may attend, although in the north it is not uncommon for a novice to take the first part of his vows in the *bot* before he goes to the *vihara* for the principal, public ceremony. It is also customary in the north for a group of monks to hold a special ceremony in the novice's house on the day he goes in procession to the temple. This is the *poi luke keo*, literally, "ceremony for the novice candidate." The monks partake of the family's noon meal and later hold a short religious service in the house; afterwards the other villagers hold a feast. It appears to be the same as the *chalong phra*, which in central Thailand is a festival at the novice's home on the day after ordination.[4] Many early accounts of Thailand have erred in describing the ordination of novices, apparently by confounding their ordination with the ordination of monks.

BECOMING A MONK

The ordination of a young man as a full-fledged Buddhist monk, or *bhikkhu*, when he has reached the age of twenty years is much more complex than his ordination as novice. Almost every aspirant to monkhood has already served in the temple as a novice for several years; if, at the age of twenty, he decides to stay on in the *wat*, and if his parents agree, plans are made for his ordination as a monk, and his sponsors are notified. If the original sponsor does not wish to continue supporting the young man as a monk, another sponsor is found. Sometimes the new sponsor will be a group of villagers or his support will come from a special fund to which all villagers contribute. On the day before ordination, the aspirant's parents and relatives call upon the abbot and ask to be allowed to take the novice home. He doffs his yellow robes and dons a white skirt and jacket over which he wears a colorful costume of gilt and brilliant colors. When the novice is once more decked out to represent Prince Siddhartha, he rides from the *wat* on a horse in gala procession through his village and perhaps neighboring villages to his home, where a feast is held for friends, relatives, and villagers from neighboring villages who have been invited some weeks before to this great occasion and who have gathered at the youth's home with food, money, yellow robes, candles, incense and other gifts suitable for a monk. The young man dismounts and is greeted by his mother and grandmother, who ceremoniously wash his feet before he is allowed to enter the house. Then, he is led onto the veranda, where the elders of the village have gathered, and is presented with new robes and other things he will need as a monk. The young man removes his garish garments and sits in his simple white dress in front of the elders on the veranda. His hands are tied with a sacred cord, and an old man or group of old men who formerly were novices or monks bless him in Pali. Old women are present, but they do not participate in this blessing.

Now the festivities begin; the orchestra plays and young people engage in rhyming-song contests while older men and women prepare the feast. The novice does not participate, but watches the dances and games from the house. At dusk four or five friends of his own age escort him back to the *wat*, where he spends the night in his white garments in the temple dormitory waiting for the ordination ceremony which takes place early the next morning. Most older villagers leave in the early evening after the feasting is over, but the young people continue to celebrate late into the evening, dancing the *ramwong*, singing, and courting. Often, the village orchestra will play all night, for even though the young women may be reluctantly drawn away by their parents at midnight, the gay young blades of the village will carry on until dawn.

Early the next morning the young man will go before a chapter of monks in the sacred *bot*. Here he will beg the abbot to allow him to become a priest or monk. The abbot questions the candidate in the form of the prescribed catechism, asking whether he is human, male, twenty years of age, free of disease, sound of mind, free of debt, free of duty to government service, and has his parents' permission. There are fifteen such questions the candidate must answer in the affirmative before he is asked the name under which he will join the order. After the chapter of monks signify their willingness to accept him, he is led to one side, where he exchanges his white tunic for new yellow robes. The chapter of monks with the newly ordained monk now proceed to the *vihara*, where relatives and friends of the youth have gathered. These villagers come, one by one, and prostrate themselves before the new monk, presenting gifts to him.

In the larger towns and cities, the family of the new monk may hold a special ceremony in their home the next morning, during which the monks who have participated in the ordination are presented with food. Northern villagers hold this special ceremony on the morning before ordination. It is customary that the new monk bless the home of his parents about two months after he has been ordained.

Only one item of dress distinguishes the monk from the novice; this is a special robe, called *pa-sang-ka-ti*, which is about eight feet long and six feet wide, folded in twelve layers and worn over the left shoulder at all religious ceremonies. Novices are never permitted to wear this robe. At all ordinary times monks and novices wear the same garments.

LIFE IN THE MONASTERY

Life in the village *wat*, while not physically arduous, is not idle. Early accounts describing the idleness of a monk's life are very misleading, and even so acute an observer as the late Ruth Benedict fell prey to the exaggerations of early writers when she reported that monks have no specific responsibilities, no full routine of devotions, and can give full rein to lassitude in the *wat*.[5] A more erroneous picture of village monastery life could not be drawn. Possibly in the large wats of Bangkok a monk's life may be more unexacting, but in a village *wat* there is little time for lassitude.

The day begins for monk and novice shortly after dawn, when, about five o'clock, the abbot begins to chant a prayer of loyalty and thanks to Buddha. All monks and novices recite this prayer aloud upon arising. This takes about fifteen minutes. Then, until six o'clock the *wat* is quiet. At this time the monks begin to leave to collect food in the village, or, if food is brought to the *wat*, villagers now arrive with laden baskets. A special early morning service for temple boys and novices, starting at six and lasting about ten minutes, is conducted in the northern temples. Novices and temple boys gather before the altar in the dormitory, and one of the novices presides at the service. Breakfast is served to the monks and novices by the temple boys between seven and half-past seven. From eight to eight-thirty the first of the regular Buddhist services for monks and novices is held in the dormitory in a room where there is an altar. Afterwards, small tasks in the *wat* are done; the compound is swept, rooms are cleaned. Monks and novices study, or may be given permission to visit relatives in the village. At eleven preparations for the midday meal are begun; this must be eaten before noon, for monks are forbidden food after that hour. Novices serve the monks at this meal, for the temple boys are at primary school.

There is a period of rest for the novices until two o'clock, at which time they attend novice school in the temple, which lasts until four. Not every *wat* has a novice school. In the commune of San Pong, for example, only the village of San Pong has this school, so that novices from the other villages of this commune must set out for the school by about one o'clock.

Novices study the Buddhist dharmas, the history of Buddhism, and Pali. In a small novice school, like San Pong's, there is only one grade or class. If a novice wants to take advanced studies, he will be sent by his abbot to a larger temple in the market town or the provincial capital, where novice schools may have as many as three grades. No fixed time is set for a novice to pass the course; bright novices finish it in one year, others take several years to pass the examination. If a novice cannot pass the examination at the end of five years, he cannot continue in the novice school, and almost always he voluntarily gives up novicehood. These temple schools, not to be confused with the government's primary school, which also may be held in the *wat*, run from the end of June to the end of December, at which time there will be an examination on the year's work. The examination in Pali for all novice schools is prepared by the Ministry of Education in Bangkok and is given at the end of the year in the local *wat*. Examination papers for grade one are sent to the provincial capital, where they are graded by a special committee of monks designated by the abbot of the province, but test papers for the second and third grades of novice school are sent to the Ministry of Education in Bangkok for grading. January through June is vacation time for the novices.

Learning consists largely of memorizing scriptures, dharmas, and conventions. Since novices have already finished the four required grades of primary school, only Buddhist topics are taught. In the north, novices are required to learn the archaic northern script in addition to Pali, for the scriptures are written in the old local script on the palm-leaf manuscripts. In the central and southern area, novices learn only Pali. The school is in the charge of one or more monks; a small school will have only one teacher.

The late afternoon is used for bathing and resting. At evening, lamps are lit in the dormitory, and novices and temple boys study their school lessons until half-past seven, when temple boys, novices, and monks gather in the dormitory room containing the altar for the evening service. The first ten minutes of this service is conducted by the temple boys, who chant the five Buddhist commandments; the novices and monks then chant the "Three Gems." After this, the monks, led by the abbot, chant one of the various legends of Buddha which are written in Pali in two sets of ancient books, one set consisting of seven books, the other of twelve books. Village monks usually learn only the legends of the first seven books, for the final set is long and difficult. Only one book is chanted at a service, which lasts about thirty minutes. Often, though, when this general service is concluded, the monks hold an additional worship service sometimes lasting another hour. Between nine and eleven temple boys and novices study. Since they chant their lessons aloud the temple is a babel until about eleven, when the temple boys and novices retire, long after the rest of the village has gone to sleep.

Life in the temple dormitory is not uncomfortable. Though the novice or monk cannot eat after midday, he can take tea with sugar, chew betel, and smoke at any time. Although he takes a vow of poverty, the novice in actuality often has more money, received in the form of gifts, than he possessed when he was an ordinary boy of the village. Each novice and monk will have his own small cubicle in the temple dormitory unless space is limited; then, two novices may share a room. The novice or monk is not allowed to use a mattress but uses instead mats which are placed on low wooden beds. Mosquito nets and pillows are used.

Novices and monks may visit their families in the morning between nine and eleven without permission from the abbot. Permission must be secured if they wish to go into the village after noon or if they wish to visit a family not their own. Rules governing novices are not quite as strict as those for the monks. If a family member is ill or some special emergency arises, a novice may secure permission to stay with his family for a period of seven days, after which he must renew the permission from the abbot. At times the novice or monk may visit the provincial capital or large market town to see friends or make some purchase. Often, he stays overnight or a few days at a *wat* in town. During Lent, a monk and novice are not allowed to leave their *wat* but must always sleep there at night. The novices and monks participate in many ceremonies in the villages. Funerals, house warmings, as well as special holy day ceremonies, all require the presence of a group of monks from the *wat*.

LEAVING TEMPLE LIFE

When a novice or monk wishes to leave the temple, he consults his parents, and if they agree, he informs the abbot of his decision, presenting a tray of puffed rice, candles, incense, and flowers when he makes this request. The abbot does not accept his resignation immediately but talks to him and advises him to reconsider his decision. A few days later, if the novice or monk still wishes to leave, he goes with the abbot before the statue of Buddha in the *vihara*. After worshiping the Buddha, he again declares his intention to leave the temple. He changes into ordinary dress and meets again with the abbot to receive his blessing and to listen to the Buddhist commandments. Then he is ready to return to his home and begin life again as a common villager. In ancient times, a monk who had decided to leave the monastery would wear a white robe for seven days prior to his departure, but nowhere in rural Thailand is this old custom followed at the present time.

According to ancient custom, he must return to the *wat* for the next three days, either in the morning or in the evening, and do some temple work, such as filling the water jars of the monks or sweeping the *wat* compound. When leaving a village *wat*, the monk or novice takes his individual money fund with him, for this belongs to him, and he will need it to buy clothing. Usually, the retiring novice or monk gives his robes and other temple equipment to friends who are still serving as novices or monks.

Only ordinary village monks can ask for retirement from their local abbot. The village abbot or a monk who has been appointed by the Council of Buddhism in Bangkok as a *Upachar* monk (one who has the power to ordain) cannot leave the priesthood unless he is granted permission by the Buddhist Council. Rarely, however, will a village monk who has reached this position ask for retirement, for by this time the priesthood will be his life's vocation.

There would appear to be, proportionally, a smaller number of monks in the northern areas of the country than in the other parts of Thailand. The northern temples have few full-fledged monks but have a fair number of novices: central and southern Thailand tend to have fewer novices and more monks. The main reason for this is that, as already noted, the northern areas do not often observe the custom of ordaining young men as monks for short periods, and although central Thai villagers do not ordinarily follow this practice either the custom is observed in the urbanized farming areas around Bangkok and in the south. In the northern areas, only novices who intend to dedicate many years of their lives to the temple will apply for ordination as monks, whereas in other areas it is the custom to serve a short time as a monk without going through the preliminary novicehood. At any given time, then, the temples in lower Thailand will be likely to have a larger number of monks than novices.

RELIGIOUS LIFE OF THE WOMAN

The village girl cannot enter into monastery life, but she early acquires a deep and lasting devotion to the Buddhist faith. Daily, with her mother, she prepares the food that will be presented to the monks. Long before she knows how to cook this food, she will be allowed to put rice into a monk's begging bowl or accompany her mother when food is taken to the temple. The great majority of offerings of flowers and incense presented continually to the statue of Buddha in the temple are taken there by women.

It is possible for a Thai woman to join a Buddhist order of nuns, but the group is very small, consisting of elderly women who wear white robes and are attached to some large temple. Most of the Buddhist nuns are in Bangkok, and few if any are ever seen in the rural areas.

COST OF MAINTAINING A MONASTERY

Every household in Thailand contributes food to the *wat*. These contributions are made either by giving small amounts to the monks or novices when they come begging, by sending occasional voluntary gifts to the *wat*, or, in the north, by assigning sections of a village to feed the *wat* in turn. Under the old custom, most households of a village make small but frequent offerings; under the "northern innovation" a few households make large offerings for several days. Under both systems the amounts given over a long time are about equal. It is impossible to estimate exactly what amount of food is given to the *wat*, but conservatively, each contributing family probably gives enough to feed one person each day. All of this will not necessarily be placed in the monk's begging bowl; the estimate includes food sent to the *wat* at noon, on special holy days, and on important ceremonies at homes throughout the village.

The 1937 census gave a quarter of a million monks and novices and more than 100,000 temple boys for the country; in other words, one in every 30 males was either a monk or novice and, including temple boys, one in every 20 males at that time was in the *wat*. There is no indication that the proportions have decreased since 1937, so that today one may estimate that there are probably 400,000 Thai males in *wats*.

The economic cost of supplying them with rice is great. For each farm household, the food contribution to the *wat* over a year is probably equivalent to the cost of feeding one additional person. The average daily rice consumption for Thai peasants was computed by Zimmerman to be 553 grams for the nonglutinous-rice eaters of the central and southern regions, and 693 grams for the glutinous-rice eaters of the north and northeast. The present survey indicated that the adult male consumed roughly one pound of rice a day, approximately the same amount computed by Zimmerman. On this basis, an average farm family would contribute annually a minimum of over 360 pounds in rice alone, and this in cash value would amount to well over 200 *ticals* at the retail market price of rice. Villagers' own estimate is that 20 *tang* of rice is the bare minimum required for one adult for a year. Probably much more rice than this is given when all of the special food offerings on religious festivals are taken into consideration. Each family's rice contribution amounts to a significant amount of the rice consumed in a year, and it must be borne in mind that rice is only the basic food offered, for curry, vegetables, fruit, and other foods are also presented.

The daily food offerings are only one of a series of ways in which the farm household contributes to the support of the *wat* and its inhabitants. Zimmerman estimated that roughly 27 per cent of the farm household's cash went for merit-making activities. Andrews' follow-up survey in 1934 indicated that Zimmerman had underestimated cash expenditures for the upkeep of the *wat*. For all farm households in Thailand at that time, the cash expenditure for the *wat* per family was considerably higher than that spent for home and food supplies.[6]

An average family will spend several hundred *ticals* in cash annually for money and other gifts to the *wat*. Cash gifts to the *wat* are voluntary contributions usually given a few *ticals* at a time. Families give proportionally to their income. These small donations are given all through the year and larger amounts are presented on special festivals such as New Year, Buddhist Lent, and other holy days. A wealthy family averages much more, for not only will it give proportionally to its income, but in all probability it will be underwriting the annual upkeep for a novice or monk whose ordination the family originally sponsored. On the other hand, a poor village household, except for donating food and laying out a small amount to buy candles and incense, may have a limited cash disbursement for merit-making.

The actual cash outlays of farm families for merit-making contributions vary tremendously according to economic status, the devoutness of the household, and special circumstances, such as whether the family sponsored the ordination of a novice or monk during the year. The village study of San Pong, in which the household expenditures of 108 farm households were analyzed, showed a wide range. Strictly cash outlays for merit-making, for one year's time, ranged from a high of 1,000 *ticals* ($50) to a low of 15 *ticals* ($.75). In this village the household giving 1,000 *ticals* actually spent 78 per cent of its major cash expenditures for the year on religion, or about 55 per cent of the total annual cash income of the household. This unusually high expenditure was brought about by the fact that the family had sponsored the ordination of a novice who was not a member of the family. The cost of the ceremony, the feast, and robes

Typical wat of the north

Village boy dressed as Prince Siddhartha before ordination as a novice

Monks and temple boys

and equipment for the novice necessitated this large outlay. In this northern village the cash outlays for merit-making ranged from 7 per cent to 84 per cent of the total cash expenditures of each family for the year. Only three families, and these very poor households (two without male heads), had no such cash outlays. The average for all households in percentage of merit-making costs to total cash expenditures was 25 per cent. This was for the year 1948, when no extraordinary major repairs for the *wat* were needed; in 1947 and 1949 there were much higher outlays, for two large special funds had to be raised.

Not all the disbursement listed as cash expenditure goes in the form of cash gifts to the *wat*. The amount includes items purchased for offerings—incense sticks, candles, tobacco, betel, and other supplies, and for extraordinary food costs incurred when sponsoring an ordination or at a funeral. Thus, the village family which spent 1,000 *ticals* or 55 per cent of its total cash income on merit-making actually spent half of this amount on food for the ordination feast and half on the ordination itself.

Two kinds of cash gifts are made—for the monks' personal use, and for the general upkeep of the *wat*. If the money is meant for a specific novice or monk, it is handed to him by the family member in a cone of flowers and betel leaves, usually before the opening of service in the temple. Offerings to individual novices and monks are known as *pat jai*. Gifts of one or two *ticals* meant for the general *wat* fund are also placed in cones of flowers but are left before the statue of Buddha in the *vihara*. Wealthy farmers who give larger amounts may present the money to the abbot of the *wat*. In northern villages, two additional regular cash contributions are made by the villagers. At the basket-offering festival in October, each family will give a larger amount of cash than usual as part of their basket offerings. Many villages also collect a special robe fund from the villagers at this time.

A small village *wat* does not have a special treasurer; the abbot takes charge of the general temple fund, and the monks and novices keep their own funds. Often, a novice may place his money for safekeeping with the abbot. The monks and novices use individual money gifts to buy robes, umbrellas, soap, matches, and for other minor expenses. If a monk comes from a very poor family, or if his parents are old and cannot work, he may use part of his money to buy clothes and gifts for them.

Monks and novices have control of their own money, but according to Buddhist rule, they are not supposed to handle it. When a monk goes to the market town or provincial capital, a temple boy accompanies him, carrying his bag and acting as treasurer, paying for the bus tickets and purchases. In the towns monks are much more sophisticated, and in Bangkok it is not unusual to see monks paying for their own purchases and handling money in the public markets. The country monk is conservative and obeys the rule much more punctiliously. Within the confines of the village *wat*, monks and novices pay little attention to the rule, however, and when they make purchases from the itinerant Chinese peddler, they handle the money themselves.

In addition to their regular money contributions for the upkeep of the *wat* and its inhabitants, villagers are called upon at irregular intervals to make sizable contributions for repairs or for erecting new buildings. In 1947, the *wat* in San Pong needed a new dormitory. Even though some of the old lumber was used, it was necessary to raise a fund of 17,000 *ticals* (at that time roughly $1,000) for the new building. This amount was raised by the abbot in less than a year. Neighboring villages and landlords of the region who live in Chiangmai contributed, but the bulk of the money came from the 108 households of the village.

The need for repairs to the *wat* is ever present. If the abbot does not have enough money for the repair job in the temple fund, he informs the village headman and the village religious lay leader who call a meeting of the villagers to ask for special contributions. Thus, in the village of San Pong at the end of 1949 it was necessary to repair the main *vihara;* 20,000 *ticals* were needed for lumber, cement, carpenter labor, and decoration. This fund was raised within a year, mainly from San Pong and nearby villages. When the amount needed for repairs or new buildings is greater than the village can raise, word is sent to neighboring villages. Villagers do not feel imposed upon when asked to contribute to a building fund of a *wat* in another village.

Wealthy villagers will contribute large amounts for any major repair work. Other villagers may give only small amounts but contribute in kind, making bricks and donating them to the temple. An ordinary household contributes from five hundred to one thousand bricks. When major repair work to the temple requires scores of thousands of bricks, a village will be dotted with homemade brick ovens. Wealthy villagers who contribute bricks may buy them from some enterprising neighbor who makes them to sell. All repair work, except that which requires specialized carpentry, is done voluntarily by the village men.

The size of cash contributions and the proportion of the outlay to total cash expenditure reveals the strong social importance of the *wat* in the peasant's life. An important feature of this giving is that it is voluntary. No person asked to make a contribution is under any social pressure to do so; the villager makes these gifts freely.

THE YEARLY FESTIVAL CALENDAR

All the important religious holidays are calculated by the lunar calendar. Most of the ceremonies will fall on one of four days of the lunar month: the eighth day of the waxing moon, the day of the full moon, and the eighth and fifteenth days of the waning moon.[7]

The Buddhist sabbath, *Wan Pra,* fixed according to the lunar calendar, falls on different days of the week, there being forty-eight *Wan Pra* days in the lunar year. In the Thai lunar calendar, six months of the year have thirty days and six months have twenty-nine days, for alternate months will not have the fifteenth day of the waning moon. Hence, to correct the calendar, an intercalary "eighth month" is added from time to time.[8] The Thai religious New Year begins in April, which in the central area is the fifth lunar month. Northern Thailand uses a somewhat different computation which makes April the seventh lunar month. But this is the only difference between the two major areas of the country, for each Buddhist holy day is celebrated in the same month throughout the country. To avoid confusion in the description of the lunar festivals of the villagers, the lunar month is referred to by name, not by number.

Villagers rarely have calendars in their houses, but there is always one in the house of the village headman and in the temple dormitory. The Thai, like the Chinese, use the twelve-year zodiac cycle of animals; the year of the Rat, Cow, Tiger, Rabbit, Big Snake or Dragon, Little Serpent or Snake, Horse, Goat, Monkey, Chicken, Dog, and Pig. This cycle is so arranged that every twelve days and every twelve years it is repeated. A host of superstitions surround combinations of the day, the number of the month, the animal, and the cycle.

The times of important ceremonies, such as housewarmings, funerals, and ordinations are never set without consulting the abbot of the local *wat* who makes lunar calculations to ensure an auspicious date. The times of unlucky dates are not consistent, for not only are they controlled by the lunar calendar, but they will vary according to the month, year, and cycle of birth of each person. An unlucky day for a man born in the year of the Goat might not be an unlucky day for a man born in the year of the Dog. In November, March, and July, Tuesday is considered an unlucky day on which to start an important undertaking, whereas for the other nine months it may not be so. Certain specific dates are lucky or auspicious, such as the thirteenth, fourteenth, and fifteenth day of every month. The determination of lucky and unlucky days is so complex that only the monks with their books of astrology and charts can make the proper calculations. In almost every incident of daily life, the animal zodiac cycle and the lunar calendar will be consulted. Certain animal-year combinations bring happiness in marriage, other combinations will doom it to failure. A woman born in the year of the Rat, for example, should not marry a man born in the year of the Dog, if a happy marriage is desired. Much of this old superstition is waning, but elements of it still cling tenaciously in the rural areas.

The traditional lunar cycle is to some extent being broken up. Sunday as a legal holiday and a day of rest is observed by government offices and the schools, and the new national holidays are fixed by the Western calendar. The official year now opens on January 1, which is a national holiday. Rural Thailand thus has two sets of holidays, the religious holidays determined by the lunar calendar and the new national holidays fixed according to the Western calendar. All major holy days are also national holidays. To the peasant, though he recognizes the official calendar, the lunar year beginning in April is important from a religious point of view.

THE LUNAR CYCLE OF FESTIVALS

April: The Buddhist New Year.—The Thai Buddhist New Year opens on the day of the first full moon of April, usually about April 12, and is one of the most important of the religious festivals for the peasant. In the northern regions, five or more days are devoted to its celebration. Preliminary arrangements for the festival may begin on the day of the full moon, which is known as *Wan Dar,* or "preparing day," but the festival proper begins the first day of the new lunar period, known in the north as *Sankranti,* and in central Thailand as *Maha Songgram.* The New Year festival is called in the northern regions *Pi Mai,* and in the other areas *Songkran.*

On the morning of *Sankranti,* the opening day of the festival, the peasant family takes special food to the temple, and presents food to the old people of the village. In the north, special cakes of brown sugar and rice flour are presented, and peasants may send these to friends and neighbors. It was once the custom to put food and water in bamboo tubes tied to the trees so that roving spirits would also be fed, and to fire guns to frighten away evil spirits; a remnant of this custom is the exploding of firecrackers during the festival.

On the second day—*Wan Nao*—villagers bring sand to the *wat* compound, each family shaping its sand contribution in the form of a *chedi* (stupa) in the courtyard. Later this sand will be distributed throughout the compound.

On the third day—*Wan Phya* in the north, and *Wan Ta Loen Sok* in the central area—special food offerings are presented to the monks. Lustral water (*som poi*) is taken to the temple by the monks to wash or sprinkle the sacred images of Buddha, and a morning service is conducted there for the congregation.

The anointing of the Buddha with holy water has its counterpart in the custom of villagers sprinkling each other. For the young people, dousing each other has become largely a mirth-making occasion, but the older villagers retain remnants of the older religious character of the custom.

On the fourth day—*Pak Pi*—villagers pay their respect to the abbot, commune headman, village headman, and the old people of the village. They carry a silver bowl of lustral water, incense, flowers, puffed rice, and other offerings, and the person visited sprinkles the visitor with the holy water and gives a blessing. Services are held in the temple by the monks from eight to ten in the evenings.

Much the same sequence of events is followed on the next two days, *Wan Pak Pi* and *Wan Pak Tuan*. According to the lunar calendar, the festival ends on the fifth day, but in the northern areas, young people continue dousing each other and keep up other festive activities for several additional days.

During the five-day period of the festival a host of other ritual observances are carried out, the meanings of which have been forgotten. Some are survivals of animistic customs, others are Brahmanistic; the very festival of *Songkran*, for example, is Brahmanistic in origin. On the opening day of the New Year, villagers wash their hair and clothes, and clean the house compound of the dirt of the past year. On the second day, any caged pets in the household are freed. On the third day, in addition to presenting food at the temple, the villagers also place paper flags on poles in the temple compound. These paper flags are similar to the bamboo flags erected as spirit offerings in the rice fields.

May.—The three-day festival of *'Visaka Buja* is observed at the time of the full moon, about May 22, to commemorate the birth, enlightenment, and death of Buddha, three events reputed to have occurred at the full moon of this month. Villagers present special food offerings to the *wat* and attend *Visaka Buja* services conducted at evening by the monks in the *vihara*. Young people march in torchlight processions in and around the *wat* while the services are going on and later set off many fireworks and rockets.

June.—This busy month—the beginning of the planting season in most of Thailand—has no principal religious festival, but if the first rains are late, the Buddhist ceremony of praying for rain may be held at the end of the month. Every household is represented at the temple service by at least one member, and offerings of special food and money are given to the *wat*.

June to October: Buddhist Lent.—The three-and-a-half month period of Buddhist Lent opens ordinarily about the middle of June, when the moon begins to wane. The most important days are *Khao Wasa* and *Ok-Barnsa*, respectively the first and last days of the lenten period. Many religious observances are celebrated by the monks, but among the laity only older villagers attend special ceremonies. On the morning of the days when regular lenten services are held in the *vihara*, villagers come bearing gifts of food, money, incense, and flowers to the *wat*. After presenting food to the monks, they retire to the temple. The old people, who spend each lenten *Wan Pra* in the *wat*, sit in the front of the congregation. All Buddhists are expected to display unusual devotion during Lent—to sleep in the *wat* on the eve of each *Wan Pra* and to pass the holy day in the *wat* in attendance at the services. White garments are supposed to be worn on *Wan Pra* throughout the year but particularly during Lent. However, it is only old people who observe the regulations about sleeping in the *wat* and wearing white clothing (which even this devout group wears usually only during Lent), and usually only old people, women, and girls attend the *Wan Pra* services, for the lenten season falls at the time when villagers are busiest in the fields. Old people who sleep in the *wat* on the vigil of the twelve *Wan Pra* days of Lent also sleep there on New Year's Night (*Wan Paya Wan*) and on the eves of the festivals of *Visaka Buja, Loi Katong, Makka Buja,* and the offering for new rice.

The lenten *Wan Pra* begins with an early morning service in the *vihara* conducted by old men who were once monks. After this service, the younger women and girls return home, leaving the old men and women in the *wat*. After lunch people gather in the *vihara* for another service conducted by the monks. The first and last days of Lent are national holidays, on which special services are conducted by the monks, and on the evening of the last day the devout light many candles and tiny lamps in their homes and in the *wat*.

Previously, the important ceremony known officially as *Tot Kathin* (literally "laying down of the holy cloth") began at the second half of the lunar month of October and continued for one lunar month. During this time robes and other gifts were presented to the *wat*. This was a very elaborate ceremony at court and among the urban aristocracy, but comparably elaborate rites were never held in the villages. Today, robes are presented at various times of the year, and the *Tot Kathin* ceremonies are not so important nor widespread as they once were, although at some time during this period villagers hold a special ceremony at which gifts are presented to the *wat*. In the north and northeast this period is known as the time of the basket offerings. The presentation of these baskets is no longer fixed; the abbot of each village *wat* arranges a date agreeable to other *wats* in the commune so that offering days will not coincide, since many villagers make offerings not only to their own *wat* but to neighboring *wats* as well. The northern Buddhist monks say that this basket offering ceremony is not the same as the old central Thai custom of *Tot Kathin*, but since it always occurs in October, sometimes before the end of Lent, sometimes after, it would appear to be related to the ancient *Tot Kathin*. In the north, where the basket offering days have become very important, they are known as *tarn koey salark* (*tarn*, "offering"; *koey*, "basket"; and *salark*, "chance" or "number"). A similar custom in central Thailand is known as *tarn sa-ka-pa-tra*, literally, "the offering of gifts."

On the morning of the day designated for the basket offerings, villagers march in procession carrying special trays of food and the gaily decorated baskets to the *wat* compound. Families vie to outdo each other's basket decorations. Tobacco, cigarettes, soap, salt, betel, matches, belts, notebooks, bags, fruit, sweetmeats, and other small gifts for the monastery are placed in the basket. In the center of each basket is an elaborate bamboo tree, to the branches of which *tical* notes are pinned to resemble leaves. Young men beat the drums and gongs of the *wat*, and the village orchestra plays. The villagers wait in the resthouses of the *wat* until the monks have eaten, and then a ceremony is held in the temple which all villagers attend. Following this the baskets are presented to the abbot, who distributes the contents according to the needs of the temple boys, novices, and monks. Sweetmeats and most of the school supplies are given to the temple boys.

In the northern areas, individual villagers rarely present robes at this time, but the village religious lay leader and headman often collect a special robe fund. Families contribute voluntarily according to their ability. In the village of San Pong, in 1948, the lowest contribution for the robe fund was 50 *satangs,* the highest 10 *ticals,* and the average about 2 *ticals.* The lay religious leader goes to the market town and buys robes in shops that specialize in Buddhist religious articles; the robes are presented on a tray to the abbot, who distributes them to novices and monks who need them. Novices and monks who need additional robes during the year have to purchase them with their own money unless they are given robes at funerals.

November: The Festival of Lights.—This three-day festival, which is one of the most colorful in Thailand, occurs on the full moon a month after the end of Lent. Its Thai name is *Loi Katong,* from *loi,* "to float" and *katong,* a small tray or dish of banana leaves, and is derived from its principal event—the floating at night of tiny boats of paper and bamboo filled with offerings and coconut-shell lanterns or candles. This festival, like so many others in Thailand, is a mixture of animism, Brahmanism, and Buddhism, and has many explanations, some based on Hindu, others on local legend. Originally it was a Brahman ceremony; today, some Thai contend that it is performed to atone for the sin of boating over the footprints or images of Buddha which may be imbedded in the sands of the waterways; others that it is a ritual to appease the river spirits. It is no longer celebrated widely in the Bangkok region but is still a major festival in the north. In 1948, the royal government sought to revive the festival in regions where it had become moribund by sponsoring contests in the provincial capitals and awarding prizes for the most original and beautiful boats.

All villages where the festival is held decorate houses and the *wat* with colored streamers and lights. Villages that are not on rivers or canals stress this part of the festival and make elaborate lamps shaped like animals, birds, dragons, airplanes, and so forth; these villages also float illuminated boats on irrigation ditches, and young people often trek to the nearest large waterway to float their boats. Villages on waterways are also gaily decorated, but they give particular attention to their boats, making them in the shape of battleships, gondolas, rafts, airplanes, dragons, or whatever image happens to catch the maker's fancy.

On each of the three days of *Loi Katong* the monks (who are forbidden to take part in the floating of the boats—though this rule in villages on waterways is honored more in the breach than in the observance) conduct morning, afternoon, and evening services in the *wat*. The village elders, the women and girls attend all of these services, but men and boys usually attend only the evening service, at which time the *wat* takes on a festive air. Drums and gongs are beaten before and after the service; firecrackers are exploded in the *wat*, and the faithful gossip, flirt, and court, and drift in and out of the temple, where the monks chant until midnight. Festivities go on until dawn.

January.—A few localized areas have pilgrimages in this month to shrines where *phrabat*, or sacred footprints of Buddha, are found, and about the thirteenth day, special thanksgiving offerings for the new rice will be made at the *wat* and a service held in the temple.

February.—The important holy day of *Maha Buja* comes on the full moon, about February 24. Next to the *Visaka* ceremonies, this is the most important Buddhist holy day of the year, for it commemorates the occasion three months before the death of Buddha when a series of miracles occurred. Popularly, it is known as the Buddhist All Saints Day, and is a national as well as religious holiday. The villagers bring special food offerings to the temple in the early morning, and the old people spend the entire day in the temple. The main service is in the evening, when the monks conduct the *Maha Buja* services in the *vihara*.

Other holy days concern only the monks who live in the *wat*. Housewarmings, funerals, ordinations, and other occasional family affairs have an important religious character and are festivals for the family or families involved, but have nothing to do with the regular Buddhist year. In present-day Thailand there is some regional variation in the number and kinds of religious festivals, but all of rural Thailand follows to some degree the cycle described in the preceding paragraphs.

AGRICULTURAL RELIGIOUS OBSERVANCES

Though the Thai peasant is officially a Buddhist, as a farmer he retains much of the ancient animism of all men who dwell close to the soil. He reverences the crop he grows as a sentient being; he marks its stages of growth by ceremonies; and he propitiates the spirit of the soil in which it grows and the good and evil spirits that may help or harm it. He considers rice to possess a life spirit (*kwan*) and to grow much as a human being grows; when it bears grain, it has become "pregnant" like a mother, and the rice is the seed or child of the Rice Goddess.

Widely described in all historical accounts of Thailand is the Brahmanistic "First Plowing Ceremony," which was celebrated in Bangkok by the king or his deputy until the present decade. The extent to which the peasant practiced this rite is problematical, for the elaborate royal rites were unknown to the great mass of rural farmers although remnants of animism connected with this ceremony are still found in the villages. Some peasants still make offerings to the "spirit of the land" before starting to plow by erecting a crude post in the corner of a field and placing food and other offerings on this, but beyond this, few remnants of the elaborate ceremony of the "First Plowing" can be found anywhere in rural Thailand.

The next important offering to the spirits—one that is much more prevalent—is made to the Rice Goddess when the seedbed is prepared. Bits of food, flowers, betel, tobacco, and other items are put in a cone of banana leaf and placed in one corner of the seedbed. At transplanting time offerings are made to the Mother Earth Goddess.

Most farmers make no more spirit offerings until threshing

time. In a few areas, e.g., around Ayuthia, offerings used to be made to the Rice Goddess when the grain began to form on the stalks; at the close of this elaborate ceremony, the farmer stuck little rectangular bamboo flags in his fields to signify to his neighbors that his rice was "pregnant" and was not to be disturbed. The bamboo flag is common throughout the rural areas of the country as a spirit offering in itself, propitiating the evil spirits. Thus, this custom has both animistic and practical values; it notifies neighbors not to trespass in the fields and serves as a magical charm which wards off evil spirits who might harm the "pregnant" rice. The elaborate offerings to the Rice Goddess have faded away, but bamboo flags are still found in the fields all over the country when the rice grains begin to form.

The next spirit offering is made when the rice is ready for threshing. Spirit offerings to appease the Rice Goddess are placed on the post in the center of the threshing floor, but the elaborate ceremony in which the Rice Goddess was invited to leave the fields and allow her children to be threshed is no longer observed. In earlier days, after the rice had been threshed, a celebration might be held. For this, the Buddhist priests held a service on the threshing floor during which the leader of the monks sprinkled holy water upon the "rice of the goddess," that is, a small quantity of rice that had been set aside for the next planting season. This custom has died out, although an attempt to revive it in a slightly different form is now being made by the government.

A variety of other spirit offerings were made in the past, such as a special ceremony to invite the rice to enter the granary. In addition to the numerous rites, many prohibitions existed as to when to plow, transplant, reap, harvest, and thresh; careful calculations according to the lunar calendar were made to find the most auspicious day for such activities.

Only remnants of the elaborate rites concerning rice cultivation remain, but in some form, most peasants still make offerings to spirits at seeding, transplanting, and threshing. The government has attempted to revive certain of the old Brahmanistic ceremonies, and at the present time sponsors a Buddhist ceremony of blessing seed rice. This ceremony is a blend of certain elements of the old Brahmanistic "First Plowing Ceremony" and the Buddhist ceremony of "Blessing the Seed Rice" (*Bidhi Miji Mangala*) which is said to have been initiated by King Mongkut as an adjunct to the Brahman plowing ceremony. The new ceremony, if it can be called this (it is more of a government service in which monks participate than a religious rite), has been performed for ten years without having had much effect on the peasants.

District officers now distribute rice seeds which have been blessed by the Buddhist priests. Before the time for planting the seedbeds, the district officer buys rice seed of the best quality and prepares a small bag for each village in his district. The headmen and *kamnans* are invited to attend the ceremony of blessing the rice, held in the office of the *nai ampur*. The bags of rice are placed on a table, and a chapter of monks chant a service and sprinkle bags of rice seed with holy water. Each headman is given a bag of the "blessed rice" to take to his villagers to mix with their own rice seeds. Villagers in the northern areas pay little attention to this new custom. In 1949, in the district of Mae Rim, the district officer spent 200 *ticals* for seed to be blessed, and every village received a bag, but few villagers bothered to get this "blessed seed."

ANIMISM AND ITS EFFECT ON DAILY LIFE

Many traditional animistic beliefs and practices have died away or been modified to fit changing situations, but in almost every incident of a peasant's daily life, from his birth to his cremation, the spirits, or *pi*, are still propitiated. Spirits exist in many forms—ghosts of the dead; wandering astral spirits of the living; spirits of trees, the ground, the house, and a host of natural objects. The variety is great, but the one common element is that the spirits are evil or will become so if not properly propitiated. Thus, even the spirit of a dead parent can become a thing of evil.

To the devout Buddhist peasant, belief in spirits does not conflict with his belief in the teachings of Buddha. He believes that man has two spirits, one a soul, living in a man's heart, that upon death will reside in heaven if a man has been righteous and good, or in hell (*narok*) if a man has been bad, the other a spirit, living in various parts of the body, that may become a free-roving element after death and often turns into an evil being. In actuality, the two so-called spirits of a man are not kept rigorously separate in folk belief. A peasant, upon being questioned as to how a man's spirit can become evil and haunt the house compound or village, since, according to Buddhist doctrine, it should go to heaven, will reply that what goes to heaven is a man's soul, not his spirit, but in the next breath he will explain that the light kept burning on a coffin is to guide the soul to the next world so that it will not become lost and turn into an evil spirit. Yet this apparent contradiction in belief is not much different from that of the Christian who believes that the redeemed soul goes to heaven and yet firmly believes in the existence of ghosts.

SPIRIT DOCTORS

Since "spirit worship" plays so important a role in the daily life of the peasants, spirit practitioners or "spirit doctors" are to be found in almost every village. Much of the practice of the "spirit doctor" is in exorcising an evil spirit out of a sick villager, for the ancient belief is that illness is caused by evil spirits. When a man is sick, the first thing the family will do is to make offerings to the spirits of the house compound. If a family no longer has a spirit house of its own, it will take an offering to a communal spirit house in the village. To be doubly certain of placating the offending spirit, a spirit doctor, an elderly villager who knows how to prepare magic water, will be called in.

In remote areas, peasants may still believe that severe illness is caused by a ghoul sending his spirit to take possession of a man's body. In the old days, families of such reported ghouls were stoned and driven from their home villages, and although the law today decrees that ghouls do not exist and forbids villagers to use force to drive them out, many northern peasants still hold that ghouls are real. Village women suspected of being ghouls are shunned and always shown a healthy respect; other village women avoid quarrelling with suspected ghouls, they do not try to beat them down in market bargaining, and do not refuse their requests. The belief in ghouls is dying away, and today peasants talk about ghouls of the old days or about those "in other villages."

When a patient or family believes a ghoul has entered a sick person's body, special measures must be taken. The spirit doctor chants his magic charms over the sick person and calls upon the hidden ghoul to reveal its name. If the sick person believes some enemy or reputed ghoul has bewitched him, he will call out its name. The spirit doctor then asks the ghoul why it has taken possession of the sick man's body. More magic spells and charms are chanted, and finally the spirit doctor takes a cane that has been given magical powers by his charms and beats the sick man, crying out to the ghoul to depart. This beating continues until the patient becomes quiet or vomits, a sign that the evil ghoul has fled.

CHARMS TO WARD OFF EVIL SPIRITS

Small children wear pieces of rolled-up paper with a magic charm written in Pali and wrapped in a lead tube to ward off evil. These charms used to be made by the spirit doctor and were often later blessed by the Buddhist monk; often the monks themselves made the charms. Today, monks are forbidden to make magic charms, but those in rural areas occasionally still do.

In lower Thailand, little boys often wear a tiny ivory or wooden phallus on a string around their waists, but this custom, of Hindu origin, is not common in the northern areas. As a Hindu custom, it always has been more prevalent in the towns of lower Thailand and is now becoming rare in the peasant area of the region. Even within the *wat,* the phallus may be encountered, although it is more prevalent in urban than in village *wats.* Some Bangkok *wats* contain phallic stones upon which barren women place offerings.

BUDDHISM AND ANIMISM

The close interrelationship of Buddhist and animistic practices is demonstrated constantly: the Buddhist amulet worn by children offers the same protection as does the magical Pali charm prepared by the spirit doctor; Buddhist lustral water, given its sacred nature by the chanting of dharmas by monks who sit in a circle around the bowl of water, is the same as the magic water (*ka-ta*) prepared by the spirit doctor who blows magical Pali charms into ordinary water, and is used in the same way to drive off evil spirits. Buddhism frowns upon spirit worship and in the exorcising of evil spirits, but some Buddhist rituals are themselves interlaced with elements of animism.

In recent years an attempt has been made by the Buddhist church to discourage the strong dependence of the peasant on spirit worship. By order of the Supreme Patriarch of the Buddhist Order in the late 1930's, Buddhist monks were forbidden to dabble with the occult powers that control the *pi*, or spirits. But a country monk is still a villager, born and raised in a rural environment, and he comes to the monkhood firmly believing in the existence of a spirit world. He will change little in this attitude unless he stays many years in the monastery. The few monks that devote their lives to the priesthood may try to discourage open spirit worship, but only if they possess very dominant personalities will they have much success. The village of San Pong illustrates the influence of a strongminded abbot on spirit worship. Here, only six households possessed small spirit houses. In his forty years of actively opposing spirit worship, the abbot of the village *wat* had trained the present generation of villagers to dispense with certain of the older customs. Overtly, in other ways, the villagers of San Pong seem to place less reliance on spirits, as seen in their funeral customs and practices when contrasted with the same practices of neighboring villages in the same commune. Yet almost every San Pong villager who planted rice made offerings to the Rice Goddess and to Mother Earth, and no housewarming in San Pong is held without spirit offerings being made. Not as spirit-ridden as his ancestors, the modern peasant still plays safe by making offerings to the spirits as well as being a devout Buddhist.

6 Changing Scope of the Villager's World

Local government in Thailand is today a modification of that of ancient times. The fundamental administrative units within the district—the commune (*tambon*) and the village (*muban*)—have remained much the same throughout Thai history, but the degree and effectiveness of local self-government have changed radically. Before the Ayuthia era, headmen were chosen locally;[1] during the Ayuthia era they were appointed by the governor of the province. In 1896, Prince Damrong, the Minister of the Interior, directed a reorganization of provincial, district, and village government which largely restored ancient self-government. Graham contends that the reorganized village government was partly copied from the system prevalent in

---
[1] For notes to chapter 6 see pages 217–218.

Burma in 1890.[5] In 1932, the village headman system was again reorganized and in 1934 made officially a part of the royal government by granting headmen monthly stipends and making them specifically answerable to the district officer, who is appointed by the national government. These measures reflect the centralizing tendencies of the present government of Thailand, under which the villages enjoy a limited self-government.

Whenever possible, the political community is correlated with the functional, or natural, community. In the delta area there is less correlation between them than in other parts of Thailand; for example, in the Bangchan area, one functional community, which encompasses a two-mile-wide area around a central *wat* and primary school, consists politically of three of the twelve hamlets of one district and of four of the ten hamlets of another district.[6] Whether the arbitrary splitting of a natural community is typical of the delta region is uncertain, but the delta is much more susceptible to the arrangement than other areas of Thailand, for the commercialization of agriculture has resulted in large farms and widely separated hamlets so that the traditional, integrated, self-governing village has largely disappeared. Sharp's study revealed that the headman system was ineffective in a delta community of separated homes loosely clustered into small hamlets over a wide area of farmland. He found that in the Bangchan area, only the Buddhist priests were capable of sponsoring and carrying through any consistent local community action.[7] The author's study of the commune of San Pong indicated that the village headman is a strong local political figure and the headmanship the crucial agency through which consistent community action is initiated and carried out. A survey of fifty other compact villages in north, northeast, and central Thailand indicated the same effectiveness of the headman system.

The *wat* is politically and socially important in the new as well as the old type of Thai village. No community program can succeed without its approval. Some sort of religious service accompanies the announcement of any new measure by the central government to gain for its decrees and programs the aura of the *wat's* sanction.

The community organization of the delta region is dominant in the economy of the country as a whole: it is the peasant of the Menam Plain who supplies the surplus rice on which Thailand's economy rests, and hence he indirectly affects the life of every peasant throughout the country. The social and economic behavior of the delta peasant determines to some extent the economic and social behavior of the self-subsistent farmer. When paddy sells for 7 *ticals* a *tang* in the Menam Plain, the glutinous rice of the northern and northeastern farmer, though sold only for regional consumption, is pegged at the same level. Both pay the same general prices for commodities; both suffer from the fact that the strict government control of the price of nonglutinous export rice keeps farm income low while the price of manufactured goods has greatly increased in recent years.

VOTING AND POLITICS

In the villages and communes of Thailand there has never been an emphasis upon "electioneering" for local offices comparable, for example, to the heated campaigns between rival candidates for headman that have been characteristic of Burmese villages. Therefore, the institution in 1932 of national elections, with an emphasis upon campaigning by the candidates for the national assembly and upon the obligation of the voters to cast their ballots, was a wholly new experience to the Thai peasants. Accounts of the first national election report that only one-tenth of the adult population voted.[*] Lack of transportation and communication together with the short time allowed to acquaint the people with the nature of the new assembly make it obvious that few of the votes cast were by villagers. Since then the percentage of voters who exercise their right of suffrage has increased remarkably (in February, 1952, approximately 39 per cent—an appreciable percentage in a country where at least half of the adult population is illiterate and where many live in isolated villages) but except in villages near urban centers, few Thai peasants see or hear the candidates, read newspapers, or take a real interest in national elections.[*] Statistics on rural suffrage suggest a much greater active interest than exists; actually, most peasants who vote cast a perfunctory, uninformed ballot, much as they passively accept other new strange ways of the modern government to which they have gradually become conditioned.

A few weeks before an election each district officer instructs the headmen of his village and communes to encourage their villagers to vote; the headmen assemble the villagers, urge them to vote, instruct those who have never voted in how to cast a ballot, and assign a registration number to each person eligible to vote. A registration list is sent by the headman to the local polling place (which is often the nearest primary school), and watchers and checkers are appointed for the polls. On the day before the elections the headman sends his assistant to all households to remind them that the election will take place on the morrow. Thus, even though the villager sees, hears, or reads nothing of the candidates, he is constantly reminded of the election during the several weeks preceding it.

In 1949, in a by-election for assemblyman, 49 per cent of those eligible voted in the village of San Pong—72 per cent of the eligible males and 25½ per cent of the eligible females. None of the candidates visited the village, no campaign literature was distributed, and since they do not read newspapers, few of the villagers had any clear idea of the campaign issues. The villagers made their choice partly on the basis of what the headman and the schoolteacher said about the candidates, partly on the basis of the nearness of the candidate's home town. A man from the closest town, even though he was personally unknown to the villagers, was regarded as a "local" man, a consideration which made him a better choice in the eyes of the villagers than his rivals from more distant parts of the province.

Eligibility to vote consists simply in being older than twenty-one. Since so many adult villagers are illiterate, a technique has been devised to allow those who cannot read and write to vote. Each candidate is assigned a number. These numbers are printed in Thai numerals and also in large dots on perforated paper. When the voter comes to the polls he is told which number corresponds to which candidate; he enters the voting booth, tears off the piece of the ballot which contains the number of dots for his choice, seals this inside an official envolope which is given to him when his name is checked on the registration list by the polling inspectors, and drops it in the ballot box. For his vote to be valid the envelope must be sealed, for Thailand voters enjoy the privilege of secret ballot. At the end of the day ballot boxes are sealed and sent to the district office in charge of the commune election committee, often under police escort. Votes are counted by the committee and the results telephoned, telegraphed, or otherwise relayed to the capital of the *changwat*.

The villager's indifference to national elections is matched by his ignorance of and lack of interest in current political events in Bangkok. Villages have no radios, and only headmen, abbots, and some schoolteachers read newspapers. (Typically, a headman may subscribe to a Bangkok weekly, which is sent to him in care of a coffee shop in the nearest market town, and perhaps a weekly provincial paper also. Schoolteachers often share the cost of a newspaper subscription.) In 1948, few of the villagers of San Pong knew that Premier Pibun had returned to power or had more than a vague notion of the circumstances surrounding the mysterious death of the young King Ananda. The highly publicized trial of persons charged with regicide then being held in Bangkok was unknown to all villagers except the headman and a few schoolteachers. In 1949, the attempted coup d'état of Pridi and the brief but bloody fighting that followed caused scarcely a ripple in San Pong; only the headman, his assistant, and the schoolteachers followed the event of Pridi's attempt to regain power; general village opinion on this national crisis amounted to the comment that it was disgraceful that Thai should be fighting Thai like dogs.

In contrast to the apathy and ignorance of San Pong, villagers in the Bangchan area took an active interest in the Pridi affair. Two men of this area are reported to have made a trip to Bangkok solely to find out for themselves the true facts of the attempted coup. Greater interest in the affairs of the capital is explained not only by the proximity of Bangchan to Bangkok but also by the fact that the several radios of the Bangchan area can pick up the government broadcasts. According to Sharp, the peasants of the Bangchan area had the same general estimate of the affair as those of San Pong—a berating of both parties for "fighting like dogs'"—but the former were able to distinguish between the parties and personalities of the affair, to take sides and to support actively the Pibul regime.

The apathy of San Pong toward events in the capital, an apathy typical of most Thai villagers, cannot be accounted for by distance or isolation from the capital. It is true that San Pong is much more distant from Bangkok than Bangchan, which lies only twenty miles outside the city limits of the capital, yet physically San Pong is the less isolated of the two. A main highway runs through the district and buses (which stop at a crossroads only one-quarter of a kilometer from the village) are frequent; by bus the villager of San Pong can be in Chiangmai, the second largest city of Thailand, in less than an hour. The explanation seems to lie rather in the peasantry's conception of itself as a single, national group under the throne and in the traditional deference of the Thai peasant to higher authority. In rural Thailand the monarchy still enjoys a reverence that has been sharply modified in urban centers; whenever the King pays a visit to the rural parts of his domain, the peasants line the road kneeling as the royal car passes. In contrast to the continued reverence for the person of the king, however, one may note that the Thai are acquiring a more sophisticated sense of political responsibility and criticism. Benedict pointed out that Thai villagers have never lodged any outright protests against the measures of the central government and regarded this as a strong cultural tradition.[8] Within the past decade, however, delegations from the farmers have petitioned the central government in matters that directly concerned them. For example, in October, 1952, a delegation from seven districts of the province of Pathun Dhani protested to Field Marshal Pikul against the appropriation of lands for military purposes, and protest by the tenant farmers of the Bangkok area against excessive rents have been reported. In 1949, farmers all over Thailand refused to pay a land tax ordered by new tax officials against those who could not show a receipt for taxes paid in 1946; it was contended that in 1946 many tax receipts had not been issued because of a paper shortage and that the government had no right to collect a second tax simply because peasants could not prove they had paid the first time.

ADMINISTERING JUSTICE

There has been a major shift in the manner of administering justice in Thai villages. Previously the villages themselves were responsible for law and order, with the *kamnan* in charge of administering local justice in the commune; this is now completely in the hands of the district officer and his police department. A villager who commits a crime is arrested by a policeman from the district office. Significantly, even if the policeman knows where the offender lives, he reports first to the headman and they go together to present the warrant of arrest. The provincial court files suit against the offender and the trial is held at the *changwat* capital, for district seats do not have courts. An individual who is arrested can put up bail and report at a later date for his trial. For minor offenses, e.g., bootlegging, which is one of the most frequent crimes in Thai villages, he is fined, but usually the fine is cut in half if he pleads guilty.

Minor disputes within the village are still settled by the village headman, or by the *kamnan* if the dispute concerns individuals from different villages of the commune. Disputes concerning land boundaries fall within the jurisdiction of the district officer, for land titles now are legally registered.

The central government has also increased its control over the villages through conscription—which has been expanded because of the events of the past several years in southern China and Indochina and the return to power in 1948 of Field Marshal Pibun—and through the registration of wills (if a will is made, it is posted at the district office at the time of death, and any member of the family who wishes to protest it must do so within a stated period of time) and of marriages and divorces. Many villagers do not abide by the last regulation, but because of the posting of wills, many marriages formerly not registered are now being registered for later inheritance purposes. There is no fee for registering a marriage or a divorce if the couple go to the district office. If a clerk is requested to go to the village to do the registering, a fee of 20 *ticals* is charged.

THE EFFECT OF NATIONAL HOLIDAYS ON VILLAGE LIFE

National holidays have helped the central government to extend its influence into the village.* The government's programs commemorating these days have a strong nationalistic tinge, since the new holidays were designed primarily to instill a feeling of nationalism. New Year's Day (January 1) is the first official national holiday of the year in modern Thailand, but it has little meaning for the villager. The district officer and his staff hold a special program on this day and usually a chapter of monks is invited to chant a service, but *kamnans* and headmen do not have to attend. Many other national holidays are celebrated by special programs in which the village school children, the village schoolteachers, and the village headmen participate. On Chulalongkorn Day, for example, all schools within walking distance (5 to 6 kilometers) of the district seat must send their classes to attend a mass ceremony at the district officer's headquarters. Schools farther away hold their own memorial services and later send a report of them to the district officer. Every national holiday program includes a Buddhist religious service, not only because the Thai are devout Buddhists, but also to give an air of religious approval to even the most chauvinistic program. On the king's birthday and some other national holidays the *kamnan,* the village headmen and the school children must attend a special service at the district office.

Not only does the central government require all village school children to participate in these programs, but it has prescribed proper dress. School children are expected to wear Western-style clothes; for the little girls, proper uniform is a blue *pasin* skirt and a white blouse, which is the regulation school costume. Actually, village girls attend school in ordinary, everyday *pasin*, which may be black, green, or some other color, but for national holidays they are supposed to wear blue skirts,

---

* Appendix VI gives a list of national holidays.

and if a headmaster rigidly enforces this regulation, a little girl who does not own a blue *pasin* must stay at home. Little boys must wear Western-type shirts, shorts, and hat. The programs are much the same regardless of the occasion. The district officer reads the official proclamation of the day, at the end of which the school children cheer three times. If the holiday is an important one, there will be speeches, a service by the Buddhist monks, and singing.

In addition, special days have been designated by the central government to impress certain government regulations on the villagers. November 27 is National Health Day. This is not an official national holiday, but children are given a half-day holiday to help their parents clean up the house and compound. The village doctor is responsible for making an inspection of the house compounds to see whether the villagers have complied with government instruction as to sanitation and cleanliness of house compounds. He must turn in a report to the district health officer if he finds any flagrant violations.

WINTER FAIRS

One of the most important traditional rural customs of Thailand is that of holding a winter fair, a festival that opens about December 5 and continues for several days. These fairs, which come after the harvest when the farmer is eager to relax and enjoy himself, were originally local agricultural festivals, held in and around the village *wat,* but today the central government has taken them under its sponsorship, expanded them, and linked them with Constitution Day, an official holiday that falls on December 10. The fairs are now held on the grounds of the district office, and each village is invited to set up stalls displaying its agricultural produce and handicrafts. Prizes are awarded for the best stalls, and for the best displays of rice by individual farmers. Stalls are often put up coöperatively, the well-to-do farmers of a village underwriting the cost; the stalls sell food or other products to try to meet expenses. There are, besides, restaurant booths, cockfights, boxing matches, fireworks, movies, plays (*likay*), and song contests. Admission to the fairground is free during the day but costs half a *tical* at night; in addition, there are admission fees to the cockfights and boxing matches. *Ramwong* dancing is held nightly, for which a fee is charged to the men. The *ramwong*, a stylized dance by couples, is a cultural borrowing from central Thailand, and has been introduced by the central government as a national dance; it has displaced many of the ancient folk dances of northern Thailand, although these are still sometimes performed at the fairs. The *ramwong* has not become prevalent among young villagers. Fees charged for the *ramwong* and other contests and sports go to make up a district welfare fund.

Under government sponsorships the winter fairs now have their climax in Constitution Day. For this occasion there is a special program by the teachers of the district, a guest-speaker, and perhaps a visit by the governor of the province or one of his assistants. Emphasis on patriotism and national unity, which have been made important motives of the fairs, is particularly strong on Constitution Day.

The winter fairs, although popular throughout Thailand, are most popular in the north where compact integrated village life links itself best to the coöperative activity necessary for these fairs. Attendance is good: in the Mae Rim district of north Thailand, 98 per cent of the school children and village youth attended every night of the fair and most of the older villagers went at least once or twice during the week. Schoolteachers are very active in the fairs; they serve on committees, organize stalls, play in the orchestra, act in the dramas, or undertake some other chore. Young women schoolteachers also act as salesgirls in the booths and so automatically participate in the beauty contests, which in Thailand are concomittant with fairs and markets, for choosing the most beautiful salesgirl.

EFFECT OF GOVERNMENT TAXATION ON THE PEASANT

Formerly, the Thai peasant was subject to heavy taxation and forced labor for the king. All male villagers were subject to military or corvee labor, and in feudal times every male Thai was supposed to devote one-third of the year to the king's service. In addition, he was also subject to various agricultural levies and taxes. During the Sukodhya period he paid taxes known as *akara,* which consisted of a levy of one-fourth of the total gross yield on agricultural produce, and a small tax on fish and forest products. Payment of these taxes tended to be in kind, and without doubt were evaded as often as possible. Later, in the Ayuthia period, the *akara* were replaced by a definite land tax. La Loubère describes this land tax as a money tax assessed at 0.25 *ticals* for each rai.⁹ Half of this was kept by the provincial lord and half was supposed to be sent to the royal treasury. This apparently was the earliest land tax in Thailand. By the first part of the twentieth century, the Thai peasant paid only a head tax, a land tax, a small tax on fruit trees, and a few other tiny miscellaneous taxes, mainly on special agricultural products.

Zimmerman reported that the various forms of direct taxation paid by the peasant amounted in 1930 to about 7 per cent of all expenditures in the central area and about 5 per cent in the other areas.¹⁰ In cash, this amounted to an average expenditure for each family of 27 *ticals* in the central region, 9 *ticals* in the north, 7 *ticals* in the south, and 4 *ticals* in the northeast. The poll or head tax at this time amounted to approximately 4 *ticals* a head, but the head tax was abolished after 1932 and the land taxes greatly lowered, so that the Thai farmer has had the unique experience of having had his taxes drastically reduced rather than increased. The land tax, which amounted to one *tical* a *rai* in 1930 now is less than one-third this, and proportionally is even smaller because of the devaluation of the *tical.*

Direct taxation on villagers today yields very little revenue. The main direct tax, a land tax levied on farmers who own paddy land, is a very small tax of about 20 *satang* per official *rai,* which amounts to less than five cents an acre. Since the landholding of the average peasant is relatively small, this land tax is a very meager item in his cash expenditure today.

Few if any Thai villagers holding paddy land attempt to evade the small land tax. Villagers who live close to the district seat usually pay the tax to the revenue section of the district office themselves. In villages some distance away, the villager may give his land tax to the headman or to the *kamnan* who pays it for him and has the receipt made out to the landowner. If villagers do not pay their land tax, the headman is notified by the district revenue office through the *kamnan*. Land holdings are registered, and the district revenue office has a list of landholders in each commune; the village headman sends a demand to the delinquent villager. Neither the village headman nor the *kamnan* is held responsible for collecting delinquent taxes. If the tax is not forthcoming in a year or so, the district revenue office sends a list of delinquent villagers to the headman with a notice that on a certain date, a clerk from the district revenue office will come to the village to collect delinquent taxes. The headman sends a notice to each delinquent taxpayer requesting him to be at his house at a certain time to pay his tax or to produce evidence that his tax has been paid.

There are a few other incidental taxes—for slaughtering pigs, cutting down of certain types of hardwood trees and bamboo trees over a certain height, and draining private fish ponds.

The extremely light taxation affects any large-scale government program to improve conditions for the peasants. It is evident that not until the government has assurance of steady and increased income from local taxes can it expect to support large-scale farm-improvement projects. The most important single source of the country's revenue comes today from various indirect taxes, such as import and export taxes, which in 1952 provided almost half of the government's revenue. These, with approximately 12 per cent contributed from government enterprises and 9 per cent from the rice monopoly provided the major source of revenue for the country. Two potential sources of revenue, income tax and land tax, are relatively unused. Income tax would not in any event affect the peasant, but an increase in paddy-land tax and other farm taxes would.

India charges a special water tax of 3 rupees per acre to the farmer who directly benefits from any irrigation project; applied on the same scale in Thailand, such a tax would be 5 *ticals* per *rai* in the major irrigated areas of the country. As yet the government has not come to the conclusion that at least partial support of such a project should come from equitable taxation of the peasants. Any program designed to aid the farmer, such as large-scale irrigation, is recognized now only as a national investment and a responsibility of the government. That this policy sooner or later must change is self-evident, for without local taxation the peasants' demands for agricultural, educational, health, and transportation improvements can not be met. The few large-scale programs of this nature now under way in Thailand are at present being supported by the Thai government with the aid of substantial financial support from the United States' and the United Nations' mutual aid programs. This support will come to an end in the foreseeable future, and the Thai government must then face the problem of how to continue these projects.

MODERN TRANSPORTATION AND THE FARMER

Even in the past, Thai villagers had considerable contact with the outside world. In the most isolated villages there were always individuals who spent considerable time away from their homes. In the north, men went to the teak forests or to the *changwat* capital in search of work; in the northeast, large numbers went to the Menam Plain to work on the big farms during the rice harvest; in the central area, village men ventured to Bangkok. This is a sharp contrast to many peasant areas of eastern Asia, where villagers seldom went any appreciable distance from their home village. This greater degree of mobility stems in part from the mendicant habits of the original Thai Buddhists and the ancient custom of the *taharn,* or military service, and the corvee labor for the king. The Thai villager has always been willing to explore the outside world, and today the modern transportation gives him even more opportunities to do so.

There are over 2,000 miles of rail lines in Thailand, and the Thai railway system, which has been regarded as one of the most reliable in the Orient, annually carries well over a million passengers. The 2,000 miles of rail line, 1,000 miles of feeder roads, a few trunk highways supplemented by numerous dry-weather cart roads, and the rivers and canals of the Menam Plain make up the transportation system of the country. If this seems fantastically little for a country the size of France, it must be kept in mind that only 10 per cent of the country is cultivated and that the largest concentration of people is in the low-lying river plains. The rail lines, roads, and cart tracks, and the network of navigable canals crisscrossing the delta region, assume much greater significance if they are considered within their proper physical framework.

The number of roads, although still proportionally small, is increasing even in the Menam Plain. Road construction has high priority in the government's program of modernization, both for economic and military reasons. The present state of military unrest in South China, Indochina, and Burma is hastening the road-building program. Although there is no continuous highway from Bangkok to Chiangmai, the northern capital, it is possible, though arduous, to drive all the way to the north, a feat which could not have been accomplished twenty years ago. Most roads are not part of a connected system, having been built originally as "feeders" at right angles to the rail lines. Connecting links for these feeder roads are rapidly being constructed. To speed the Thai government road-building program, the United States, through the Mutual Security Agency, in 1952 supplied over a million dollars for road-building equipment, the largest single item of expenditure in the agency's program for Thailand.[11]

The completion of trunk roads connecting the "feeders" will bring urban life even closer to the peasant. Only a few parts of the low-lying delta area and remote sections of other areas are out of the reach of these "feeder" roads. The importance of the bullock-cart roads leading from villages to these "feeders" should not be underestimated; built and maintained by village communal labor, crude, washed away annually, or made impassable during the rainy season, they are, nonetheless, for nine months of the year an important connecting link to the main road. Motor travel on them is difficult and dangerous, but they are traversed by trucks and busses that reach into the villages to bring certain features of urban life to the peasant's door. On the branch roads, for example, have gone the traveling "tent cinemas" showing Thai movies and Western films to the villagers, and dealing perhaps the fatal blow to the rapidly declining local companies which formerly plied the countryside in the dry season performing Thai classical drama.

Better transportation has increased contact between the village and the city. Most of it so far has been the result of trips by the villager to the town or provincial capital, but contacts in the opposite direction are increasing rapidly; for example, traveling dispensaries bring not only Western drugs but the latest songs, news, and fashions of the city.

Twenty years ago Andrews noted that motor transportation was one of the important expenditures in a household budget except in the Menam Plain.[12] Today the situation has been changed measurably by the expansion of the road system in the Menam Plain, and in other areas the bus has become commonplace for the villager. The farmer and his family make frequent shopping trips to the market towns, the district seat, or even the provincial capital on business or for recreation; the winter fair at the provincial capital will bring villagers from many miles away to spend a day in relaxation.

Fifty years ago San Pong was an isolated northern village, some distance from the nearest river and one-half a kilometer from a caravan road leading from Chiangmai to the Burmese border. It took a whole day to walk to the provincial capital along a dirt trail (the river was navigable during only parts of the year). Then the dirt trail became a gravel road and later a surfaced road; it was about twenty-five years ago that trucks and buses began to traverse it regularly. If a San Pong farmer catches a bus at the crossroads today, he can be in Chiangmai within the hour. As a result, except for a few of the very old women and the very young children all the villagers have been to the capital. Only two old women of the village have never ridden in a bus.

Sharp has reported frequent visits to Bangkok by Bangchan villagers who also travel long distances to attend an important festival, make a pilgrimage to a famous Buddhist shrine, or engage in some other recreation.[13] Roads and bus transportation enable a villager to have more regular contact with the city, but villagers in more remote areas have better transportation than those of the Menam Plain. Some sections of the delta region, though near Bangkok, have few roads, and a villager in such an area is fairly isolated, for canal travel is slow and tedious. Thus a peasant of the delta area may have less actual face-to-face relationship with the town than a peasant of other regions of the country. For example, he probably sees fewer films than his more remote countrymen, since he is less accessible to traveling companies. The delta region presents an interesting blend—it has adopted certain Western laborsaving devices in farming and uses many Western commodities, and at the same time has retained a number of the older customs.

ADAPTATION TO A MONEY ECONOMY

A generation ago a Thai peasant could transact almost all of his business by barter and meet nearly all of his obligations in kind or by work. He could even pay his taxes by labor on the government's public works. Today rural Thailand has become accustomed to a money economy, although payment in kind has by no means entirely disappeared even in the delta. The delta farmer sells all of his rice crop except the part he retains for his family's consumption; the farmer elsewhere sells his secondary crop of tobacco or soybeans. In general, the delta farmer has a much larger cash income than farmers of other parts of Thailand, but he also has proportionally higher disbursements; rent, wages, and the many imported goods he must buy consume nearly all of his income.

A Thai farmer rarely has enough permanent surplus cash to merit opening a savings account in one of the banks of the provincial capital or the district seat. Whatever surplus cash he may have from time to time is invested in land or used to purchase "luxuries." In former times, Thai peasant families usually bought jewelry whenever they had any extra money, for it was in this form that the family kept its savings. The modern Thai family is likely to invest less of its money in jewelry and more of it in foreign imports, which range from such trivial items as matches and cosmetics to more expensive items such as bicycles and sewing machines. These "luxury" purchases, in addition to the disbursements for necessities, keep most Thai farmers from ever accumulating surplus cash. A prosperous farmer of San Pong has an annual cash income of from perhaps 2,000 to more than 5,000 *ticals*, or 100 to 300 dollars. (This, of course, is only his cash income, derived from the sale of secondary crops, pigs, and surplus rice; he produces almost all of his own food and many of his other needs are taken care of by barter.) For a self-subsistence area this is a high cash income, but the farmer's disbursements are proportionally high: he may give as much as 500 *ticals* to the *wat;* he will probably want to buy a sewing machine or a bicycle, which will cost him several thousand *ticals;* and he will have many other comparable disbusements.

The notion of what a luxury is varies from one region to another. In central Thailand, for example, where kerosene pressure lamps are standard household equipment, a Bangchan headman who had bought three Mitsubishi sewing machines for his daughters and two gasoline pumps for his fields aspired to the "luxury" of owning an electric generator to illuminate his house at festivals.[14] A prosperous headman of San Pong, where pressure lamps are relatively scarce, aspired to buy the biggest available kerosene pressure lamp for much the same "luxurious" purpose. The Thai peasant has a double purpose in mind when he buys foreign imports and luxury goods: snob appeal and utility. Sewing machines, bicycles, pressure lamps, etc., have a status value, but they are also means of increasing the family's income or lightening its work load. Even prosperous families that have bought sewing machines often set mother and daughters to work sewing for other village families; bicycles save teachers, headmen, and other villagers much time in commuting to work or making necessary visits, thus allowing them more time for their farm chores.

The change from a barter to a money economy has destroyed some old customs and practices, particularly the coöperative work group which has largely disappeared in the delta and which in other areas is no longer used to plant and harvest secondary crops. On the other hand, the change has helped to retain other ancient customs: the traditional gift and dowry giving, for example, has been retained in the delta, where the farmers have more cash; in other parts of the country is has disappeared. Janlekha notes that in the Minburi region it is common for the bride's parents to give land, a water buffalo, and plowing equipment to the young couple when they set up their own household.[15] The traditional marriage charge—a sum given by the bridegroom or his family to the bride's family—is also still paid in the delta. In the north, this is no longer done, and only wealthy families make sizable gifts to a young couple at their marriage.

EFFECT OF PUBLIC EDUCATION ON THE VILLAGER

A somewhat misleading and erroneous description of education and literacy in Thailand has resulted from incomplete and inaccurate observations in the past. European writers of the nineteenth century attributed to the villages of Siam an educational pattern which did not exist. Early reports commonly state that all boys learned to read and write in the temple schools and that free education for all existed long before it was established in Europe. Using such inaccurate reports, writers, as late as 1943, stated that all Thai boys went to temple schools and that literacy was practically universal among men and common among women of the traditional regime.[16] (How literacy could be common when women were excluded from the temple schools was not explained.) Contrary to these reports and to popular notions about Thailand, only a small number of Thai males were literate. Before the compulsory education act of 1921 the only schools available to the villagers were the temple schools run by the monks. Only a relatively few boys, whether of the city or the countryside, attended these, and of this small number only a very few—those who remained in the temple as novices and monks—attained more than the rudiments of reading, writing, and arithmetic. Almost all Thai women were illiterate.

When public schooling was first established in Thailand, nearly all of the school buildings were in the *wat*. There were several reasons for this: the *wat* had the only available buildings, it was centrally or strategically located, only the monks were qualified to teach. Today the monks no longer have any role as teachers in the primary schools. Temple schools run by monks for novices are entirely for religious education and have no connection with the government primary-school system. In 1931, over 80 per cent of the government primary schools were located in the *wat*, but this percentage declined as the government and local communities built permanent school buildings. By 1944 only 60 per cent of the primary schools were in the *wat*, and in 1950 this had fallen to approximately 48 per cent." The Ministry of Education pays only a small part of the cost of putting up a school; it is up to the local school authorities to raise money from the village. In villages too poor to raise funds for new buildings schools are usually in ramshackle buildings in the *wats*. The government has attempted to standardize primary-school buildings by having architects draw up a number of designs for elementary schools. New schools must now follow one of these standardized plans.

The original primary-school act of 1921 required a three-year primary course for children between the ages of seven and fourteen and stipulated that a child who did not go on the secondary course must have an additional two years of vocational training. The plan to set up vocational schools throughout the country was not carried out and the compulsory education act was gradually modified. In 1935, the elementary-education act was proclaimed, and two years later a new scheme of education was put into effect. Attendance at a primary school of four grades, plus a "beginners class," was made compulsory for all children between the ages of eight and fifteen or until they had successfully passed grade four.

By 1935 almost every village in Thailand obeyed the compulsory school law, although there was great variation in the degree of conformity. At this time only half of the village children entered school at the age of eight; the other half did not enroll until they were nine or ten; enrollment at eight did not become universal until the end of 1952. Individual cases of children enrolling at later ages still exist, but these are relatively few and are today regarded as evasions of the required school law. It is recognized that the compulsory school law cannot be put into effect in remote and isolated areas where there are no schools. Accordingly, children who live more than 2,000 meters from a school are exempted. Today, however, there are very few village children who do not attend the government primary school. In 1951, out of 2,936,647 children in schools in Thailand, over 2,500,000, or 89 per cent of the total, were in village primary schools.[12]

Although it is possible for a child to pass through the required curriculum in five years and graduate at thirteen, few do this, for they must stay in a class until they have successfully passed the government examination. It is not unusual for village students to spend several years in each grade. The beginners' class may have students from seven to fourteen years old, and an advanced grade may contain students from twelve to eighteen. Students who continually repeat the grades rarely finish the entire program, for they usually drop out of school when they reach the age of fifteen. (This is not generally mentioned by government officials when they discuss the effectiveness of the primary school system). Generally, only those who wish to become village schoolteachers or are children of well-to-do farmers finish the entire course. Lack of adequate teaching staff is the main reason why a village child cannot pass the yearly examinations.

Instruction in the primary school must conform to the standard government curriculum, and all school texts are prepared by the education department in Bangkok. All school children throughout the country are taught in the central-Thai dialect, which has been made the standard dialect of the country. The central government prepares the textbooks and distributes them through the district educational office to the village schools but does not provide them free of charge. Village children must buy their own texts (they usually buy them second hand at from 2 to 4 *ticals* a book) and must supply their own exercise books, slates, chalk, pencils, and other equipment. A village parent must spend at least 15 to 20 *ticals* annually to keep a child in school supplies, and this does not include cost of clothing. School rules now stipulate that a boy must wear shorts and a Western-type shirt, and a girl must wear a white cotton vest and a skirt.

The central government supplies village schools with only a bare minimum of equipment, such as blackboards, school record books, desks for teachers. The local community almost always has to supply desks and benches for the children. Few schools have libraries or any books except the textbooks. In 1940 only 745 primary schools out of approximately 16,670 had libraries; most of these were in the cities or towns, and the library consisted of a few worn-out books and old magazines.

The schools offer some vocational training. There are craftsmanship classes that teach methods of cutting down bamboo trees, how to choose the right kind of wood for various purposes, how to make twine from bark, how to weave baskets, make trays, brooms, and other household objects—all of which was formerly learned by the child at home. Much of it he will still learn there, but to an increasing extent the village school is taking over the role of the parent in teaching the children these home crafts which will be so important in their household economy in later years. Domestic science training has not yet reached the village schools, and girls still learn the old traditional ways of keeping house from their mothers. Many village schools have small truck gardens, in keeping with the central government's program of encouraging the growing of vegetable crops. The vegetables raised by the village school children are sold in the nearby market, and the cash proceeds go to buy miscellaneous things for the student body.

ROLE OF THE VILLAGE SCHOOLTEACHER

The typical rural schoolteacher is a man or woman from the village who has completed the required public education and perhaps one or two years at a government teacher-training school in the provincial capital. The head teacher of a school in a larger village often has a bit more training and often comes from some other part of Thailand, but even his level of education is likely to be low. In 1950, nineteen per cent of the teachers in Thailand failed to meet the prescribed qualifications.

Between 1932 and 1949 the number of village schoolteachers increased more than five-and-a-half times (from about 12,000 to more than 68,000, distributed among some 18,000 rural schools).[12] This increase has been not only in total number of teachers but also in number of teachers from the villages. In

1934, Andrews' study of forty-one villages revealed only seven villagers who were schoolteachers—fewer than one for every six villages.[20] Today, every Thai village boasts several men or women who have become teachers. In 1932, there were only some seven hundred women teachers in rural Thailand (about 6 per cent of all village teachers); today about 25 per cent are women.

Teachers are paid according to their academic training, so that all village schoolteachers except the head teachers fall into the lowest pay bracket. In 1950, this called for a minimum salary of 330 *ticals* a month, but many rural teachers received even less than this (280 to 300 *ticals*). However, despite this poor pay most rural teachers are better off than urban teachers since the self-subsistent rural areas have not felt the increased cost of living so much. (Living costs in Thailand have increased 16 times over what they were in prewar days; salaries are only 11 times greater than they were.) Most village schoolteachers own bicycles, wear good clothes, and live in reasonably good houses; some own rice land, and others live with their families.

Though he is economically much better off than his urban counterpart, the rural schoolteacher has to work much harder. He may teach as many as thirty hours of classes a week in all subjects; he must maintain the building and do all routine administrative work. In some parts of the northeast teachers have as many as 100 pupils in their classes.[21] Besides these regular chores, the teacher is expected to take an active role in public affairs—to serve on committees, to be an inspector at elections, to take part in the winter fairs and in programs on national holidays. The teacher, as an educated person, is respected by the villagers, even though many teachers are quite young. He is influential in persuading the villagers to obey the government's programs and policies, and in introducing Western ideas and products.

VILLAGE LITERACY

Even though primary education did not become widespread in the villages until 1935, the 1937 census reported 31 per cent literacy for all Thai women and about 47 per cent literacy for

Thai males.[a] The 1947 census gave the literacy rate for all Thai over ten years old as 54 per cent, an increase of over 20 per cent in one decade. This increase seems disproportionally high, in view of the fact that much of the decade was a war period when education was greatly curtailed. It is, however, the latest official figure released by the census office, and must be taken at face value. Almost without exception recent accounts of the educational situation in Thailand, even those issued as late as 1950 by the United Nations, have used the earlier 1937 census figures which obviously, in the light of advances made in rural education in the past ten years, are no longer accurate. Whether one credits the 1947 figure of 54 per cent or the 1937 figure of 31 per cent, the literacy rate in rural Thailand is still vastly higher than Thailand's neighbor, India, where the standard of literacy is less than 12 per cent. Literacy rates at present in Thailand seem to be close to those of the Philippines, where roughly half of the population are literate. But statistics do not tell much about the functional literacy of the villager. A person who attended school and learned to read and write may be listed as literate even though he has lost most of this learning. Many Thai villagers are only nominally literate, for usually only teachers, novices, and monks retain any effective measure of their schooling. Adult education has had a very limited effect in rural Thailand despite a vigorous wartime effort by the central government to increase literacy among the peasantry. In 1941, an adult-education division of the Ministry of Education was set up, and in 1943 an act was passed making it mandatory for all Thai from twenty-four to forty-five to learn to read and write. The law called for an annual fine of five *ticals* a head on all who remained illiterate and specified that all heads of families must register their illiterate members at the beginning of each year or incur a fine of fifty *ticals*.[a] But the vociferous protests of the people and the government's realization that compulsory adult education was impossible when even compulsory primary school education was still so limited caused the law to be repealed before it was ever put into effect. Currently there are fewer than 45,000 adults enrolled in school in Thailand and all of them are in urban centers.

Though compulsory primary education is relatively new in village life, it has had strong influence on the present generation and the potentiality of the primary school as a unifier of village patterns is important. The formal education the village children receive is rudimentary, but the experience is valuable in terms of other social influences. All children of both sexes receive this education, limited though it may be, in contrast to the previous generation, of which only a small part of the village boys had the opportunity to attend the temple school. Children now come in contact with classmates from neighboring villages, form close associations with them, and so broaden the scope of their contacts. All village children receive a common education in the standard Thai dialect, and through studying Thai history and Buddhist ethics acquire a sense of nationalism that their parents did not have. The school is an agency for teaching the child the ideas which the government approves.

In 1950, the Ministry of Education drew up a reorganization plan for compulsory education, by which a seven-year program of study was to replace the present four-year one. A modification of this plan now is being tried in one provincial town. The central government, with the collaboration of UNESCO, the Food and Agriculture Organization, the International Labor Organization, and the United States Mutual Security Administration, has undertaken an intensive educational experiment at Cha Choeng Sao, sixty miles east of Bangkok. Here United Nations and Thai educational experts are redesigning the entire educational system under a seven-point program.[a] Ranging from the introduction of pre-primary education for children from five to seven to the establishment of rural vocational schools and adult-education centers for the villagers, this Cha Choeng Sao experiment has been under way since 1950. The central phase of this reorganization program as it will affect village children lies not only in extending compulsory education by another three years, but also in the reorganization of teaching methods and curricula and stressing of agricultural vocational education. With Cha Choeng Sao as the pilot area, the experiment will be expanded gradually, until the entire province has been brought under the scope of the program by

1955. Then the results of the program will be evaluated and it will be decided whether it should be adopted on a nation-wide scale.

It is estimated that to initiate such a program for the country, the first year's cost alone would be close to a billion *ticals*, which is almost half of the national budget. Consequently, if it is decided to put it into effect all over the country, it can only be done over a period of many years. The original plan called for a five-year study in Cha Choeng Sao after which the plan or a modification of it would be expanded throughout the country in the next five years: a twenty-year period of expansion would be more realistic. The Cha Choeng Sao experiment, though likely to have far-reaching results, will not affect the present generation of school children. The experiment at present is being conducted in ten primary schools in the town and in one rural vocational school in the province. Even when extended throughout the province of Cha Choeng Sao, it will reach only 36,000 children. For the next generation of children, at least, the rural education described in this report will be typical.

CHANGES IN RECREATION

Rural pastimes have changed very little; villagers still play the old card and chess games at funerals and ordination ceremonies, and gambling of various sorts is still the chief national recreation. The newest form of gambling is the national lottery, which has penetrated into even the most remote village. There is scarcely an adult villager who does not buy one or more chances in the lottery every year. Not only are the national lotteries held at regular intervals, but they are supplemented by special lotteries sponsored by various government ministries for welfare purposes. Concerted effort is made to get villagers to buy lottery tickets for these special welfare benefits. Books of tickets are distributed by the district officer to the village headmen, who receive five per cent of the receipts for all tickets sold. Since these special lottery tickets are expensive (as high as 20 *ticals* a ticket) the village headman often sells shares in a ticket. In addition, "outlaw" lotteries can be found in every village area.

These are organized on a commune level by some enterprising villager who puts up a pig or a bicycle as the main prize. Thousands of these unauthorized lotteries are held in the northern villages every year, where they are popularly known as "pig lotteries."

Cockfighting and its attendant gambling is still one of the most popular pastimes of the men during the dry season from December to June. Cockpits are licensed by the government in the larger market centers, but many smaller "bootleg" pits are run throughout the village areas. Every village will have one or two men who specialize in breeding fighting cocks, and other men may purchase a young bird from them; but most village men go to the market cockpits, not to match their own birds, but to watch the fights and bet on the outcome. In the south, proportionately more village men raise fighting cocks. The south also has a special form of bullfight, which might be better described as a "shove-of-war" between two bulls. The betting that goes on at these southern bull fights is more important than the entertainment value of the fight itself. Other contests in which the betting is the most important factor include fights between fish, crickets, goats, and kites. Kite-flying contests are primarily urban events. Village women rarely attend these animal matches, nor do they play cards for money, as do prosperous Thai women of the town.

Whenever a group of Thai village men congregate, within a short time a coin-tossing game will be started. This form of gambling, in which coins are tossed at a hole in a ring on the ground, has many local variations, and the stakes can be adjusted to suit different groups. Little boys use stones instead of coins, temple boys toss for copper *satangs* in the *wat,* and their older brothers and fathers play for paper *ticals.*

The great emphasis on fighting in recreational sports has led an ardent exponent of Thai superiority to claim for the Thai people a love of fighting,[35] but actually the Thai are a peace-loving people, whose interest in sports and games centers around betting and gambling, not around the combat.

The element of contest permeates all Thai recreational activities. In the old days, on harvest and religious holidays, boat contests, tug-of-war contests, and rhyming-song contests were held. Many of these are gone today, although the winter fair with its contests among village stalls, beauty contests, and boxing matches, carries on the older, traditional behavior in a more modern form.

New forms of Western recreation are beginning to affect the villager. The radio has had little influence upon him, for except in a few villages near Bangkok, Thai peasants do not own radios and are likely to hear them only by chance in a market town or a city. Movies, on the other hand, have considerable influence. Landon, writing eighteen years ago, remarked that the movies had invaded every market town of any size and had become one of the most popular forms of entertainment.[*] The cinema is even more prevalent today, for the traveling tent-cinema has gone deeper into the village area with the advent of better roads. Young people, particularly, are coming in contact with both Thai and Western movies and are aping the behavior they see in them. For them, the movie in the nearby market town has an ever-increasing attraction. For the older villagers the movie has not yet replaced the traditional *likay* drama, but it has shoved the *likay*, even in the provincial capitals and larger market towns, into the background.

The rapidity with which village youth have taken to the cinema may be seen in an example from the village of San Pong. Before 1948, films were shown in Mae Rim (the district seat; four kilometers, or an hour's walk, from San Pong) only on special occasions; in 1948, a film unit from the provincial capital started showing films—usually American movies put on 16 mm. film for showing at military posts in World War II—in Mae Rim and other district seats regularly during the dry season. On nights when the unit was in Mae Rim, young villagers came from miles around; going to the films immediately became one of the most popular recreations in San Pong. Both Thai and American films are shown in the villages during the winter fairs, so that older people see movies at least once or twice a year.

CHANGES IN WAY OF LIFE

Apparent to all observers of the Thai is their characteristic enjoyment of life. The life of a Thai peasant may be hard or sorrowful but it can be enjoyed, whether it involves the backbreaking planting of rice or the mourning rites for a relative. These occasions are made lighter by music, games, eating, drinking, chewing betel, and smoking. Even important religious festivals are occasions of much gaiety and enjoyment.

So deeply ingrained is this tendency to take life as it comes and enjoy it, that even drunkenness (which in other cultures often changes personality by releasing tensions ordinarily suppressed) tends only to accentuate the Thai peasant's feelings of gaiety. A Thai farmer may become noisy under the influence of drink, but rarely or never is he quarrelsome or despondent. Cheerfulness, easy conviviality, nonviolence, and self-reliance characterize the behavior of the peasant. The changes in his economic and social life have not sensibly modified his behavior.

The comparatively relaxed, convivial, carefree manner of the Thai peasant has deceived many foreign observers into regarding him as indolent and far less industrious than peasants in other nations of Asia. Actually the Thai work as hard as most farmers, put in long, hard hours in the field to eke out a living, and, especially in northeast Thailand, struggle constantly against the disadvantages of poor soil and inadequate rain. The charge of indolence may also arise from the leisurely manner in which the Thai peasant goes about his chores. One reason for this leisure is that most Thai still reckon time in old-fashioned methods, that is, by relative phases. The day is marked by periods—"before breakfast" and "after breakfast." Thus, a headman's meeting called for "after breakfast" may get under way anytime between eight-thirty and nine in the morning. The Thai, most of whom own neither clock nor watch, have not acquired the vice of punctuality. They note the passage of time by various means: position of the sun or moon, crowing of cocks, the temple drum (regularly beaten at eleven o'clock to remind villagers to prepare dinner for the monks), the cast of a shadow. The *wat* is likely to own an alarm clock or a wooden, Swiss-type clock made in China. The primary school, which has regular class periods, is making Thai children more time-conscious, but away from school they slip back into the old, relative ways of thinking about time.

EFFECTS OF MODERN HEALTH PROGRAMS

By the standards of other countries of Asia, the level of health of the Thai peasant is relatively good, although considerable regional variation does exist. Central Thailand, which is relatively free of malaria, has the highest level of health, the northeast has the lowest. Villages near the provincial capitals and district centers have readier access to modern health facilities and show a higher level of health than isolated villages. If malaria, dysentery, childhood and maternal diseases, yaws, and other debilitating diseases can be brought under control, the level of health of the Thai peasant will be remarkably good, considering the environment in which he must continue to live.

There are only 2,000 doctors in all of Thailand, or one doctor for every 9,000 inhabitants. This is a considerably smaller ratio than that of the Philippines, which has one doctor for every 4,000 inhabitants, the highest ratio of southeast Asia, and although the Thai ratio is considerably better than the one doctor for every 50,000 inhabitants in nearby Indonesia," the nation should have at least five times as many doctors as it has. Except for the district health official and one or two private doctors in each provincial capital, few Thai doctors are willing to work in the country nor could they make a living even if they desired to do so. The Thai peasant has little or no contact with trained physicians, but still depends on local remedies, spirit practices, and a few Western drugs dispensed by the village "doctor." Only when the illness becomes critical is he likely to go to the medical officer in the district health office, and by that time it is usually too late. His child comes into the world with the aid of an untrained village midwife.

Yet his level of health has been steadily climbing. Much of the change that has come about has been the result of the public health programs of the last fifty years, which indirectly or directly have affected the villages. The earlier elimination of epidemic disease has been notable. Smallpox and cholera, which were constant scourges in the past, have been brought under almost complete control. Smallpox vaccination, introduced in 1840 by American missionaries, was slow in taking hold, but once it was made compulsory in the early part of the twentieth century, smallpox was quickly wiped out. Vaccinations are now made regularly during the year by the district health officer or his representative. Babies are vaccinated by the registered village doctor, who gets the vaccine from the health officer. Death from cholera is rare today but in former times epidemics wiped out scores of thousands throughout the country, always spreading from Bangkok and other urban centers. Safe water supply and modern methods of sanitation in the cities have brought cholera under control.

MALARIA CONTROL

The great epidemic killers of mankind—cholera, smallpox, and plague—have been overshadowed in the tropical countries by the much more deadly and insidious endemic malaria. Thailand has battled this crippling disease for thousands of years, and its vast northern areas, lying in a semitropical mountain region, have had to struggle with a malignant form of the disease. Malaria, as an endemic disease in Thailand, has always been the leading killer among the rural population, causing from 30,000 to 50,000 deaths annually. Over 40 per cent of all deaths in the country are from malaria, ranging from a high of 60 per cent in the north to a low of 20 per cent in central Thailand. Conservative estimates have placed the death rates at one death for every 60 cases. On this basis, somewhere between 1,800,000 to 2,400,000 Thai annually suffer from malaria. The economic losses to the peasant because of work stoppages have been serious.

Malaria in Thailand is, to a large extent, seasonal in nature; its incidence is also closely correlated with the periods of rainfall, topography, and type of irrigation. Extensive rice cultivation does not necessarily mean a high incidence of malaria; most of the vast rice-growing area of the Menam Plain has relatively little malaria. The annual malaria epidemic starts after the beginning of the rains early in June, rises to a peak in July, and gradually tapers off in September. Unfortunately for the farm family, this is the plowing and planting time, so that the crippling effects of malaria coincide with the farm family's busiest time of year. Between September and November there is little malaria, but a second epidemic flares up again in November and lasts until March; this coincides with the rice harvest. Malaria not only cripples the peasant but does so at the times that will cause his family to suffer most.

Malaria is not widespread in central Thailand and, more important, when it appears it is not the malignant type. The annual overflowing of the Chao Phya River, which spreads silt-laden water over the fields, particularly where broadcast rice is planted, prevents extensive breeding of the anopheline mosquito. In northern Thailand, where the incidence of malaria is high, the method of irrigation, that of paddy fields being irrigated continuously from field laterals and ditches, provides favorable breeding places for the malaria-carrying mosquito. For this reason a malaria-control program in conjunction with any large-scale irrigation program is essential.

In 1930, the department of health tried to exert some sort of control over malaria by making quinine available at cost to the village headmen for resale to villagers at a nominal price, but the high cost of quinine, even under these conditions, soon brought the program to an end. In the northern malarial region, oiling streams to destroy mosquito larvae has been neither practical nor feasible. Response to an educational program to convince the villager to use mosquito nets was slow, but nets are now so commonly used by northern villagers that it is only the very poor who sleep without them. The cutting of quinine supplies during World War II spread the crippling effects of the disease, and deaths caused by malaria jumped to over 50,000 a year during this period. Drastic and widespread action was needed. Malaria control on a large scale was undertaken in 1948 by the central government in collaboration with the World Health Organization. The antimalaria campaign was started by setting up control centers in the north to demonstrate how the disease could be controlled by proper methods. The district of

Sarapee near Chiangmai, with a farming population of 36,592, and the Hong Dong section of Chiangmai, both malarial spots, were chosen as control areas. Survey of the areas revealed that approximately 5 per cent of the farmers in the district had malarial fever. This was approximately 50 cases for every 1,000 persons. After a year and a half, the number of malaria cases had dropped to 7 per 1,000 in the control areas, showing what medical prophylactic treatment and an almost complete eradication of the adult and larva anopheline mosquito by spraying DDT could accomplish.[28]

A nation-wide control program was then started, the initial World Health Organization study being taken over by the central government aided by the United States Mutual Security Program. In 1951, over 200,000 village houses in northern Thailand were sprayed with DDT. Aralen, a new drug which has both prophylactic and curative value, was distributed to all fever cases. By the end of 1952, a million and a half villagers had been brought under the control program, and by the end of 1953, over three and a half million peasants in the worst malarial regions of the north and northeast were reached by the DDT-spraying and prophylactic program. A check of the spraying program of 1952 revealed that there was no malarial infection among the infants born in the villages that had been sprayed, an event new in the history of northern Thailand.

The results of a program of malaria control are obvious. Although the cost of this program is slight, compared with the benefits gained, the outside financial support for the pilot project will soon cease, and the problem of how to continue it has yet to be solved. Extremely effective ways of fighting malaria are now known, but new drugs for treatment are not yet within the price range of the ordinary village household budget. For the immediate future, if malaria is to be brought and kept under control, the central government must subsidize not only a program for eradication of the anopheline mosquito, but also a preventive and prophylactic program for the villagers. Malnutrition is a contributing cause in the high malaria death rate of villages, so that improvement of the diet of the people is also necessary.

The effects of control of malaria on health standards of the peasant of the north and northeast will be far-reaching. Already scores of thousands of peasants formerly stricken each year by malaria are now free from attack. If the control program continues to be effective, significant results will soon be seen in the reduction of general and infant mortality. In Ceylon, an effective malaria-control program has in the last few years reduced general mortality by one-third and infant mortality by one-half.[29] Similar results in Cyprus and Sardinia demonstrate clearly how rapid increase in population growth is correlated with modern health-control programs. Continuance of widespread malaria control in northern Thailand should begin to show the same results. The potential effects of such population growth will be discussed later in this chapter.

CONTROL OF INTESTINAL DISEASES

Next to malaria, intestinal diseases are the worst menace to the peasant's health. Sanitary facilities, both for water supply and sewage disposal, are primitive in the villages. The peasant has learned by experience that canals and rivers are polluted, but he still drinks water from shallow wells and ponds without boiling it first, and as a result develops dysentery and other intestinal afflictions. The current effort to improve health standards in Thailand calls for the digging of new wells in the villages; in 1952, Mutual Security Aid included materials for constructing 4,000 village wells and for boring 500 wells at least 100 feet deep in regions where surface pollution and ground seepage were serious. But so far dysentery goes virtually unchecked, and takes a fearful toll of life, especially among infants. Villagers are becoming aware of the dangers of pollution, but they lack the means to correct them.

MATERNAL AND INFANT HEALTH PROGRAMS

For whatever they are worth, the official statistics on infant and maternal mortality in Thailand are as follows: 65.9 infant deaths at birth for every 1,000 live births; 7.1 maternal deaths for every 1,000 births.[30] Like all statistics about a peasant population, these are unreliable and are probably far too low. Infant mortality and maternity deaths rank sixth among the first ten killers of the nation; conservative estimates reckon more than 15,000 maternal deaths and more than 100,000 infant deaths a year in rural Thailand. By Western standards these are appallingly high figures, but relative to the rest of southeast Asia they are quite good—far better than the estimated average for the whole area of 100 deaths per 1,000 in the first year of life, or the approximately 123 deaths for every 1,000 births that was reported for India in 1949.

Using the rough data available, we can estimate that less than twenty-five years ago infant mortality in the Bangkok area averaged 220 deaths for every 1,000 births. Infant mortality is usually higher in an urban area than in a rural region, but considering conditions a quarter of a century ago in rural Thailand, it is likely that the rate there was about the same. Before 1920 health statistics are almost meaningless, but health and medical workers in the twenties estimated that one-third of all the babies of the country died before they reached the age of one year. This was more than three times the infant mortality of western European countries for the same period.

Though the present 1952 figure of 65.9 deaths for every 1,000 births given out by the Economic Statistics Bureau is without doubt too low, it does indicate a sizable decrease in infant mortality. The decrease in the rural areas has taken place largely without modern curative or preventive work; it must be attributed partly to the cumulative effect that the limited use of Western medicine and health practices have had in curtailing the death rate, partly to the abandonment of certain childbirth customs—for example, "mother roasting"—which both directly and indirectly affected the newborn child. If such a drastic reduction can be brought about by the indirect effects of modern medicine, the immediate effect of a modern maternal and child health-training program would be even more tremendous. Hence, an important coöperative health program of the United Nations International Children's Emergency Fund, World Health Organization, and the Thai government is in this field.

Thailand, like the other countries of southeast Asia, is desperately in need of doctors and public health nurses to instill better methods of infant and child care at the village level. Ninety per cent of all Thai births, and nearly all rural Thai births, are still handled by untrained midwives; incorrect and inadequate feeding and ignorance of preventive health precautions are responsible for the serious intestinal diseases of children. In 1952, in the most important province of the north, Chiangmai, there were only eight trained midwives among a population of 500,000 and most of these eight were in the capital.[31] At least one hundred professional midwives are needed, and this figure is low when difficulty of rural transportation is considered. Approximately five thousand trained midwives are needed for the country.

The training program for midwives now under way will provide eighteen months of training, after which the midwife will return to the village or town from which she was recruited. Up to the end of 1952, the hospitals were able to turn out only a few score trainees a year and as yet the program has had little effect on the rural population. Consequently, eighteen maternal and child welfare centers were organized in 1952, primarily to train nurses and midwives.[32] But at the present rate of training it will be many years before the effect of this program will begin to infiltrate the village areas.

CONTROL OF YAWS AND OTHER DISEASES

Yaws, one of the most infectious skin diseases, has crippled many villagers, especially in the northeast and south. Roughly 6 per cent of the entire peasant population is infected with the disease, the percentage varying sharply from region to region. The north has been relatively free, having shown in the past less than one-fourth of one per cent infection, central Thailand has had about 5½ per cent infection, but the northeast has had 9 per cent, and the south as high as 15 per cent infection.[33]

A yaws-control program was started under the joint auspices of UNICEF, WHO, and the Thai government. In 1952 antiyaws teams operated in five provinces in the northeast, and examined 600,000 persons, treating over 100,000 with penicillin. The cost of detecting and curing each case of yaws amounted to approximately $2.35 (35 *ticals*) per case, but of this only half was for treatment, the other half being for the initial campaign expenses. Future cost of the program, if continued, would be about 17 *ticals* per case. At present about a quarter of a million infected persons are being treated annually, and it is estimated that by 1956, when the pilot program will end, over a million and a quarter yaws sufferers will have been cured. Since a cure renders the individual immune from further attacks, yaws is well on the way to being stamped out among the present generation. If the central government continues the program in the future, yaws can be kept at a minimum or perhaps completely wiped out.

Tuberculosis ranks third in the list of the most important causes of death. Though largely an urban disease, the high death rate indicates a sizable rural incidence. Some 10,000 people die every year from tuberculosis in Thailand. Until recently there was little or nothing in the way of a control program for this serious disease. In 1952, UNICEF, WHO, and the Thai government began an antituberculosis program which will in the next few years include every rural school child. Approximately one million children were given tuberculin tests in 1952 and all those who showed negative signs were vaccinated with BCG. Tests on a million and a half children a year will be continued until 1955, when the six million children of the country will have been tested. Mobile units are working with district health officers and school officials in testing the children. Testing and vaccination are only part of the program, for with a large percentage of the population infected, curative treatment is also necessary. Plans to set up treatment centers are under way but these obviously will not affect the peasants for a long time to come.

Other widespread diseases such as trachoma are being attacked by similar jointly sponsored programs. If all these serious diseases can be effectively brought under control, the present generation of peasants will face a totally different over-all rural health picture from that of the previous generation.

More and more the peasant is relying on Western drugs, although he may still dose himself indiscriminately with local cures and Chinese remedies as well. The startling effectiveness of the newer drugs which control malaria and of the sulpha drugs have convinced the villagers of the usefulness of modern preventives, and they feel somewhat cheated if they are not given at least a few pills when they call on the local practitioner. The high cost of such modern drugs is the main factor that limits their use. Even the villager who may still believe that spirits cause illness and who may call in a spirit doctor will also take modern drugs to be on the safe side.

CHANGES IN NUTRITION

The basic diet of rural Thailand—which is principally rice and dried fish—is by no means unnourishing, but it is low in vitamin and mineral content, and seriously lacks fats. However, compared to that of other parts of southeast Asia, Thailand's diet is good; the few professional studies that have been made of Thai diet rate it as adequate but in need of improvement. There is also considerable regional variation; the northeastern Thailand diet is poorest, and since this region contains some 30 per cent of Thailand's population, its low level of nutrition poses a serious problem. However, the Thai peasant is hardly the "poorly clothed," "badly fed," and "diseased" creature that many a copywriter sitting in Bangkok has made him out to be.

It is one of the misfortunes of the Oriental diet that its primary food, rice, becomes more appealing in taste and appearance in proportion as it becomes less nutritious, for it is the pericarp, which is removed when rice is polished, that contains most of the food value. Fortunately for the Thai, most of them eat rice that has been milled at home by a wooden pestle in a wooden mortar—a method that cannot grind the rice to the highly polished and quite worthless food demanded by discriminating Asiatic palates. Also, the Thai cook rice by using very little water, steaming, rather than boiling it, and keep the water in which the rice has been cooked; by this method most of the mineral value of the rice is retained rather than thrown away as garbage. Unfortunately, in the delta many Thai farmers have taken advantage of the proximity of commercial rice mills to have their family's rice supply milled by them. The result is that delta farmers enjoy a fluffy, pure white rice—and have the highest incidence of beri-beri, which ranks tenth among the causes of death in Thailand.

Throughout Asia, an attempt is being made to induce the people to eat either unpolished or parboiled rice. The former is simply rice in which all or most of the pericarp is left intact; theoretically, it matters little whether the rice is milled at home or commercially, by hand or by machinery, so long as its food value is not destroyed. (Home-milled rice can be ground to much the same degree of polish as machine-milled rice by the use of a stone pestle and mortar; the difference is that home-milling breaks the kernels, but machine-milling keeps the grain intact). Parboiled rice is steamed before milling to drive the vitamins into the innel kernel, thereby retaining most of its food value, but has an unattractive color and a disagreeable odor. The consumer who is accustomed to polished rice finds neither unpolished nor parboiled rice palatable, nor is he readily persuaded by talk about nutritional values and vitamin-B content. Until technical improvements in making nutritious kinds of rice palatable can be effected, it seems unlikely that the urban dweller can be persuaded to change his dietary preferences, and since reforms and innovations usually move from the city to the country, any improvement in rural rice-eating habits will have to await urban changes. There have been no technical improvements in rice milling in the past thirty years, and until the present system of small, independent, Chinese-owned rice mills is replaced by some sort of government-controlled, standardized mill system there is little likelihood of any progress. Even if this step were taken, it would be a long, slow task to overcome the habit and inertia of the people.

Some rural areas have large supplies of fresh vegetables and fish, but other areas, particularly the northeast, are lacking in these staples. The peasant of the northeast lacks sufficient water to grow vegetables and must depend on dried fish (which lacks important vitamins) during most of the year. In the northeast, as well as in the commercialized farming areas of the Menam Plain, dietary deficiencies are a constant menace to health.

EFFECT OF MODERN AGRICULTURAL PROGRAMS

Not until the last decade were any large, integrated programs for the economic development and social improvement of the farmer undertaken by the central government. Many have been started only in the postwar years, when international organizations such as the Food and Agricultural Organization of the United Nations began to give technical service and financial support. Since 1950, these pilot programs in economic development have been underwritten by joint collaboration of the central government and the mutual aid programs of the United States. Some of these newer agricultural-advancement projects—plant breeding, animal and poultry breeding, fertilizer experiments, and diversified farming experiments—are in an experimental stage and have had little effect on the peasant; others, such as large-scale irrigation programs and animal-disease control programs, have already affected millions of peasants in all sections of the country.

CHANGES IN LAND TENURE FOR THE PEASANT

In ancient times land had little monetary value for the peasant. Since there was so much free land, any freeman could gain squatter's rights by clearing the land, planting a crop, and paying a small land tax. This land might, in turn, be abandoned, once its fertility began to decline. In traditional Siam, tenant farmers worked for shares for a prosperous local landlord, and all villagers, whether freeholders or tenants, were subject to military and corvee labor. In ancient times, large individual holdings of land were accumulated by the upper classes through the practice of officials' being granted land by the king in lieu of salary. This system, known as the *sakdi na,* defined the wealth and status of the nobility. *Chao Phyas,* with important posts, could hold from 1,000 to 4,000 acres, while subordinate officials held 160 acres or more. With this granted land went a toll from the produce of the farmers cultivating it. The *sakdi na* was officially abolished about 1900.

Traditionally, a freeman could secure land by clearing it and cultivating it, but his holdings were limited to 25 *rai* (approximately 10 acres) and he did not hold permanent title, for by usufructuary action the king could claim the land by right of expropriation.[34] Not until the twentieth century were official government land titles instituted, the first being issued in 1901. The peasant today holds his land by a system of regular land titles (*chap chong*). The old system of squatters' rights (*bai yiap yam*) which gives virtual possession, can still be practiced, but only on specific types of public land, which in most areas is not suited to rice farming.

The Thai government has made little or no attempt to control rental rates. However, in 1952 a royal decree controlling rice-land rental was put into effect in eighteen provinces of the Menam Plain. But this decree did not take subletting into consideration. The law has been ineffective, for landlords simply sublet the farms to brokers who in turn demand the former high rent from the tenant farmer.

RURAL DEBT AND CREDIT COÖPERATIVE ASSOCIATIONS

Many conflicting generalizations have been made about rural indebtedness in Thailand. Many of the data on farm indebtedness have come from specialized sections of the delta, where the family-operated farms of 8 to 10 hectares have given way to large rented farms operated on a cash basis. Unfortunately, observations from this special area have been applied to the rest of the country, giving an erroneous picture of the debt situation. Actually, the majority of the peasants are rarely deeply in debt.

Zimmerman's 1930 survey showed that in the central area average indebtedness was ten times greater than in the self-subsistent sections of the country; 49 per cent of the families he studied were in debt.[35] Andrews, making a follow-up survey four years later, found that 80 per cent of the total indebtedness of rural Thailand was concentrated in the lower Menam Valley, and most of this was in the delta zone of intensified rice farming. Of the remaining 20 per cent, northern Thailand had 8 per cent of the total, northeastern Thailand 7 per cent, and southern Thailand 5 per cent.[36] After careful analysis, Andrews reached the conclusion that the greater part of the farm debt, even in the central area, was not basically detrimental since relatives and friends held most of the loan contracts and usually charged interest rates that did not exceed the legal limit of 15 per cent. His general conclusion was that, except in the marginal region of the delta, farm debt was of minor importance. Since his observations were drawn in a period of relative depression, it can be assumed that in today's period of relative prosperity, debt is not a significant factor in the life of the average peasant. The only available data on present conditions tends to substantiate this. Janlekha, making an economic survey of rice-raising costs of 104 farmers in the Bangchan area in 1949, found that when loans were made, the maximum legal rate of interest was often ignored and interest rates as high as 50 per cent were charged.[37] But he gives no indication of the prevalence of such extortion, nor does he indicate how many of the 104 households were in debt. The obvious conclusion is that the debts were so few and insignificant as to be unimportant in his sample.

In Thailand, local credit associations like those in Japan, China, and Vietnam, have not been developed. The peasant in need of a loan has had to turn to relatives or to a prosperous townsman, a Chinese shopkeeper or rice dealer, or some other moneylender. When the poor farmer borrowed money he placed himself in an economic trap. It was not so much the amount of interest charged by the moneylender as the way the loan was repaid that hurt the peasant. Merchants and brokers advanced commodities to the peasant on credit and demanded payment in paddy rather than in cash; by fixing the amount of paddy to be paid by the debtor, the broker reaped a sizable profit.

It was also common in the past for a moneylender to insist on a written contract in which rice land was offered as security. The small landowner, who put up his land for security and was not able to pay the loan plus the high interest, lost his land. A tenant farmer who wished to secure a loan had to wait until his paddy showed signs of a promising yield, and was then charged a high rate of interest, amounting in the delta region to 50 per cent for the work season of approximately 5 to 6 months.[38]

The government has made no effort to regulate interest rates or to control private moneylenders, but it has expanded government-controlled coöperative credit associations in an attempt to solve the problem of rural indebtedness. In 1919 the Thai government embarked on a program of setting up a coöperative credit movement; today there are some 8,482 credit associations in 216 of the country's 411 main districts, with a membership of 156,000.[39] But only farmers who own land can join these associations, and as a result the tenant farmers, who need help more than any other group, have not yet been helped by the coöperative program.

Since the end of World War II, new credit coöperatives have been established under government sponsorship at the rate of 1,000 a year. Yet, the coöperative credit movement, in spite of aggressive government policy, touches at best only 8 per cent of the country's land-owning farmers. The local coöperative credit associations obtain loan funds from the government, for which they pay an interest rate of 6 per cent a year. In turn, the local credit association loans out money to its members at the rate of 8 per cent for long-term loans and 10 per cent for short-term loans. Interest rates charged by money-lenders in the past have been six or seven times this amount. The government-sponsored credit associations are popular among the small landowners, who borrow money to pay off long-outstanding, high-interest debts to brokers and professional moneylenders, to purchase work animals and farm implements, and to acquire additional land. Most of the credit coöperatives are in central Thailand, where they are most needed.

In the past few years the central government has established land-hire-purchase coöperative associations to enable the landless farmer to buy land on a hire-purchase basis. But in all of Thailand, in 1950, there were only 21 such hire-purchase coöperatives, involving only 820 families and taking in only 3,000 hectares of paddy land.[40] The landless peasant is not being reached by the coöperatives to any appreciable extent.

The number of coöperative marketing societies dealing with the sale of paddy is even smaller than the land-hire-purchase associations; up to 1950 there were only about a half dozen for the entire country. Since it is in the sale of paddy that the farmer loses much of his profit to the middleman, coöperative marketing associations would greatly benefit all peasants raising large crops of rice for sale. So far, the central government has not had enough money to underwrite an ambitious program of marketing coöperatives, and there seems little likelihood of any great expansion of this type of coöperative in the foreseeable future. The farmer will continue to sell his paddy in small lots to the middleman and continue to take a smaller share of the profits of rice-raising. Modern consumer coöperatives are unknown in rural Thailand.

ANIMAL HEALTH PROGRAMS

Next to his land, his water buffalo is the farmer's most important possession. Without it he cannot work his fields; if it dies, he may go in debt to buy another; he tends his buffalo carefully, and shows great interest in the government program designed to safeguard its health. In the past, he followed the instructions of the district veterinarian regarding the health of his animals more readily than those that applied to the health of his family. When a water buffalo dies in the village, the house compound of the stricken owner quickly fills with his neighbors who come to see if it was a natural death or one from an infectious disease that might strike their animals as well. District regulations require that its death be reported at once after an inspection by the headman.

Rinderpest always has been the major disease attacking water buffalo as well as other cattle, and up to eight years ago there was little effective control of it in the country although it was confined largely to the two northern areas and was kept out of central Thailand by quarantine stations along the stock routes. The supply of tissue vaccine and serum then used was so limited that it was impossible to combat the disease effectively. During the war the disease got out of hand, and by 1946 over 200,000 water buffalo had been stricken: the infected bullocks of the Japanese ox-drawn transports had spread it throughout the country in the course of the Japanese retreat from Burma. The situation became so desperate that a stringent eradication program had to be undertaken on a national scale. Laboriously, and at tremendous cost, the country was finally cleared of rinderpest by 1950.

The peasants had no choice but to coöperate with the drastic government control program of 1946–1948, although many objected to the use of goat virus as an immunizing agent. This virus provided good, durable protection but always caused a serious reaction in cattle and water buffalo, rendering the animals unworkable for a considerable time. Farmers did not always take kindly to the idea of having a healthy animal immunized.

In 1948, experiments were started in Thailand using lapinized rinderpest serum; by the end of 1949 lapinized serum was in production, and it is now used almost exclusively throughout the country. In contrast to goat virus, lapinized virus does not cause symptoms of ill health in a normal animal. Villagers have quickly seen the value of this new vaccine, and as a result of its widespread use, the country, for the first time in centuries, is free from rinderpest; the isolated cases that appear are brought in by animals coming across the border.

Water buffalo and other stock are periodically vaccinated in the villages. The district officer sends word to the *kamnan* that on a certain day a *changwat* veterinarian will vaccinate animals, and each headman must see that every villager with animals receives the notification. Immunization is not yet compulsory, but since the great rinderpest scare of 1946 almost every adult water buffalo in the country has been vaccinated. Villagers do not have to pay for this vaccination, another reason for their ready acceptance of it. Since previously villagers in the two northern areas lost over 25,000 animals every year to this disease, they have benefited immensely from the government program of immunization, and the program is popular among the villagers. If mass immunization were to be carried out in neighboring regions of Burma and Indochina, rinderpest could be wiped out in all of southeast Asia.

The other diseases striking the farmer's work animals have not yet been brought under control. Villagers still lose water buffalo and cattle from an enzootic disease (haemorrhagic septicaemia) which now ranks first as a cause of death among water buffalo. Anthrax is found occasionally, but fortunately its incidence has been so small as to be unimportant. Vaccines for the enzootic disease now are in test production at the government's experimental station at Pak Chong. Poultry disease has never been a problem in the villages as the peasant farmer raises few chickens.

MODERN FERTILIZER PROGRAMS

The only chemical fertilizer used at all widely in Thailand has been ammonia sulphate, and this is used only by the commercial vegetable growers near Bangkok, who are Chinese. Rice-farmers do not use inorganic fertilizers. In various sections of the country, the central government has attempted to show the farmer the benefits of using chemical fertilizer by setting up test plots, but nowhere has the attempt been successful, even in the delta region where, conceivably, a well-to-do farmer could afford to buy fertilizer. Chemical fertilizers would benefit the northeastern region greatly but since this is a noncommercial farming area, the farmers here cannot afford them, and with over five million peasants in the region, the government can not afford to underwrite, now or in the future, any sizable chemical fertilizer program. Thus, any discussion of a modern fertilizer program is somewhat academic, although it may have potentialities for the commercial rice growers of the delta. A factor not often taken into consideration by agricultural experts who stress the use of chemical fertilizers is that only a long, slow period of demonstration can convince the peasant that he will benefit from such a drastic new measure. Also, in other parts of southeast Asia where large-scale chemical fertilizer experiments have been attempted, not enough attention has been paid to analyzing types of soils and local types of plants. Simply dumping a load of chemical fertilizer on a paddy field does not ensure higher yield; it may even decrease it. The Thai peasant is a long way from being able to use the techniques of scientific farming without direct supervision. This supervision the government is not prepared to give, even if it had the chemical fertilizer, for an agricultural extension program is almost nonexistent.

FUTURE OF MECHANIZED FARMING FOR THE PEASANT

Rising costs of production in the Menam Plain are already creating serious problems for the rice farmer: the use of labor-saving devices to keep production costs down seems to be the only solution. Mechanized rice production has been suggested, but this does not fit the present economic or social structure of the area.

Mechanized equipment can be used economically only in large fields. Over 80 per cent of all rice in Thailand is transplanted and grown in small, irregular shaped paddy fields surrounded by *bunds*, or dikes. Only in the broadcast-rice area of the Menam Plain would the use of tractors be practical, but even here the average holding is less than 10 hectares. A peasant farmer owning or renting such a limited farm area could not possibly buy a tractor, much less pay operating expenses. "Custom plowing," in which the farmer pays for tractor plowing on a contract basis, might overcome this obstacle but this also would necessitate a sizable cash outlay at the beginning of the planting season, when a rice farmer's cash surplus is lowest. Further, experiments conducted by the government during the past twenty years at the government's rice experimental station have demonstrated that it is not possible to do without water buffalo in plowing. Plowing out corners, carting, and other odd jobs can be done more economically by animals than with a tractor, even on fairly large farms."

The greatest obstacle to the mechanization of rice farming, however, is the inadequacy of existing methods of harvesting. A large rice farm could be plowed by tractor and planted by hand in the broadcast method with a minimum of labor, but harvesting a large area by hand labor would be too costly. The obvious solution would be machine harvesting, but only a standing crop can be harvested mechanically, and to produce a standing crop it is essential that the depth of water in the paddy fields be rigidly controlled, which can not be done under present conditions. Water must be kept at a depth of not more than 40 or 50 centimeters or later the plants will not stand, but flatten out when the water recedes.

There has been some mechanized rice production on the large commercial farms of the Bangkok delta area ever since the First World War, when great demands for rice and high prices encouraged a few operators to introduce mechanized equipment, but mechanization on a large scale is far off in modern Thailand. Serious doubts exist that it could ever find a place, even in commercial rice-farming areas, unless the whole cultural pattern of the farmer was changed. For the other 80 per cent of Thai peasants who are living mainly in a self-subsistent economy, it has no foreseeable future.

IRRIGATION, RECLAMATION, AND FLOOD CONTROL

Though the area under rice cultivation has increased in fair proportion to the increase in population in the last forty years, rice yield per unit acre has decreased by 60 per cent.[a] This has led the central government, with the assistance of outside technical and financial aid, to institute in the past five years a far-reaching program of irrigation, land reclamation, and flood control, in an attempt to increase rice yield.

Since annual inundation in central Thailand restores much of the fertility of the soil, the decrease in yield per acre under cultivation shown by the government's figures cannot be attributed alone to infertility, although there is no doubt that intensive use of the soil for centuries has cut down its productivity. The main reason for the statistical decrease in rice yield is that the growth of population and the increased demand for rice for export has caused more and more land in the upper reaches of the Menam Plain to be put under cultivation; here flood water is irregular and insufficient, and rainfall is not adequate for proper irrigation. The low yield of this land has caused the national average yield of paddy per unit acre to decline.

The northeast needs more water before it can produce additional rice, but the soil is so poor that even with irrigation the amount of rice available for export will not be measurably increased, since over 70 per cent of all rice grown there is of the glutinous, nonexport variety. The north, raising glutinous rice, is primarily a self-subsistent area, and because of the difficulty of transport can not be considered as a surplus-rice producing area. The central plain must meet the demand for increased production.

Yet the Menam Plain does not receive adequate rainfall for wet-rice cultivation. Commercialized rice production has been made possible only by the annual flooding of the Chao Phya River network, which, coming a month or so after the rains begin, makes up the rainfall deficiency. The entire Menam Plain is channeled with canals that carry the flood waters to the fields. This flood water is spread by gravity, for the canals are also the waterway thoroughfares for the delta region, and there has been no artificial control of the water. It has never been possible to control the duration or the depth of flooding, and the risks involved in rice farming have always been great. Either there is too little water at the beginning of the planting time, or too much or too little during the growing season. Records kept over the past thirty years indicate that from one-fourth to one-third of the rice planted annually does not reach maturity because of floods or of water shortage. The annual inundation has been important in maintaining the fertility of the Menam delta, but at the same time the continual flooding has silted channels and caused drastic shifts in the location of the most reliable rice-growing areas. Parts of the central plains have been built up by sedimentation until they were above the ordinary flood level and hence have had to be abandoned by the rice growers.

An extensive controlled-irrigation system is the answer but only recently has work on such a system begun. Though an irrigation control program for the Chao Phya watershed was started in 1880, it proceeded by fits and starts. Because there was never enough money to construct a major dam at Chainat, where the main reservoir basin should be located, this essential keystone of the entire irrigation scheme for the region was never built. Instead, a series of smaller dams across the lower tributary streams were constructed. The Chao Phya irrigation system has in effect worked backwards without a secure foundation and has been a makeshift affair; some areas that previously had ample water now feel occasional water shortages, for without the main dam, distribution as well as conservation and storage of water have been faulty."

In 1952 a loan of $18,000,000 from the International World Bank made it possible to begin construction of the Chainat dam and fourteen other major projects designed to modernize the central-plain's irrigation system. When this work is completed in 1957, eighteen provinces of the Menam Plain will have much better water distribution, and it is hoped that the annual rice yield of the area will be raised from its present annual average of 885,000 tons of paddy to over 1,800,000 tons. Over 400,000 hectares of rice land in the lower reaches will be reopened to cultivation, and in the upper areas 160,000 hectares, which can be used in the dry season for secondary crops, will be opened to rice growing for the first time. The effects of this on the rice-export economy will be significant, but as yet the life of the average farmer of the Menam Plain has not been affected by the over-all irrigation program.

The northeast poses a serious problem. Although some 300,000 tons of inferior nonglutinous rice are sent annually to the central area for local consumption, thus releasing more rice there for export, the northeast has few potentialities as a surplus-rice producing area. It has been for centuries an area of bare subsistence living: in the more arid parts of the Korat Plateau thousands of peasant families have barely scraped out a living from the dry, infertile soil. The northeastern peasant has adapted remarkably well to his environment, but as he does not have enough river water he has not been able to develop an irrigation system. The northeast received little attention from the government until 1933, when construction of eight small dams on the main rivers was begun. These dams were only partly finished when World War II brought the work to a complete standstill, and they were not finished until late in 1952.

To provide for some of the driest areas, the central government after the war began a program of construction of small earthen dams, each capable of irrigating about 200 farms. In collaboration with the MSA, this was expanded in 1950 into a long-range program calling for the construction of over one thousand small storage reservoirs throughout fifteen of the northeastern provinces that annually suffer from a water shortage. But the Korat peasant needs help at once, and a storage-tank project was designed to help farmers in localized village areas as quickly as possible. These small storage tanks (the size depends on local needs and storage facilities) will store sufficient water to irrigate from 300 to 10,000 *rai* of land. Although only twenty-two tanks were completed during the first eighteen months of operation and only some twenty more begun by late 1952, immediate effects were evident. Forty-seven thousand *rai* of land in twenty different places were put under rice cultivation for the first time, and the estimated rice yield on this land alone will be over 12,000 tons. The eventual plan is to establish local irrigation coöperatives to control and operate the tanks and construct the small ditches needed for the distribution of water.

When all the irrigation projects are completed, the rice yield of the northeast will materially increase and the standard of living will be raised measurably. But this is a potentiality, since only a few dams and fewer than a hundred of the storage tanks have been constructed. If construction does not proceed at a faster rate, it will take another twenty years to complete the project.

For the first time in the history of the northeast, emergency crop aid for the peasant was put into effect in 1952, as a joint operation of the Thai irrigation department and the American mutual-aid program. Powerful pumps installed on trucks were sent into drought-stricken areas where the farmers had no means of getting water from the streams to the stricken paddy fields. Some twenty of these pumps were put into operation in 1952, each capable of giving emergency irrigation to more than 200,000 *rai* of paddy land annually. Theoretically, over 2,000,000 *rai* of land can be irrigated by them, or in other words, the holdings of more than 250,000 peasant families—approximately one quarter of all peasant families of the region. Designed to move into areas where shortages of rainfall endanger the crop, these mobile pumps have proved remarkably effective.

In the north, inadequate rainfall, sandy soil, and markedly sloping terrain has always made irrigation a necessity for the growing of wet-land rice. By irrigation the northern peasant has been able to build up a relatively high standard of living in a self-subsistent economy, although maintenance of the main canals and division weirs has always been a serious problem. Private concessionaires usually constructed the main weirs and canals, and farmers paid these private operators a water fee either in cash or rice. The result was confusion until the government's irrigation department took over control and maintenance of all main canals and weirs. Within the commune, the villages are still responsible for building and maintaining local networks.

In the past seven years, a few large modern water-control projects have been started in the north. The main problem of the peasant of the north has not been to bring water to his fields—for crude local irrigation systems have effectively accomplished this—but to prevent floods and drought. Any unusual spring flooding brings disaster to a farmer's fields; about one-fourth of all rice planted in the north does not reach maturity because of floods. The small, communally created irrigation system can do little to check this flood damage or to conserve water as a safeguard against drought. A few large dams to give some protection against flood and drought are now being built, but even when these are completed they will affect only a limited area. Controlled irrigation for the north is a long way off.

The next generation of peasant farmers all over the country should benefit immeasurably from these government-sponsored irrigation projects. Standards of living will be raised. The potentialities are promising, but their realization depends upon continual expansion and maintenance of a large-scale program.

FISH CONSERVATION

The increasing decline of both the salt- and fresh-water fisheries in the past quarter century has seriously alarmed the central government. Without sufficient fish to supplement his rice, the Thai peasant's diet would quickly fall below an adequate nutritional level, for most of the farmer's protein comes from fish he himself catches. Only in the last decade has there been any serious nation-wide planning to remedy the situation. The government has set aside as a reserve the lake of Bung Borophet near Paknampo, where the northern rivers meet to form the great Chao Phya River. Bung Borophet, formerly a swamp, was converted into a vast lake covering 400 square kilometers and today serves as the spawning ground for the millions of fish that annually spread throughout the Chao Phya and its complex of tributaries. In 1948, when it was discovered that the annual catch of both fresh-water and salt-water fish did not exceed 100,000 metric tons annually, and that normally the country, with a population of 17,000,000 would consume locally five times that amount, the first serious efforts were made to plan for the future. In the past few years, with the help of the WHO and the MSA, the central government has embarked on a program of experimental work in fish breeding for fresh-water fishing as well as planning for the commerical fishing industry of the country. Fish-breeding stations have been set up on the central reaches of the Chao Phya, Nam, Yom, Thachin, and Meklong rivers, and in the Chiengrai and Chiangmai areas of the north. The peasant is not aware of this conservation program, but it will eventually have a great effect on his daily life; the next generation will reap its benefits.

POPULATION GROWTH

The progress made in the past half century in improving the general health of the country has resulted in a significant population increase which is beginning to demonstrate its potential effects on the peasant economy. Thailand's population grew from an estimated 8,000,000 in 1900 to over 17,000,000 in 1947; that this is a result of a reduction in mortality is shown by the birth rate for 1947—23.7 per thousand population—which is not significantly high. Reliable statistics for earlier periods do not exist but according to figures compiled by the Public Health Department between 1921 and 1926, the annual birth rate for that period was 29.5 per thousand. The average general mortality rate in Thailand a quarter of a century ago was 17 per thousand population; it is now 10.5 per thousand."

The effects of large-scale health projects on population trends pose a significant problem for most of the underdeveloped countries of southeast Asia. Fortunately, Thailand is one of the few countries there where rapid growth in population is an asset rather than a liability, for it is thinly populated (87 persons to a square mile) and still has vast areas of undeveloped land that can be cultivated. Only in the low-lying valleys has there been extensive cultivation; roughly 16 per cent of the central plain area, but only 7 per cent of the land of the rest of the country, is cultivated. Of the vast uncultivated area of the country about 70 per cent is forest.

As a result of the increase in population the area under cultivation has steadily increased, land being reclaimed from the jungle largely through the efforts of the farmers themselves. In 1910, over half of the Menam delta was still jungle land, and much of what is now the richest rice land of the country, near Bangkok, was a jungle swamp. In the delta region alone over 5,000,000 acres of farm land have been put into cultivation since 1900; fertile land in the higher regions lacks only water to turn it into good rice land.

The Thai came originally as migrants from the north, and there has been a steady drift from the northern regions towards the fertile Ayuthia and Bangkok delta regions. This ancient shift southward continues on a limited scale; from 1937 to 1947 the only two provinces of the country that showed declining populations were Mae Hong Son and Chiangmai of the north, and the other six northern provinces showed less than a 10 per cent increase in population compared to the average 20 per cent for the country as a whole.

The highest rural population density is in the Bangkok delta (250 persons to a square mile) and the lowest (50 persons to a square mile) is in the western mountain zone of the central area; the northeast and north have population densities ranging between 50 and 100 people to a square mile." But these figures give only a rough idea of concentration, for most of the Thai peasants are crowded in the fertile river valleys. Since the Bangkok delta is a surplus-rice producing area with larger farms than elsewhere, it has actually the lowest nutritional density, that is to say, the lowest number of persons per cultivated square mile, of any region in Thailand. It is for this reason that the region with the greatest population density can produce the greatest amount of surplus rice for export.[46]

NUTRITIONAL DENSITY IN THAILAND

Region	Population per cultivated square mile
Delta Region of the Menam Plain	550
Western Edge of the Central Plain	630
Middle Central Thailand	730
Korat Plateau (N.E. region)	1400
North Thailand	1930
Southern Thailand	3400

The controlled-irrigation system in the Menam Plain, now nearly completed, which will double rice yield, means that the standard of living will continue to rise and more surplus rice will be produced, in spite of the great increase in population. Agricultural economists have estimated that Thailand can support a population of at least 100,000,000, although intensified farming, adequate irrigation programs, and other improvements would be necessary in order to maintain a reasonable standard of living for such a population. As her population increases, so can her rice production, so that for the next half century at least, there is no danger that Thailand will suffer from population pressure; rather, the reverse will be true, for the standard of living of the peasant should rise as his numbers increase.

SUMMARY

Like all peasant societies which have come into contact with the Western world, Thai peasant society has changed greatly within the past half-century. Some of the changes are the direct result of government supervision and control: for example, the compulsory school system, conscription, and the government's political, economic, and agricultural programs. Concomitant with these have been the changes caused by the transformation of a barter economy into a money economy; these changes have been most pronounced in the Menam Plain, but the transformation has also affected all other parts of the country, for nowhere in Thailand today can a peasant farmer get along without some cash outlay.

The old agricultural practices have not changed basically in the past half-century. Some machines are now used in the cash-crop economy of the delta region, but elsewhere machines have no place at all in the agricultural techniques of the peasant. He has, however, adopted many of the Western modes of dress, and uses many Western commodities.

Many of the traditional patterns of village life have undergone great change. Certain ones, such as the top-knot ceremony, mother roasting, and tattooing have almost entirely disappeared, as have most of the elaborate spirit practices of the past. A host of other cultural practices have been greatly modified: traditional costumes are worn only on special occasions, the older marriage customs are observed only perfunctorily, piercing of women's ears and betel chewing are no longer universal. But in spite of the outward adaptation that peasant life has made to Western influences, the old basic patterns of life, in agriculture, in religion, and in social life, remain strong and secure. Thai peasant society shows none of the signs of disintegration that are so often evident when a peasant group is brought rapidly into contact with modernization and Westernization.

APPENDICES

APPENDIX I

A: POPULATION GROWTH IN THAILAND, 1911–1951

Year	Population in thousands	Rate of increase in per cent
1911	8,266	....
1919	9,207	1.36
1929	11,506	2.20
1937	14,464	2.96
1947	17,443	1.89
1948	17,666	....
1949	17,987	2.00
1950	18,313	2.00
1951	18,836	3.00

B: BIRTH AND MORTALITY RATES IN THAILAND, 1925–1949
(Per thousand)

Year	Birth rate	Death rate	Infant mortality rate
1925–9	29.9	15.5	.....
1930–4	34.6	16.3	93.0
1937	36.7	17.8	100.8
1943	36.5	18.4	97.4
1944	32.0	17.6	98.7
1945	25.9	16.5	105.6
1946	24.2	15.2	94.6
1947	23.8	13.5	79.8
1948	24.1	10.8	68.1
1949	28.1	10.6	68.2

Demographic Yearbook, 1952. New York: Statistical Office of the United Nations, Department of Economic Affairs, 1952.

APPENDIX II

Chart of Provincial and District Government

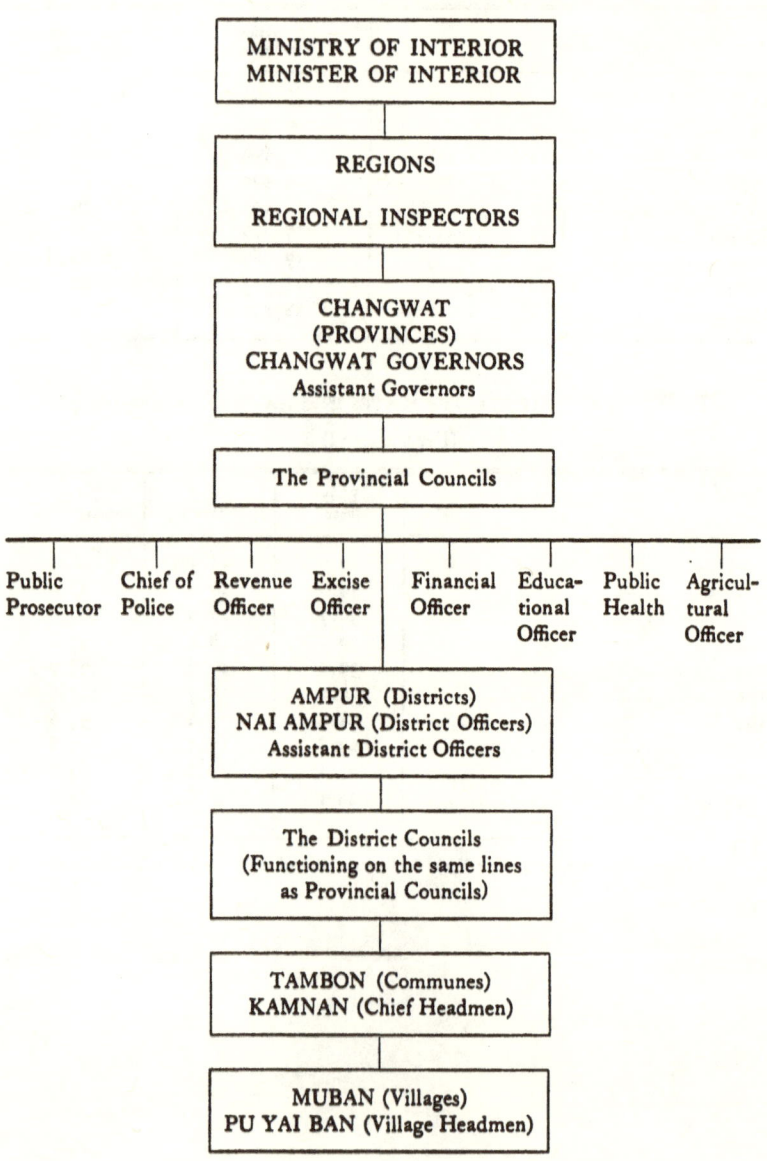

APPENDIX III

Common Vegetables, Food Plants, and Fruit Trees Found in the House Yards of North Thailand

Vegetables and Food Plants

1. Chili
2. Egg plant
3. Cucumber
4. Lettuce
5. Cabbage
6. Onion
7. Garlic
8. Green pea
9. Green bean
10. Groundnut
11. Sugar cane
12. Bamboo (shoots)
13. Corn
14. Ginger
15. Tumeric
16. Pumpkin
17. Sponge gourd
18. Water gourd
19. Hyacinth bean
20. Pigeon pea
21. Basil
22. Tomato
23. Long pepper
24. Lemon grass
25. Galanga
26. Rospelle
27. Acacia

Fruit Trees

	Name	Frequency	Time of bearing
1.	Banana	Almost all yards	All year round
2.	Betel palm (areca)	Almost all yards	Green nuts, August–December
3.	Coconut palm	About 50% of all yards	All year round
4.	Mango	Occasionally	June
5.	Pomelo	Occasionally	September–December
6.	Papaya	Occasionally	All year round

(Many others, such as pomelo, jackfruit, custard apple, lime, and tamarind, are found, but their occurrence is not frequent.)

APPENDIX IV

Provincial Breakdown into Land Area and Administrative Units

Changwat	Square kilometers	Per cent of total area	Ampur	Tambon	Village
Krabi	3,960	0.77	4	39	252
Kanchana-buri	19,472	3.79	10	74	488
Kamphaenghet	8,887	1.73	4	25	199
Khon-kaen	15,896	3.09	7	58	1,239
Chantburi	6,023	1.17	6	58	566
Cha-choengsao	5,649	1.10	6	82	1,234
Cholburi	4,473	.07	8	61	512
Chai-nat	2,807	0.55	6	43	432
Chayaphun	7,589	1.48	6	42	588
Chumphorn	5,703	1.11	6	55	462
Chiengrai	15,204	2.96	11	74	1,037
Chiangmai	22,920	4.46	17	159	1,441
Trang	4,973	0.97	5	84	582
Trat	2,789	0.55	4	29	235
Tak	13,644	0.66	6	35	335
Thonburi	394	0.08	9	40	425
Nakhornayak	2,161	0.42	4	30	461
Nakhornpatham	2,231	0.43	5	91	1,083
Nakhornphanom	9,706	1.89	7	56	750
Nakhornratchsima	20,360	3.96	13	117	1,825
Nakhorsrithamrat	10,222	1.99	13	122	1,149
Nakhornsawan	9,772	1.90	8	83	859
Nontburi	622	0.12	5	44	490
Nara-thiwat	4,172	0.81	9	58	368
Nan	14,821	2.89	7	67	612
Nong-khai	7,519	1.46	4	39	408
Buri-ram	5,951	1.87	7	37	637
Pathum-thani	1,568	0.31	7	59	873
Prachuap-Khirikhan	6,272	1.22	5	23	164
Prachinburi	11,971	2.33	8	87	1,302
Pattani	1,948	0.38	8	101	704
Phra-Nakorn	889	0.17	13	73	925
Phang-nga	3,958	0.77	8	45	341
Phatalung	4,414	0.86	4	30	395
Phichit	4,468	0.87	5	46	404
Phitsnulok	9,548	1.80	6	69	547
Phetchbun	12,695	2.47	5	40	447
Phetchbur	6,308	1.23	6	52	494
Phrae	5,952	1.16	6	56	395
Phuket	533	0.10	3	24	181
Mahasarakham	15,265	2.97	11	65	1,526

Provincial Breakdown (Continued)

Changwat	Square kilometers	Per cent of total area	Ampur	Tambon	Village
Mae-hongson.	15,278	2.98	5	27	312
Yala.	4,902	0.95	5	48	267
Roi-et.	6,310	1.23	9	55	1,247
Ranong.	3,522	0.69	4	26	141
Rayong.	3,761	0.73	3	25	191
Ratburi.	4,660	0.91	7	86	1,143
Lopburi.	3,687	0.72	5	60	749
Lampang.	12,501	2.43	10	65	482
Lamphun.	4,506	0.88	5	40	337
Loei.	11,238	2.19	5	32	402
Srisaket.	8,909	1.74	6	91	1,007
Sakonnakhorn.	10,250	2.00	5	59	650
Song-khla.	6,502	1.27	10	116	1,063
Satun.	3,086	0.60	3	29	197
Samutprakan.	911	0.18	5	46	741
Samutsongkhram.	1,004	0.19	3	34	289
Samutsakhorn.	761	0.15	3	35	343
Sara-buri.	5,866	1.14	9	98	1,020
Singh-buri.	844	0.16	4	40	482
Sukho-thai.	7,014	1.37	7	47	450
Suphanburi.	5,218	1.02	7	95	924
Surat-thani.	13,536	2.64	10	76	601
Surin.	9,197	1.79	7	64	985
Ayuthya.	2,529	0.49	15	206	2,037
Ang-thong.	1,072	0.21	5	62	735
Udorn-thani.	11,894	2.32	6	47	760
Uttaradit.	7,706	1.50	6	38	428
Uthai-thani.	6,326	1.23	5	41	374
Ubonrat-thani.	23,172	4.51	16	185	2,289
Total.	513,521	100.00	506	4,538	49,832

APPENDIX V

POPULATION OF THAILAND BY MAJOR REGIONS

I: CENTRAL THAILAND
MENAM PLAIN

Provinces (Changwat)	Population
Bangkok (Phra-nakhorn)	889,538
Ayuthya	373,889
Suphanburi	341,039
Thonburi	289,343
Nakorn Pathom	273,683
Cha-choengsao	242,898
Phichit	236,905
Sara-buri	207,051
Lopburi	202,041
Phitsnulok	202,113
Sukhothai	189,153
Chai-nat	170,962
Samutprakan	163,137
Ang-thong	150,515
Pathum-thani	142,488
Nontburi	133,623
Singh-buri	115,669
	4,324,047

REGION OUTSIDE MENAM PLAIN

Nakorn Sawan	379,077
Ratburi	301,563
Prachinburi	225,636
Cholburi	210,513
Phetchburi	180,251
Uttaradit	171,549
Phetchbun	162,627
Kanchanaburi	140,812
Nakhornayak	117,004
Samutsakhorn	113,673
Chantburi	114,076
Uthai-thani	104,550
Tak	105,712
Rayong	84,461
Kamphengphet	67,515
Samutsongkhram	126,592
Prachuap-khirikhan	73,400
Trat	45,040
	2,724,051

Demographic yearbook, 1952. New York: Statistical Office of the United Nations, Department o Economic Affairs, 1952.

II: NORTHEASTERN THAILAND (KORAT)

Ubon	856,373
Nakhornaratchsima	371,722
Khon-kaen	590,368
Roi-Et	536,278
Srisaket	472,378
Surin	438,474
Maha Sarakham	399,553[a]
Udornthani	386,116
Buriram	334,561
Kalasin	307,793
Nakorn Panom	313,953
Chayaphum	291,598
Sakon Nakorn	270,442
Nongkhai	144,240
Loei	136,161
	5,850,010

III: NORTH THAILAND

Chiangmai	535,664
Chiengrai	485,080
Lampang	331,956
Lamphun	180,360
Prae	213,203
Nan	210,858
Mae-hongson	66,389
	2,023,510

IV: SOUTH THAILAND (PENINSULA)

Nakhornsrithamrat	487,743
Songkhla	350,687
Surat-thani	211,679
Pattani	203,155
Nara-thiwat	168,714
Patalung	151,964
Chumphorn	118,460
Yala	80,770
Pang-Nga	60,355
Krabi	58,799
Phuket	49,104
Satun	46,326
Ranong	21,305
Trang	151,739
	2,160,800

Total population .... 17,082,418[b]

[a] Originally listed in 1947 census as 707,346, but formation of new province of Kalasin in 1947 removed 307,793 inhabitants and 6,316 square meters from Maha Sarakham.
[b] This is the adjusted figure published by the United Nations in 1952; official Thai sources at list the figure, 17,343,714, given in chapter i.

APPENDIX VI

List of Thai Official Holidays (1953)

Date	Occasion
December 31, January 1–2	Official New Year Holidays
Two days (February or March, depending on lunar calendar)	Ma-Ka-Buja
April 6	Chakri Day
April 13–14–15	Songkran (Buddhist New Year)
May 5	Anniversary of King's Coronation (Chakri-Mongkul)
Two days (May or June, depending on lunar calendar)	Vi-Sa-Ka-Buja
One day May or June	Harvest Festival
June 23–24–25	National Days
July 20–21	Beginning of Buddhist Lent
August 12	Queen's Birthday
October 23	Chulalongkorn Day
October 24	United Nations Day
December 4–5–6	King's Birthday
December 9–10–11	Constitution Days

NOTES
BIBLIOGRAPHY
and INDEX

Notes to Chapter 1

VILLAGE ORGANIZATION

[1] Credner, W., *Das Land der Thai* (Stuttgart, 1935), Ch. 1.
[2] Andrews, J. M., *Siam: Second Rural Economic Survey* (Bangkok, 1935), p. 303.
[3] Sharp, Lauriston, "Peasants and Politics in Thailand," *Far Eastern Survey*, 19 (1950), p. 159.
[4] Zimmerman, Carle C., *Siam: Rural Economic Survey, 1930–31* (Bangkok, 1931), p. 16.
[5] Sharp, *op. cit.*, p. 158.

Notes to Chapter 2

SOCIAL ORGANIZATION

[1] Embree, John F., "Thailand—A Loosely Structured Social System," *American Anthropologist*, 52 (1950), p. 184.
[2] Benedict, Ruth, *Thai Culture and Behavior, 1943*, Cornell University Southeast Asia Program Data Paper No. 4 (Ithaca, N.Y., 1952), p. 22.

Notes to Chapter 3

LIFE HISTORY OF THE INDIVIDUAL

[1] Zimmerman, Carle C., *Siam: Rural Economic Survey, 1930–31* (Bangkok, 1931), p. 16.
[2] Sharp, Lauriston, "Peasants and Politics in Thailand," *Far Eastern Survey*, 19 (1950), p. 158.
[3] deYoung, John E., *San Pong, A Village of North Thailand* (Unpublished manuscript, 1954), p. 62.
[4] Le May, R., *An Asian Arcady* (Cambridge, 1926), p. 190.
[5] deYoung, *op. cit.*, p. 77.
[6] Sharp, Lauriston, "Introduction," in Ruth Benedict, *Thai Culture and Behavior, 1943*, Cornell University Southeast Asia Program Data Paper No. 4 (Ithaca, N.Y., 1952), p. 1.
[7] deYoung, *op. cit.*, p. 79.
[8] Benedict, *op. cit.*, p. 44.

⁹ Janlekha, K. O., *A Preliminary Study of the Economic Conditions of Rice Farmers in Bangchan, Thailand* (Unpublished M.S. dissertation, Cornell University, 1951), p. 35.
¹⁰ Wells, K. E., *Thai Buddhism, Its Rites and Activities* (Bangkok, 1939), p. 160.

Notes to Chapter 4

AGRICULTURE AND ECONOMIC PATTERNS

¹ Thailand, National FAO Committee, *Thailand and her Agricultural Problems*. Bangkok, Ministry of Agriculture, 1949, p. 30.
² Zimmerman, Carle C., *Siam: Rural Economic Survey, 1930–31* (Bangkok, 1931), p. 18.
³ Sharp, Lauriston, "Peasants and Politics in Thailand," *Far Eastern Survey*, 19 (1950), p. 158.
⁴ Zimmerman, *op. cit.*, p. 18.
⁵ *Loc. cit.*
⁶ Janlekha, K. O., *A Preliminary Study of the Economic Conditions of Rice Farmers in Bangchan, Thailand* (Unpublished M.S. dissertation, Cornell University, 1951), p. 34.
⁷ Dobby, E. H., *Southeast Asia* (London, 1950), p. 277.
⁸ Janlekha, *op. cit.*, p. 34.
⁹ *Ibid.*, p. 42
¹⁰ Thompson, Virginia, *Thailand, the New Siam* (New York, 1941), p. 358.
¹¹ Janlekha, *op. cit.*, p. 49.
¹² Dobby, *op. cit.*, p. 270.
¹³ Janlekha, *op. cit.*, p. 42.
¹⁴ Zimmerman, *op. cit.*, pp. 37, 41, 44.
¹⁵ Janlekha, *op. cit.*, p. 26.
¹⁶ Dobby, *op. cit.*, p. 279.
¹⁷ Pendleton, R. L., "Land Use in Northeastern Thailand," *Geographical Review*, 33 (1943), p. 33.
¹⁸ *Ibid.*, p. 34.
¹⁹ Zimmerman, *op. cit.*, pp. 39, 43.
²⁰ Janlekha, *op. cit.*, p. 65.
²¹ *Ibid.*, p. 70.
²² Andrews, J. M., *Siam: Second Rural Economic Survey* (Bangkok, 1935), p. 136.
²³ Sharp, *op. cit.*, p. 158.
²⁴ Andrews, *op. cit.*, p. 136.
²⁵ Skinner, William G., *Report on the Chinese in Southeast Asia* (Ithaca, N.Y., 1951), p. 3.
²⁶ Coughlin, R. J., "The Status of the Chinese Minority in Thailand," *Pacific Affairs*, 25 (1952), p. 385.
²⁷ Purcell, Victor W., *The Chinese in Southeast Asia* (London, 1951), p. 195.

Notes to Chapter 5

RELIGIOUS BELIEFS AND PRACTICES

[1] Janlekha, K. O., *A Preliminary Study of the Economic Conditions of Rice Farmers in Bangchan, Thailand* (Unpublished M.S. dissertation, Cornell University, 1951), p. 5.
[2] Wells, K. E., *Thai Buddhism, Its Rites and Activities* (Bangkok, 1939), p. 5.
[3] Sharp, Lauriston, "Introduction," in Ruth Benedict, *Thai Culture and Behavior, 1943*, Cornell University Southeast Asia Program Data Paper No. 4 (Ithaca, N.Y., 1952), p. 1.
[4] Wells, *op. cit.*, p. 130.
[5] Benedict, *op. cit.*, p. 15.
[6] Andrews, J. M., *Siam: Second Rural Economic Survey* (Bangkok, 1935), p. 263.
[7] Graham, W. A., *Siam* (3d ed.; London, 1925), vol. 2, p. 242.
[8] Wells, *op. cit.*, p. 91.

Notes to Chapter 6

CHANGING SCOPE OF THE VILLAGER'S WORLD

[1] Wales, H. Quaritch, *Ancient Siamese Government and Administration* (London, 1934), p. 120.
[2] Graham, W. A., *Siam* (3d ed.; London, 1925), vol. 2, p. 322.
[3] Janlekha, K. O., *A Preliminary Study of the Economic Conditions of Rice Farmers in Bangchan, Thailand* (Unpublished M.S. dissertation, Cornell University, 1951), p. 5.
[4] Sharp, Lauriston, "Peasants and Politics in Thailand," *Far Eastern Survey*, 19 (1950), p. 159.
[5] Thompson, Virginia, *Thailand, the New Siam* (New York, 1941), p. 83.
[6] Thailand Economic Council, *Monthly Bulletin of Statistics*, Central Statistical Office, June, 1952, No. 1, p. 7.
[7] Sharp, *op. cit.*, p. 160.
[8] Benedict, Ruth, *Thai Culture and Behavior, 1943*, Cornell University Southeast Asia Program Data Paper No. 4 (Ithaca, N.Y., 1952), p. 7.
[9] Wales, *op. cit.*, p. 202.
[10] Zimmerman, Carle C., *Siam: Rural Economic Survey, 1930–31* (Bangkok, 1931), p. 78.
[11] U. S. Mutual Security Agency, *East Meets West in Thailand* (Washington, 1952), p. 2.
[12] Andrews, J. M., *Siam: Second Rural Economic Survey* (Bangkok, 1935), p. 209.

[13] Sharp, *op. cit.*, p. 159.
[14] *Loc. cit.*
[15] Janlekha, *op. cit.*, p. 75.
[16] Benedict, *op. cit.*, p. 9.
[17] Jumsai, Manich, *Compulsory Education in Thailand* (Paris, UNESCO, 1951), p. 74.
[18] *Ibid.*, p. 58.
[19] United Nations Educational, Scientific, and Cultural Organization, *Report of the Mission to Thailand* (Paris, 1950), p. 20.
[20] Andrews, *op. cit.*, p. 186.
[21] Jumsai, *op. cit.*, p. 101.
[22] Reeve, W. D., *Public Administration in Siam* (London and New York, 1951), p. 50.
[23] Jumsai, *op. cit.*, p. 83.
[24] Behrman, Daniel, *They Can't Afford to Wait* (Paris, UNESCO, 1952), p. 19.
[25] Sarasas, Phra, *My Country, Thailand: Its History, Geography, and Civilization* (Tokyo, 1942), p. 180.
[26] Landon, Kenneth P., *Siam in Transition* (Shanghai, 1939), p. 213.
[27] Balfour, M. C., and associates, *Public Health and Demography in the Far East* (New York, Rockefeller Foundation, 1950), p. 91.
[28] *Bangkok Standard*, No. 217, February, 1951, p. 6.
[29] Clements, F. W., "The World Health Organization in Southern Asia and the Western Pacific," *Pacific Affairs*, 25 (1952), p. 347.
[30] Thailand Economic Council, *Monthly Bulletin of Statistics*, August, 1952.
[31] *Bangkok Standard*, December 27, 1952, p. 4.
[32] *Ibid.*
[33] Zimmerman, *op. cit.*, p. 295.
[34] Wales, *op. cit.*, p. 122.
[35] Zimmerman, *op. cit.*, p. 195.
[36] Andrews, *op. cit.*, p. 293.
[37] Janlekha, *op. cit.*, p. 76.
[38] *Loc. cit.*
[39] *Bangkok Standard*, August 23, 1952, p. 5.
[40] Thailand, National FAO Committee, *Thailand and Her Agricultural Problems* (Bangkok, Ministry of Agriculture, 1949), p. 13.
[41] *Loc. cit.*
[42] *Loc. cit.*
[43] Janlekha, *op. cit.*, p. 18.
[44] Thailand Economic Council, *Monthly Bulletin of Statistics*, December, 1952, p. 1.
[45] Dobby, E. H., *Southeast Asia* (London, 1950), p. 280.
[46] Table adapted from material in *Thailand and Her Agricultural Problems*, and Dobby, *Southeast Asia*.

BIBLIOGRAPHY

Andrews, J. M. *Siam: Second Rural Economic Survey, 1934–35.* Bangkok, Bangkok Times Press, 1935.
Anumanrajthon, Phya. *Life of the Thai Peasant.* [In Thai.] Bangkok, 1948.
Balfour, M. C., and associates. *Public Health and Demography in the Far East.* New York, Rockefeller Foundation, 1950.
Behrman, Daniel. *They Can't Afford to Wait.* Paris, UNESCO, 1952.
Benedict, P. K. "Studies in Thai Kinship Terminology," *Journal of the American Oriental Society,* 63 (1943), 168–175.
Benedict, R. *Thai Culture and Behavior, 1943.* (Cornell University Southeast Asia Program Data Paper No. 4.) Ithaca, N.Y., 1952.
Bidyalankarana, Prince. "The Pastime of Rhyme-Making and Singing in Rural Siam," *Journal of the Siam Society,* 20, pt. 2 (1926), 101–127.
Bowring, J. *The Kingdom and the People of Siam.* London, 1857. 2 vols.
Campbell, J. G. D. *Siam in the Twentieth Century.* London, 1902.
Carter, A. C., ed. *The Kingdom of Siam.* (Louisiana Purchase Exposition, St. Louis, 1904. Siamese Section.) New York and London, 1904.
Chandruang, K. *My Boyhood in Siam.* New York, 1940.
———. "The Royal Family and Ours," *Asia,* 40 (1940), 539–540.
Clements, F. W. "The World Health Organization in Southern Asia and the Western Pacific," *Pacific Affairs,* 25 (1952), 334–348.
Cort, M. L. *Siam, or the Heart of Farther India.* New York, 1866.
Coughlin, R. J. "The Status of the Chinese Minority in Thailand," *Pacific Affairs,* 25 (1952), 378–389.
Credner, W. *Siam, das Land der Thai; eine Landeskunde auf Grund eignener Reisen und Forschungen.* Stuttgart, 1935.
Curtis, L. J. *The Laos of North Siam.* Philadelphia, 1903.
Deignan, H. G. *Siam: Land of Free Men.* (Smithsonian Institution War Background Studies, No. 8.) Washington, 1943.
deYoung, J. E. *San Pong, A Village of North Thailand.* (Unpublished manuscript, 1954.)

Dobby, E. H. *Southeast Asia.* London, 1950.
Dodd, W. C. *The Thai Race.* Cedar Rapids, Iowa, 1923.
Dubois, C. *Social Forces in Southeast Asia.* Minneapolis, 1949.
Embree, J. F. "A Note on the Vertical and Horizontal Cultural Traits in Asia," *Man,* 26 (1950).
———. "Thailand: A Loosely Structured Social System," *American Anthropologist,* 52 (1950), 181–193.
Firth, R. *Housekeeping Among Malay Peasants.* (London School of Economics Monographs on Social Anthropology.) London, 1943.
Foran, W. R. *Malayan Symphony.* London and Paris, 1935.
Graham, W. A. *Siam.* London, 1925. 2 vols.
Hutchinson, E. W. *Adventurers in Siam in the Seventeenth Century.* London, 1940.
Jacoby, E. H. *Agrarian Unrest in Southeast Asia.* New York, 1949.
Janlekha, K. O. *A Preliminary Study of the Economic Conditions of Rice Farmers in Bangchan, Thailand.* (Unpublished M.S. dissertation, Cornell University, 1951.)
Jumsai, Manich. *Compulsory Education in Thailand.* Paris, UNESCO, 1951.
Kambhu, X. M. L. *Report on the Irrigation, Drainage and Water Communication Project of the Chao Phya River Plan.* Bangkok, Royal Irrigation Department, 1949.
Kheosiplard, P. "Irrigation in Siam," *Reclamation Era,* 33 (1947), 95.
Ladejinsky, W. I. "Thailand's Agricultural Economy," *Foreign Agriculture,* 6 (1942), 165–184.
Landon, K. P. *The Chinese in Thailand.* London and New York, 1941.
———. *Thailand in Transition.* Shanghai, 1939.
———. *Southeast Asia: Crossroads of Religions.* Chicago, 1949.
Le May, R. S. *An Asian Arcady.* Cambridge, 1926.
———. *Siamese Tales, Old and New.* London, 1930.
McGilvary, D. *A Half-Century Among the Siamese and the Lao, An Autobiography.* New York, 1912.
Mills, L. A., and associates. *The New World of Southeast Asia.* Minneapolis, 1949.
Pelzer, K. J. *Population and Land Utilization.* (Economic Survey of the Pacific Area, Part I.) New York, Institute of Pacific Relations, 1941.
Pendleton, R. L. "Importance of Termites in Modifying Certain Thailand Soils," *Journal of the American Society of Agronomy,* 34 (1942), 340–344.
———. "Land Use in Northeastern Thailand," *Geographical Review,* 33 (1943), 15–41.
———. "Soils of Thailand," *Journal of the Thailand Research Society, Natural History Supplement 12.* (1940) 235–260.
———. "The Agriculture of Siam," *Foreign Agriculture,* 10 (1946).
Prasert, R. "Buddhist Lent," *Bangkok Standard,* 132 (1949), 11, 25.

———. "Kathin," Bangkok *Standard*, 145 (1949), 16.
———. "The First Ploughing," Bangkok *Standard*, 122 (1949), 10, 23.
Purcell, V. W. *The Chinese in Southeast Asia*. London and New York, 1951.
Reeve, W. D. *Public Administration in Siam*. London and New York, 1951.
Rosinger, L. K., and associates. *The State of Asia*. New York, 1951.
Sarasas, P. *My Country, Thailand: Its History, Geography, and Civilization*. Tokyo, 1942.
Seidenfaden, E. "Review of Funeral Customs in Thailand by Phya Anuman Ratchathon," *Journal of the Siam Society*, 33, pt. 2 (1941), 197–208.
Sharp, L. "Peasants and Politics in Thailand," *Far Eastern Survey*, 19 (1950), 157–161.
Siam Commercial Directory. Bangkok, 1948.
Siam Directory B. E. 2491 [1948]. Bangkok, 1948.
Siam. Division of Central Services. *Statistical Yearbook, 1939/40–1944* (No. 21). Bangkok, 1944.
Siam. Ministry of Commerce and Communications. *Nature and Industry*. Bangkok, 1930.
Skinner, G. W. *Report on the Chinese in Southeast Asia*. Ithaca, N.Y., 1951.
Smith, M. *A Physician at the Court of Siam*. London, 1947.
Smyth, H. W. *Five Years in Siam, from 1891 to 1896*. London, 1898. 2 vols.
———. *Notes of a Journey on the Upper Mekong, Siam*. London, 1895.
Sriswat, B. C. *Thirty Nationalities in Chiengrai*. [In Thai.] 2d ed. Bangkok, Uthai Publishing Co., 1950.
Thailand National Economic Council. *Monthly Bulletin of Statistics*, 1 (1952), nos. 1–7.
Thailand. National FAO Committee. *Thailand and Her Agricultural Problems*. Bangkok, Ministry of Agriculture, 1949.
Thompson, P. A. *Lotus Land*. London, 1906.
Thompson, V. M. *Thailand, the New Siam*. New York, 1941.
United Nations Educational, Scientific, and Cultural Organization. *Report of the Mission to Thailand*. Paris, 1950.
United Nations Food and Agricultural Organization. *Report of the FAO Mission for Siam*. Washington, 1948.
United States. Department of State. *Thailand: Its People and Economy*. (Far Eastern Series, 36). Washington, 1950.
United States. Mutual Security Agency. *East Meets West in Thailand*. Washington, 1952.
United States. Mutual Security Agency. *Far East Data Book No. 9*. Washington, 1952.
United States, Office of Strategic Services. Research and Analysis Branch. *Social Conditions, Attitudes and Propaganda in Thailand*. Washington, 1942.

Wales, H. Q. *Siamese State Ceremonies*. London, 1931.
———. *Ancient Siamese Government and Administration*. London, 1934.
———. "Siamese Theory and Ritual Connected with Birth," *Journal of the Royal Anthropological Institute of Great Britain*, 63 (1933), 441–451.
Wells, K. E. *Thai Buddhism, Its Rites and Activities*. Bangkok, 1939.
Wheatcroft, R. *Siam and Cambodia in Pen and Pastel, with Excursions in China and Burma*. London, 1928.
Wood, W. A. R. *A History of Siam*. 2d ed. Bangkok, 1933.
———. *Land of Smiles*. Bangkok, 1935.
Young, E. *Kingdom of the Yellow Robe*. 3d ed. London, 1907.
Zimmerman, C. C. "A Demographic Study of Eight Oriental Villages Yet Largely Untouched by Western Culture," *Metron*, 3 (1934), 179–198.
———. *Siam: Rural Economic Survey, 1930–31*. Bangkok, Bangkok Times Press, 1931.
———. "Some Phases of Land Utilization in Siam," *Geographical Review*, 27 (1937), 378–393.
———. "The Stature and Weight of the Siamese," *Genus*, 2 (1937), 295–323.

INDEX

Abortion, 49
Adolescence, 57
Age: groups, 66; terms of respect, 67; ceremony, 68
Agriculture: general description of, 75–80; shifting crops, 85; cattle raising, 90–93; fertilizer use, 93–94, 191–192; secondary crops, 95–97; spirit offerings, 141–143; mechanized, 192–193. *See also* Rice; Seasons
Animism, 143–146
Associations: informal, 23, 78–80, 115–116; irrigation, 80; credit, 186–189

Benedict, Ruth, 62, 152
Betel, 45–46, 201
Bhikku. See Monks
Birth: reporting of, 17; beliefs, 49–51; rate, 198
Buddha: house altar, 34; offerings to, 35, 46, 135, 137; birthday of, 136
Buddhism: general description of, 110, 123–128; Sabbath, 113–114; services, 113–114; monks, 114–116, 124–126, 132; temple boys, 117–118; novices, 118–120; calendar of, 133–141; festivals, 135–141; New Year, 135–136; Lent, 137; and animism, 145–146

Calendar: festival, 133–135; lunar, 134–135; zodiac, 134. *See also* Festivals
Cemetery. *See* Cremation
Change: in language, 7; in dress, 7, 201; in government, 148, 153; due to transportation, 159–162; due to school, 166; in agriculture, 201

Children: birth, 48–51; nursing, 51; naming, 52–53; ceremonies, 53; toilet training, 53; clothes of, 54–55; punishment of, 54; play of, 55. *See also* School
Chinese: as peddlers, 105–107; as rice-mill operators, 106; as moneylenders, 107–108, 187; restrictive decrees against, 107–109; in agriculture, 108
Climate, 5–6
Clothing. *See* Dress
Cockfighting, 172
Coffin, 68, 69. *See also* Funeral
Conscription, 59–60, 153
Coöperation: in housebuilding, 32–33; general description of, 78–80; civic, 79–80; exchange labor, 79. *See also* Associations
Courtship, 60–62
Cremation, 69–74

Dances: *ramwong*, 61; at fairs, 156
Death: registration of, 19, 21; ceremonies for postponing, 68; beliefs, 69; general description of, 69–74; rate of, 179. *See also* Funeral
Debt, 186–189
Disease: caused by ghouls, 144–145; and spirit doctors, 144–145; control of, 175–179; of cattle, 189–191
Divorce, 66
Doctors: village, 20–21, 135; spirit, 144–145; number of, 175
Dress: changes in, 7, 201; general description of, 41–44; Western, 41–42, 154; of women, 41–42; of corpse, 68; mourning, 73

Ear piercing, 44–45
Education: national system, 55–56, 164–167, 168–171; changes in, 164–167, 170–171; adult, 169–170. See also School
Election: of headman, 17; national, 149, 153

Family: description of, 22–24; name, 25; daily activities, 36–37; size, 49
Festivals: calendar, 133–141; general description of, 133–141; lunar cycle, 135–141
Fish: in diet, 38, 39; conservation program, 197–199
Fishing, 100–102
Fishpond, 101–102
Flood control, 193–197
Food, 37–38
Friends, 27
Funeral: coffin, 68, 69; dressing corpse, 68; general description of, 69–74; cremation, 69–74; food, 70; mourning clothes, 73; coöperation at, 74

Gambling, 171–172
Ghosts. See Ghouls; Spirits
Ghouls, 144–145
Gifts: at marriage, 63; at death, 70; to temple, 133
Granaries, 90–91
Government: administration, 13–14; village officials, 17; changes in, 147; traditional, 147–148

Handicrafts, 102–103
Headman, village, 16. See also Kamnan
Holidays, 155–156
House: general description of, 29–34; types of, 29–30; plan of, 31–32; room arrangement, 31–32; cost of, 33; building ceremony, 34; spirit offering for, 35; furnishings, 36

Inheritance, 23
Irrigation: associations, 80; projects, 193–197

Justice, administration of, 153–154

Kamnan, 16–17
Kinship: family, 25; terms, 26–27

Land ownership, 185–186

Literacy, 168–171
Lottery, 171–173

Markets: morning, 12; role in women's life, 103–104
Marriage: age at, 60; trial marriage, 62; description of, 63; exchange of gifts, 63, 163–164; registration of, 63; residence, 64–65
Meals: time of, 37; at funerals, 70. See also Food
Memorial service, 72–73
Midwife, 49–50, 181
Modesty, 40
Money: as offering, 131–133; effect of, 162
Monks: general description of life, 114–116, 124–126, 132; ordination of, 121–123; number of, 129. See also Buddhism
Mother roasting, 50, 58
Movies, 60, 160, 162, 173

Names: surnames, 21; of children, 52–53
New Year festival, 135–136
Novices: general description of life, 118–120; ordination of, 119–120; school, 124–125. See also Buddhism; Monks

Offerings: to household spirits, 35, 146; at funerals, 69; of money, 131–133; at festivals, 137–140

Peddlers, 104
Police, 153
Pigs, 97–99
Pilgrimage, 161
Polygamy, 66
Population: of Thailand, 1; density, 1–2, 199–200; growth, 199
Poultry, 99–100
Priests. See Monks
Puberty. See Adolescence

Radio, 173
Railroads, 159
Religion, 110–146. See also Animism; Buddhism; Festivals; Monks; Novices
Rice: varieties of, 77; farming, 80–91; preparing seedbed, 81; transplanting, 82; harvesting, 86; threshing, 88; and spirits, 142–143

Roads, 159–161

School: system, 55–57, 164–168; curriculum, 56, 167; celebrations, 57; building, 164–165; vocational, 167. *See also* Education; Schoolteachers
School children: dress, 154; number of, 166
Schoolteachers: women, 58, 167; role of, 167–168
Seasons: rainy, 5–6; and occupations, 77
Sewing machines, 162, 163
Sex: division of labor by, 36–37, 80, 81, 89; act, 48; education, 55; separation of sexes, 55; symbols, 145
Sharp, Lauriston, 12, 148, 151, 161
Songs, 89
Souls. *See* Spirits
Spirits: houses, 31, 146; offerings to, 89, 141–143, 146; distinct from souls, 143–144; evil, 144–145

Taboos: toward house altar, 34–35; tasks forbidden men, 37
Taharn. See Conscription

Tattooing, 45
Taxes: in traditional days, 156–157; modern, 157–159
Temple boys, 117–118, 132
Tenants, 76–77
Thailand, geographical description of, 2–4
Toilet, 30, 40

Umbilical cord, 50

Vaccination, 21, 176, 182
Village: types of, 8

Wat: general description of, 111–113; novices and monks, 123–126; cost of maintaining, 128–133. *See also* Buddhism
Wedding. *See* Marriage
Women: position of, 24; in household, 36–37; life cycle of, 48; religious life of, 128; schoolteachers, 58, 167. *See also* Birth; Marriage

Zodiac, 134

www.ingramcontent.com/pod-product-compliance
Lightning Source LLC
Chambersburg PA
CBHW021703230426
43668CB00008B/708